NEW FORMATIONS

CW01559034

EDITOR:
Judith Squires

EDITORIAL BOARD:
Homi Bhabha
Lesley Caldwell
Tony Davies
Simon Frith
Jim Grealy
Stuart Hall
Dick Hebdige
Maria Lauret
Kobena Mercer
Graham Murdock
Ali Rattansi
Denise Riley
Jenny Bourne Taylor
Valerie Walkerdine

OVERSEAS EDITORS:
Ien Ang
Angelika Bammer
Tony Bennett
Jody Berland
Victor Burgin
Hazel Carby
Iain Chambers
Joan Copjec
Lidia Curti
Ian Hunter
Cora Kaplan
Noel King
Colin Mercer
Edward Said
Renata Salecl
Gayatri Chakravorty Spivak
John Tagg

ADVERTISEMENTS:
For enquiries/bookings contact S
Lawrence & Wishart

SUBSCRIPTIONS:
For 1997, subscription rates to L
are, for 3 issues
UK: Institutions £70, Individuals £35.
Rest of world: Institutions £75; Individuals £38.
Single copies: £14.99

CONTRIBUTIONS AND CORRESPONDENCE:
Send to:
The Editor, *New Formations*
Dept. of Politics, University of Bristol,
12 Priory Road, Bristol BS8 1TU.

BOOKS FOR REVIEW:
Send to:
Alasdair Pettinger
Scottish Music Information Centre
1 Bowmont Gardens
Glasgow, Scotland G12 9LR

Prospective writers are encouraged to contact the
editors to discuss their ideas and to obtain a copy of
our style sheet.
Manuscripts should be sent in triplicate. They will
not be returned unless a stamped, self-addressed
envelope is enclosed. Contributors should note that
the editorial board cannot take responsibility for any
manuscript submitted to *New Formations*.

ISSN   0 950 2376
ISBN   05315 838 X

Text design and setting by Art Services, Norwich
Printed in Great Britain at the University Press,
Cambridge.

New Formations is
published three times
a year by
Lawrence & Wishart
99a Wallis Road
London E9 5LN
Tel: 0181-533 2506
Fax: 0181-533 7369

NOTES ON CONTRIBUTORS

Ien Ang is Professor of Cultural Studies and Director of the Research Centre in Intercommunal Studies at the University of Western Sydney, Nepean, Australia. Her latest book is *Living Room Wars: Rethinking Media Audiences for a Postmodern World* (Routledge, 1996).

Ian Buchanan teaches in the School of English and Comparative Literature at Murdoch University. Currently he is editing a collection of papers for a special issue of *Social Semiotics* on Michel de Certeau.

Vicki Callahan is a Lecturer in Film Studies at the University of Kent, Canterbury.

Richard Carvell is Chair of Canadian Studies at the University of British Columbia, Vancouver, Canada where he teaches in the English Department and is completing a book called *McLuhan in Space: a Cultural Geography*.

Jeremy Gilbert is currently working on his PhD in the Media Studies Department at Sussex University.

Daniel Goodman is a member of the English Department at Frostburg State University in Maryland. His recent work examines the cultural and political impact of transformation in the telecommunications infrastructure.

Drew Hemment spent many years as a practising DJ and promoter of early dance music events, before obtaining an MA in continental philosophy at Warwick University. He has written for various magazines including Mixmag, The Herb Garden and Mute. He recently organised a multi-discipinary theory conference at Leeds University called Thinking Alien and is studying for a PhD at Lancaster University.

Michael Humphrey is a senior lecturer in the Department of Sociology, Culture and Communication at the University of New South Wales in Sydney. His forthcoming publications are *Islam, Multiculturalism and Transnationalism: from the Lebanese Diaspora* (1997) and *Ethnicity and Identity in a Globalizing World* (1997).

Fiona Nicoll is a tutor in Fine Arts at Melbourne University and has recently completed her PhD entitled 'Metonymy and Metaphor: Configurations of Nationalist Subjectivity in Twentieth Century Australia'.

Albert Paolini was an associate lecturer in the School of Politics, La Trobe University. Prior to his untimely death in 1996, he wrote and researched in the areas of postmodern international relations, postcolonialism, third world studies and globalization.

John Rundell is Director of the Ashworth Centre for Social Theory, the University of Melbourne, Australia. His publications include *Origins of Modernity* (1987); *Between Totalitarianism and Postmodernity*, co-edited with Peter Beilharz and Gillian Robinson (1992); *Rethinking Imagination: Culture and Creativity* (1984), co-edited with Gillian Robinson. He is an editor of the journal *Thesis Eleven*.

Jon Stratton is Associate Professor in Cultural Studies in the School of Communication and Cultural Studies at Curtin university of Technology. His most recent book is *The Desirable Body: Cultural Fetishism and the Erotics of Consumption*. He is currently working on the experience of postassimilation Jewishness.

CONTENTS
NUMBER 31   SUMMER 1996

Uncivil Societies

Albert Paolini died on 30th September 1996, aged 33. He was diagnosed as having acute leukemia nearly six years prior, although the diagnosis then was that he would be lucky to stay alive for another six months. Throughout this long and difficult period, Albert undertook and completed a doctoral thesis at the University of Melbourne, entitled 'From International to Intersubjective Relations: Post colonialism, Globalization, Modernity and the Place of Africa'. He was awarded the Ph.D. only days before his death.

Writing a doctoral dissertation under the pressure of a terminal illness was impressive in itself, but this was merely the tip of the iceberg in terms of Albert's intellectual productions. He wrote many articles on contemporary theory, international relations and the modernity/postmodernity debate, articles which have been published in journals such as *Alternatives*, *Thesis Eleven*, *The Australian Journal of Politics*, *Arena*, *The Melbourne Journal of Politics* and (in this volume) *New Formations*. He helped organise two major conferences on international relations at La Trobe University. He was joint editor of *The State in Transition: Reimagining Political Space*, (Lynne Reinner, Boulder, US, 1995). And his doctoral thesis is now to be posthumously published as *The Navigation of Modernity* (Lynne Reinner, Boulder, US, forthcoming).

Albert Paolini's death is a cause of deep sorrow for all of those who knew him. He was a scholar of considerable brilliance. He was my greatest friend and interlocutor.

Anthony Elliott
University of Melbourne

Soundtrack to an Uncivil Society: Rave Culture, The Criminal Justice Act and the Politics of Modernity

Jeremy Gilbert

The Criminal Justice Act (1994) did many things. From revising the right to silence to criminalising male rape, it was a collection of legislation with far wider implications than attempting to clamp down on rave culture. But it is the specific set of measures aimed at restricting the free party movement which received the most attention, and perhaps not without good reason. For while none of us were surprised to see the former Tory government further eroding the civil rights of British subjects in general, it was less obvious why they should be so bothered about ravers in particular, who when it comes down to it, have never offered any threat to public order and who have singularly failed to become a cause for sustained moral panic. Those rural areas where free ravers are most potent as a perceived threat were rarely if ever in constituencies which were traditional Tory strongholds, so this was hardly a matter of political exigency. But one's instinctive reaction to the last governments' vehement opposition to free raves seemed to be an unsurprised shrug of the shoulders and some comment about Tories never approving of other people's fun. Of course, we assumed, they wanted to ban raves; banning raves is bad, therefore a Conservative government desperately in search of new policies and only capable of doing evil was bound to do it eventually. But the complete failure of any senior Labour or Liberal Democrat figure to oppose the act or its aims, and the increasingly well-documented alienation of an entire generation from the political process, demonstrate that the issues involved go wider and deeper than the Tories' traditional contempt for civil liberties.[1] Why should the government be so concerned to prevent people gathering in groups of ten or more to listen to music characterised by a series of repetitive beats? Why should opposition parties be so willing to help them, indeed, to fall over themselves in their eagerness to demonstrate their own contempt for alternative culture? What is the nature of the threat that rave poses, and to whom?

1. See, for instance, any of Helen Wilkinson's reports for *Demos*.

THE BESTIAL CROWD

Firstly, we can consider the Act itself in terms of a long history of attempts (and an even longer history of unattempted desires) to regulate the right to public assembly. This is not something new; nor even is it something relatively recent. The 'crowd' has always been a fearful sight for those who have sought to govern (wisely or unwisely, for the governed or the governors). There is a sense in which the crowd has always seemed to threaten *government* itself, to present it with its own imminent illegitimacy. Introducing his historical survey *The Crowd and the Mob*, J.S. McClelland writes:

> It could almost be said that political theorising was invented to show that democracy, the rule of men by themselves, necessarily turns into rule by the mob. Athens had been some kind of working democracy for two centuries before Plato invited us to see the Athenian demos as an ignorant and irrational crowd always likely to be turned into a mob by its demagogues.[2]

2. JS McClelland, *The Crowd and the Mob*, London, Unwin, 1989, p1.

This, then, is a tradition in the West which goes back at least as far as Plato, whose abhorrence of the Athenian mob was couched in terms similar to those with which Burke in 1790 expressed his and his class' terror of democracy in revolutionary France. Burke's notorious phrase, 'the swinish multitude', is close enough both to Plato's image of the mob as a wild beast, and to Shakespeare's 'many-headed hydra' for us to ask what exactly the nature of this fear is, that these writers separated by centuries seem to share with Michael Howard and Jack Straw?At one level the answer is obvious enough; a crowd has the capacity to become a riot which could potentially lead to a revolution.[3] But even this chain of equivalences needs examining closely before we can say just what it is that our rulers and would-be rulers are afraid of. What's more, it is not only our rulers and legislators who are afraid of this thing; we find, in fact, this same distaste again expressed in terms reminiscent of Plato's in Freud's writing on the crowd:

3. See George Rudé, *The Crowd in History*, London, Serif, 1995.

4. *ibid.*, p101.

5. Freud, 'Group Psychology and the Analysis of the Ego', *op. cit.*, p101.

6. *ibid.*, p103.

7. *ibid.*, p107.

> in a group the individual is brought under conditions which allow him to throw off the repressions of his unconscious instinctual impulses.[4]
> In a group every sentiment and act is contagious.[5]
> a group knows neither doubt nor uncertainty.[6]
> groups have never thirsted after truth. They demand illusions, and cannot do without them.[7]

This seems remarkably close to the idea of the crowd as swinish multitude, as many-headed-hydra, as wild beast.

This set of metaphors implies a number of simultaneous and at times contradictory fears about the crowd. The image which stands out most obviously and most consistently is that of the crowd as beast ('animal' would be too weak a word). In coming together, human beings are somehow stripped of their humanity; sociality is regression. This itself reveals a very specific idea of the nature of human beings and their relation to one another. The distances between us, it seems, are in some way what keep us human; bring us too close together and we lose the status of sovereign subjects, regressing both individually and collectively to a primal state. And yet, what it is about this primal state that is so frightening is still slightly unsure. On the one hand there is the fear that, all individuality having collapsed, the mob will now act as one, with a ferocious and irrepressible will. But on the other hand, it seems as if it is the very *absence* of such a unified will which is so offensive. The hydra has many heads, the swine constitute a multitude, even Plato's beast is easily swayed, having no consistent opinions of its own. It is in one sense the very refusal of the crowd to declare its intentions which makes it so worrying. The crowd, demanding illusions, cannot be reasoned with, and it cannot be reasoned with precisely because it is never absolutely One.

This apparent contradiction, between the fear of the crowd's homogeneity on the one hand and its inherent heterogeneity on the other; needs to be examined. As I have suggested, the breaking down of the barriers between the different constituent subjectivities of the crowd necessary to their homogenisation is grossly offensive to this tradition. In this, perhaps, we see manifested what can be called, following Derrida, the metaphysics of the *proper*. The proper (the correct, the *owned*) is in this sense the privileged term of philosophy. The proper is what marks the unity of the self-present subject, the boundary between self and other/s, identity and in-dividuality. Derrida writes in his very early essay on Husserl:

> Originary being must be thought on the basis of the trace....the trace is the intimate relation of the living present to its outside, the opening to exteriority in general, to the nonproper.[8]

Such thinking, as much of Derrida's work has demonstrated, is refuted (if never entirely successfully) by the whole dominant tradition of Western thought. Here we can see one reason for the fear of crowds; such a tradition must obviously be hostile to that shedding of 'burdens of distance' which Cannetti sees as constitutive of the crowd itself, for such distances are what maintain those precious distinctions between inside and outside, self and other/s.[9]

Yet at the same time, as we have seen, this fear of crowds is often a fear of their very multiplicity. It seems to be implied that were the crowd to have the unity and constancy of reason that it might not be so objectionable. This reminds me of Jean-Luc Nancy's remarks concerning the political logic of *communion*. Nancy contrasts this metaphysical longing for a hypostatic fusion with a deconstructive notion of *community* as something else, something that would seems to preserve the singularity of its constituent subjects without reducing that singularity to an individuality:

> What this community has 'lost' - the immanence and intimacy of a communion - is lost only in the sense that such a 'loss' is constitutive of 'community' itself. It is not a loss: on the contrary, immanence, if it were to come about, would instantly suppress community, or communication, as such...That is why political or collective enterprises dominated by a will to absolute immanence have as their truth the truth of death.

8. Derrida, 'Speech and Phenomena', in Kamuf (ed), *Between the Blinds*, pp26-7.

9. Cited in McClelland, *op. cit.*, p296.

Immanence, communal fusion, contains no other logic than that of the suicide of the community that is governed by it.[10]

10. Jean-Luc Nancy, *The Inoperative Community*, Minneapolis: University of Minnesota Press, 1991, p12.

It might be that we can locate this fear of the unstable crowd between these two poles (which are nothing, in fact, but manifestations of the same thought of immanent self-presence), between the logics of the proper and of communion. The unreasonable crowd refuses both of these imperatives.

This fear of the unreasoning crowd, McClelland points out, is as old in the West as political discourse itself. If that metaphysics which Derrida deconstructs has just the same history (and it certainly appears to), is it not fair to suggest that these two histories are in some sense coextensive?[11] This would at least give us some means of locating this fear of the crowd, oscillating unpredictably between unity and plurality, which cannot be reduced to a ruling class' fear of democracy. Metaphysics seems to be always most terrified of the crowd when it refuses either to coalesce into a static community or to disperse into a set of discrete units; it is the unstable mobility of the crowd which worries it most. We can, if we like, understand that the crowd constitutes a kind of ultimate refusal of the basic metaphysical imperative to *be One*.[12] Mikkel Borch-Jacobsen, analysing Freud's strained and at times hostile thinking about crowds (and - at the same time - about sociality in general), identifies this imperative at work in some of the founding texts of psychoanalysis. Commenting on Freud's account of the patriarchal Law of the Father, Borch-Jacobsen writes:

11. See Derrida, *Of Grammatology*, part 1.

12. And, by the way, can we separate this account of the metaphysical imperative to *be One* from Irigaray's account of phallocentric discourse's persistent privileging of the singular, the unitary, the Sex which is One?

> Before it has any content at all, the law announces, imperatively and categorically, that one must not identify...not to identify with the other (more precisely, not to identify the other with oneself) is the only way of respecting the other as other, without doing him violence. The law is of the Other. It is thus, by the same token, a Law of the Subject. 'Do not be like me': this is understood positively, prescriptively, as 'Be yourself', 'Be original', 'Be a subject'.[13]

13. Mikkel Borch-Jacobsen, *The Freudian Subject*, trans. Catherine Porter Stanford, Stanford University Press, 1988, p217.

Freud's objection to the crowd, it seems, derives from its members' refusal of this imperative. In fact, Borch-Jacobsen suggests that the crowd in the shape of the *primal horde*; stands for everything which Freud cannot allow himself to understand in his attempt to simultaneously maintain a coherent notion of the subject; and to wrest psychoanalysis and individual psychology away from hypnotic therapy and the psychology of groups.

What is important about Borch-Jacobsen's reading for our purposes here is that he demonstrates that, at least in Freud's case, a distaste for crowds derives from a desire to maintain a logocentric notion of the subject. Taking *The Freudian Subject* as a case study, we can apply Borch-Jacobsen's diagnosis of Freud's symptoms to all of those similarly phobic texts to which I have referred: Plato's *Republic*, *Julius Caesar* by Shakespeare, *Reflections on the Revolution in France* (Burke), and the 1994 Criminal Justice Act. And furthermore, while the various

French philosophers which I have cited often seem to locate the manifestations of 'metaphysics' solely within the pages of the texts which they deconstruct, is the CJA not evidence in itself that these discourses can operate outside of the academy as well? Borch-Jacobsen's Law of the Subject might be not merely something which occurs in the pages of Group Psychology and the Analysis of the Ego but a discourse whose constitutive interpellation of subjects-in-modernity is at times enforced by the brute strength of non-discursive forces (in this case, the police forces and the courts).[14]

All right, all right, enough; the fear of crowds derives from metaphysics, from the discourse of the proper, from phallogocentrism, from that thing - however many names we want to give it - which Derrida and the rest have argued has been going on at least 'since Plato'. But whatever recurring nightmares may trouble the sleep of metaphysics, it would obviously be a mistake to treat 'the crowd' as a homogenous phenomenon. Actual historical crowds do very different things at different times. Rioting over a single issue (the price of bread, the poll tax), storming the Bastille or the Winter Palace, instituting a pogrom or merely constituting that space of collective anonymity which Baudelaire found so intriguing, people *en masse* can mean very different things. What I think is interesting from this point of view, then, is how very closely, in certain ways, the *raving* crowd confirms all of this tradition's worst fears about what happens when people get together. It is precisely neither a purposeless mass nor a unified collective entity with a definite purpose. It's purpose is, in a sense, simply to be itself. But what exactly this *means* is never entirely pre-determined, and we can see this illustrated quite concretely in the simple fact that free raves very rarely have set finishing times, and have even been known to change location entirely in the course of an evening (and isn't the whole framework of our licensing laws aimed precisely at limiting these two variables)? At the same time, there are certain aspects of a rave which all participants would be agreed on. The ultimate end, obviously, is the attainment of ecstasy, both collective and individual. Nancy writes of the ecstatic experience:

> Ecstasy...defines the impossibility, both ontological and gnostological, of absolute immanence...and consequently the impossibility either of an individuality, in the precise sense of the term, or of a pure collective totality.[15]

The means to this end, that for which the raving crowd specifically comes together, is dancing.

MODERN MEN DON'T DANCE

Social dancing is, again, something which has troubled the defenders of public morality and individual rationality since Plato. In particular, it was the ecstatic dances of the bacchanals - whose legendary celebrations of

14. It seems to me that there is something of the logic of 'interpellation' as conceived by Althusser which is very close to Derrida's 'metaphysics of presence'. In both cases an attempt is made to fix subjectivity into a specific and unitary meaning. See Laclau, *Reflections on the Revolution of Our Time*, (p186) and Judith Butler, *Bodies that Matter*, London, Routledge, 1993, pp121-2. The notion of 'interpellation' which I would want to tentatively propose here would be one that would differ from Althusser's in two senses: it would see various 'discourses' rather than Althusser's 'ideology' as potential sources/sites of interpellation; it would emphasise, along with Lacan, Judith Butler, Laclau; and Mouffe, that such attempts to *fix* identity must always fail in a manner which is in some senses a condition of the very possibility of the attempt itself.

15. Nancy, op. cit. p6.

hedonism, pushing their participants to the edge of animality, sound uncannily like the bestial gatherings of which we have already seen so many writers down the centuries to be so fearful - that Plato wanted banned and forbidden. Here again we can see that what disturbs metaphysicians most about the dancing crowd is that it refuses to settle down into a stable and meaningful object:

> It is hard to pronounce that whole style of dance [the Baccanals] either warlike or pacific [Plato tries to fit all types of dance into one of these two categories], or to determine what purpose it has. The most correct course, I think, will be to discriminate it alike from the dances of war and of peace, declare it unfit for a citizen, and leave it so on one side.[16]

Given that it's an obvious and understandable cliché of rave culture that rave constitutes the 're-discovery' of this lost practice of primal, ecstatic dancing, we might ask if Plato's gesture is not emblematic of one of the key repressions by which the West has constituted itself? Of course, we should also be troubled by the naive and exoticising terms in which participants in rave culture imagine 'the West's others', but that's a topic for another paper.

Such speculation aside, it is certainly the case that the regulation of dancing occupies a special place in the history of British culture. Throughout the first half of the seventeenth century, the puritans tried to ban the traditional sites of public dancing on national and local levels. These sites constituted a vital part of the fabric of everyday life for centuries beforehand. Church ales (precursors, perhaps, of the twentieth century church fete, but considerably different in character - which largely revolved around drinking and dancing), traditional festivals, maypole dances etc, all of which might be seen as manifestations of the subversive tradition of carnival, all came under attack, and for explicit reasons.[17] Such public revelry, and dancing in particular, was seen as tending to undermine at the same time sexual morality, and respect for authority. In hindsight the significance of this moment for an understanding of English culture (and European culture in general) is hard to overestimate. Puritanism, it has been suggested, constituted the first historical manifestation of the revolutionary consciousness of the bourgeoisie.[18] It marked the emergence of a whole constellation of terms and meanings which we have come to see as characteristic of modernity itself. This was the moment when the first attempt was made to institute the work ethic, the worship of individual reason, the fear and hatred of the body, and the belief in rational progress as the dominant values of English culture.[19] Going hand-in-hand with the scientific revolution, the puritan ascendancy constituted an unprecedented politico-cultural project. Although it might be inaccurate to define it as the first full-blown modernising project in British history, it was certainly the first to engage in such an ambitious assault on traditional ways of life, and to treat the everyday life of the common people as a site of radical transformation. The prohibition of dancing, in

16. Plato, *The Laws*, trans. A.E. Taylor, London: J.M. Dent, 1934, p201. Interestingly, the rhetorical strategy which Plato deploys here - that of attempting to relegate a denigrated object not just to a denigrated position but to one *outside* the conceptual scheme being elaborated - is just the same as that carried out in the texts of Platonic philosophy on the interrelated concepts of femininity and matter; see Judith Butler *Bodies that Matter*, Chapter 1.

17. See J. Underdown, *Revel, Riot and Rebellion*.

18. See, for example, Christopher Hill, *Puritanism and Revolution*, London:, Penguin, 1954, chapter 4.

19. These issues are discussed in a range of works such as Underdown and Hill (*op. cit.*), many other works by Christopher Hill and, from a different but important perspective, in Max Webers' *The Protestant Ethic and the Spirit of Capitalism*.

particular the *intoxicated* dancing of the church ales, was therefore one of the key gestures by which modernity was instituted in Britain. The social pleasures of the body, of music, of intoxication and of the dance were intolerable to this new consciousness, and the memory of this intolerance and partially-successful repression is still strong enough that the word 'puritan' remains in our vocabulary today, with all of its connotations of anti-pleasure, excessive reason, and repressive regulation.

This regulation of social dancing is in part (and is part of) a regulation of social *space*. It remains the case today (and it is a legal detail which has its roots in the puritan ascendancy) that a building must be granted a special licence for dancing to be permitted on its premises. It is a clear testament to the fact that the regulation of space within British modernity is tied closely to the hostile regulation of just those types of intoxicated crowds, and all that they manifest, that licensing laws are specifically concerned with the issues of when and where people will be allowed to gather, listen to music, drink and dance. This process can itself be considered as a part of those new trends in governmental discourse which Foucault identifies as emerging in the seventeenth and eighteenth centuries:

> Discipline sometimes requires *enclosure*, the specification of a place heterogeneous to all other and closed in upon itself....
>
> But the principle of enclosure is neither constant nor indispensable, nor sufficient in disciplinary machinery. This machinery works space in a much more flexible and detailed way. It does this first of all on the principle of elementary location or *partitioning*. Each individual has its own place, and each place its individual. Avoid distribution in groups; break up collective dispositions; analyse confused, massive or transient pluralities

Do not our licensing laws on the one hand, and the Criminal Justice Act on the other, demonstrate that the government of the UK would be disposed to constitute as much space as possible, and in particular spaces of intoxicated dancing, as just such ordered places? Obviously the machinery of discipline will operate most acutely on those spaces specifically designated for punishment and for the containment and absolute regulation of specific groups (e.g. the prisons and army barracks about which Foucault here writes). But the same disciplinary logic can be seen at work in the new laws against *mass* trespass and the Act's particular attention to unlicensed places of dancing (i.e. free raves).

We should be careful here to avoid a naive conception of 'regulation' as an inherent evil, always and only a source of 'repression'. Foucault's own comments on the ambivalence of power are vividly illustrated when we consider that recently spaces for dancing (in particular rave clubs) have been deliberate objects of regulations which aim to empower and protect those using those spaces. I refer specifically to the actions taken by bodies such as Manchester city council to force rave clubs to provide facilities such as free water to their raving clientele. It's still the case that most such clubs in London charge high prices for water, sold only in bottles, and take extreme measures to prevent people getting access to cold water in toilets; here perhaps we have another issue to be considered, that of the rave as a site (or not) for commodity exchange. This contrasts with the inaction of the national government and highlights only more vividly the Criminal Justice Act as part of the disempowering discourse of regulation which Foucault identifies at work in the constitution of modern disciplinary spaces. Here again, we see that the Act is part of a long history which should be measured not in years or even decades, but in centuries.

LISTENING TO MODERNITY

We can hear much of this history in the music which has been produced in the west since the Renaissance. The classical tradition itself was defined, in a way, by the gradual detachment of music from the dance. In the various changes in form and composition which mark music from the sixteenth to the nineteenth century, we can hear the shift of the principal site of music's consumption away from the dance-floor to the concert-hall. The gradual shift from dance-related forms, the gradual move away from repetition and rhythm towards melody and complex harmony as sources of musical pleasure, all bear witness to this process.[20] We shouldn't forget, of course, that the music which has come down to us from these periods, was the music of the ruling classes. What evidence there is suggests that the distance between the music and dances of the court, and those of the peasantry, were not nearly so wide during the sixteenth century as they were to become. Also, the development of the concert hall and of a music which bore no trace of the dance - for all that it widened the accessibility of performances to members of a certain self-defining audience - was part of the process by which a distinct elite music discourse was articulated.[21] We shouldn't forget, either, that music discourse is always fissured and differentiated; dance has always remained present in music discourse, and is never entirely eradicable from it. But what is certain is that within the dominant culture of western Europe, dance became an increasingly devalued activity during these centuries, as the body and its pleasures were increasingly devalued (in ways which the medieval ascetic attention to the body cannot be said to have devalued them), and that this can be heard in the gradual expulsion of rhythm from the list of acceptably pleasurable aspects of music. Rhythm, repetition and dance have in fact always been associated with the irrational and plebeian (and, importantly, feminine) pleasures of the body in the imagination of modernity; the history of its music has at times seemed like little more than the history of their suppression.[22]

This applies principally to instrumental music, of course. While the history of modernity has been the history of music which couldn't be danced

20. See, for instance, Wilfred Mellers, *The Sonata Principle*, London, Barrie & Rockliff, 1962, pp1-9.

21. See Jacques Attali, *Noise: the political economy of music*, trans. B. Massumi, Manchester, MUP, 1985, chapters 2-3.

22. See Judith Hanna, *Dance, Sex and Gender*, Chicago, UCP, 1988, p123; John Shepherd 'Music and Male Hegemony' in his *Music as Social Text*, and also Susan McClary 'Getting Down off the Beanstalk' in her *Feminine Endings*.

to, the much older discourses of metaphysics have never actually been sure that purely instrumental music, of any kind, was such a good idea at all. Going back, once again, to Plato; his comments on the correct way to compose music are very interesting:

> We shall then adapt the beat and tune to the appropriate words, and not the words to the beat and tune.[23]

23. Plato, *Republic*, trans. Desmond Lee London: Penguin, 1974, p160.

Two thousand years later, Immanuel Kant felt pretty similar about the matter. In fact, the philosophical tradition has tended to view the whole idea of music as a very secondary accompaniment to the voice. This idea survived until the moment when Beethoven decisively demonstrated that instrumental music could be composed and performed without the slightest danger that anybody might want to dance to it (after which philosophers did start to get very excited about music's ability to offer a wholly spiritual and/or intellectual, entirely *non-physical*, experience). Andrew Bowie, in his detailed account of the changing status of music within the philosophical tradition, describes the change which occurred in philosophical attitudes to music between the times of Kant and Schopenhauer (precisely the time during which Beethoven became established as the key figure in music discourse and the concert hall became fully established as the dominant site of musical consumption) thus: [24]

24. See Barthes' essay 'Musica Practica' in Barthes, *Image Music Text*, trans. Stephen Heath, London, Fontana, 1977.

> From a union of music and language, where language is the senior partner, emerges a divorce, in which the formerly junior partner becomes autonomous and is no longer bound to represent what a verbal text can express.[25]

25. Andrew Bowie, *Aesthetics & Subjectivity: from Kant to Nietzsche*, Manchester, MUP, 1990, p179.

It is important to understand that this ancient prejudice against instrumental music is a further manifestation of one of the most notable aspects of 'metaphysics'. Derrida has demonstrated exhaustively that this tradition has consistently privileged the voice over other forms of communication. In the authority and authenticity of the living human voice metaphysics finds manifested and symbolised all that it holds most dear; the figure of hearing-oneself speak is the very figure of being-as-presence. There is a powerful sense in which Western culture itself could be described as a culture of the voice; our phonetic systems of writing attempt to mimic faithfully the voice, our notions of communication, of relation, of politics and representation are all thought in terms of metaphors of speech.[26] And very often our musics have been subjugated to what is in fact, within the dominant musical imagination of the West, the *least* physical of instruments, the voice.[27] Can we imagine, then, musics more inimical to that whole set of imperatives which privileges the voice and its song and suppresses rhythm and repetition, the body and its dance, than the various musics which recent dance culture has produced? Musics which convey no information, which have no words,

26. See, for instance, Derrida, *Of Grammatology*, trans. G. S. Spivak, Baltimore, John Hopkins, 1974, pp1-87.

27. This is discussed in Barthes' classic essay 'The Grain of the Voice' in Barthes, *Image Music Text*, trans. Stephen Heath, London, Fontana, 1977, p189.

which exist only to dance to, transgress prohibitions which at least certain people have been trying to lay down for millennia.

These things obviously cannot be separated out neatly; they are all bound up with the whole history of 'the West'. What is clear enough is that dancing, the crowd, and music with repetitive beats have been things which the dominant culture has tried to suppress and to regulate at least for the whole history of modernity, and that the philosophers and would-be legislators have wanted us to get rid of since Plato. [28]

28. This word 'suppress' (like 'repress') is always problematic after Foucault's problematisation of the notion of power-as-repressive, but I continue to use it here specifically to denote a certain denigration and devaluation which is always necessarily involved in the institution of conceptual 'violent hierarchies' such as that which actively sets out to de-value and delegitimate music-without-the voice, music-for-dancing, in the texts of philosophers from Plato to Hegel.

29. Spencer, *Society and the Dance*, Cambridge, CUP, 1985 p28.

So if the prohibition of intoxicated dancing, of social revelry, and of rhythmic instrumental music is as old as modernity itself, and if the desire to enact this prohibition is far older, doesn't this mean that to resist this prohibition we need a politics which can, in some sense, think itself beyond the limits of that modernity? I won't say a 'post-modern' politics because, apart from anything, it would invoke a critique of existing modernity which is at least as old as modernity. What I will say is that it seems clear enough that we have to understand that to oppose the provisions of the Criminal Justice Act is ultimately to oppose attitudes which are far more deeply ingrained in our culture than is often acknowledged. The opposition to dancing in intoxicated crowds comes along with the invention of the modern subject itself. The very idea that human beings are hermetically sealed units, irreducible and unitary individuals, rational agents, is challenged by the ecstasy and collectivity of the dance. As Paul Spencer writes of dancers the world over, [In] their *ecstasy* they literally *stand outside*; standing outside of oneself, especially when that means exposing one's individuality to the being of others, is what that metaphysics of the subject which has dominated European culture at least since the seventeenth century cannot tolerate. [29] But to resist that intolerance is to recognise that all of our common-sense notions about self, reason and value might also have to be put into question at the same time. It is crucial to remember that the politics of the vast majority of the left - certainly, at least, of the Labour Party and the Marxist left - is just as deeply imbedded in such conventional notions as that of the Tories.

ROCK AND THE POLITICS OF REPRESENTATION

So is rave nothing more than the re-emergence of an archaic resistance to the culture of modernity? Certainly many of those people involved with rave culture, and have a specific commitment to paganism, seem to believe so. Is rave, as my line of argument thus far might seem to suggest, a kind of essential deconstruction, an inevitable and perpetual symptom of the socio-political text of modernity deconstructing itself? Does this imply, therefore, that the Criminal Justice Act is merely an instance of metaphysics seeking to perpetuate its violent hierarchies, its binary oppositions between inside and outside, self and other, reason and madness, body and soul? Is the recurrence of this hostile attitude to dancing in crowds eternal and always the same? Are rave culture and music inherently deconstructive?

Of course not. To understand the reasons for rave culture's emergence, and the nature of the opposition to it, we must look to the specific historical circumstances of their emergence. This involves a discussion of 'youth culture' in a way which, under other circumstances, I would be radically opposed to. The 'idealised' 'youth culture' I'm going to discuss is that more-or-less homogenous, largely white, largely middle class, largely male, explicitly music-centred formation whose claim to represent the attitudes and aspirations of more than a fraction of young people has always been questionable to say the least. I don't think that this culture's dubious legitimacy actually makes it impossible to evaluate; it is a real phenomenon, the culture of the *NME* and the *Melody Maker*, whose privileged position allows it to have cultural effects disproportionate to the size of its immediate constituency.[30]

1988, I suggest, can be located as the moment of an epistemological break in at least this strand of British youth culture. Between then and the moment somewhere back in the mid-1970s when punk took hold of one part of the collective imagination and disco the other, a fairly consistent set of attitudes had remained in place (despite the many mutations they went through). Take a look at a copy of *NME* from early 1976, and we see a fairly coherent politico-aesthetic agenda in place, but one which seems very alien to what we have come to expect from the 'indie' music press. This is a critical discourse which valorises musical virtuosity over spontaneity, and American blues-forms over more characteristically British kinds of rock music. NME had obviously yet to fully encounter the shock of feminism or the radical critique of musical values which punk would instigate. Take a look at a copy from 18 months later, and you'll see firmly in place the whole set of terms and values which dominated British rock journalism up until very recently.[31] If we look at the history of British rock culture of this period 1976 to 1988, of the artists who we might describe as hegemonic within British youth culture (despite the attempts by various critical practitioners, from post-punks like The Fall to New Pop theorists such as Paul Morely, to break the status quo) we can see a fairly consistent thread running right through from The Sex Pistols to The Smiths. Despite very different aesthetic agendas, a number of crucial equivalences and assumptions rest unchallenged. The supreme good is Authenticity; artists must speak the truth of their (and others') situations. Authenticity is guaranteed by the presence of a specific type of instrumentation (rhythm guitar, bass, drums, voice) and the refusal to deploy this instrumentation in displays of excessive virtuosity (which might attract attention away from the singing voice). The singer is all-important, and it is crucial that he (it was always he) be authentic and *sincere*, because his fundamental role is to *represent* the culture from which he comes. In speaking the truth of his situation he must speak the truth of his audience's situation. Be it the first wave of anger at the realisation that the welfare-state settlement was crumbling in 1977, or the sense of resignation as the Thatcher government rolled into its second and third terms, the singer (be

30. What's more, the recent remarkable and unprecedented co-incidence of 'indie' culture with mainstream pop, has actually made it far easier to discuss it as a mainstream - even, perhaps, 'hegemonic' - formation.

31. This - admittedly impressionistic and anecdotal - evidence for this assertion is derived from my examinination of the popular music press archives at the National Sound Archive.

he Jonny Rotten, Ian Curtis, Morrissey or a dozen others) should say what *we* feel.

A number of imperatives were implicit in this particular set of terms and values. Quite obviously, the phonologocentric ideal of the pure voice, of the *logos* as the site of truth, can be seen at work here. At the same time, we see here an attempt to make this ideal coincide with a politics of representation. However little figures like The Smiths may have advertised, or even been aware of, their politicality, implicit in everything they did - indeed in the fact that they did anything at all - was a faith in such a politics. Faced with the hegemony of Thatcherite individualism, this discourse appealed to a notion of political community not at all unlike the one which Thatcherism was in the process of displacing; the one which had characterised the era of post-war security whose passing was mourned by everyone from the Pistols to the Smiths. When The Sex Pistols screamed 'we're the future; *your future!*', what was the point of this outburst, so directly addressed to those in authority, if it was not ultimately an *appeal* to The Nation (who they must, at some level, have been assumed to be listening) not to forget them? A protest always carries with it the implication that the protester and their audience share a set of values according to which the justice of the protest can be judged. This is what, in various forms, the whole dominant strand of English rock culture during this period amounted to. However nihilistic they may have seemed at the time, not even Joy Division (or their disinherited children, the Goths) can really be located outside of this discourse of protest. For just what is the point in complaining about how alienated you are, how poor you are, how bored you are, *unless you believe that someone out there might be listening and that they might actually do something about it*? As agents of protest, the singers and songwriters were therefore to be the politico-cultural *representatives* of their audience. In popular culture, as in parliament, we all had our chosen representatives, whose sincerity and realism could comfort us, assuring us that we were not alone, and whose eloquence would doubtless, someday, bring this misery to an end.

Now, the logic of representation is always ambiguous. Ernesto Laclau elucidates the nature of this ambiguity in 'New Reflections on the Revolution of Our Time':

> If the representative and the represented constitute the same and single will, the 're' of representation disappears since the same will is present in two different places. Representation can therefore only take place to the extent that the transparency entailed by the concept is never achieved.[32]

32. Laclau, *New Reflections on the Revolution of Our Time*, London, Verso, 1990, p39.

We can perhaps understand the dominant tendency in British rock discourse during the period 1976-88, as one of trying to erase this constitutive distance in the relationship between representative and represented. The voice, the

Logos as truth, was the ideal point at which this transparency would be achieved in the constitution of a hypostatic communion in which we would all be the same, speaking with one voice, feeling the same thing. Didn't we see something of this in the spectacle of fans during the 1980s not just adopting a specific *style* but dressing up to resemble their idols as precisely as possible? The armies of Morrissey look-a-likes who roamed our provincial streets in the mid-80s were only the most obvious example[33]. There are many other, less extreme examples of this logic, and the underlying faith in traditional forms of representative politics that went with it, governing the pop music discourses of this period. This was the moment of Rock Against Racism and Red Wedge, both governed by the notion that rock could and should 'speak out' on the issues of the day, and that this could have some effect. And what more vivid example of the whole set of terms and values which dominated this era than the could we ask for than the music and persona of Billy Bragg? Billy, whose guitar (barely played at all) served *only* as a marker of folk/punk authenticity spoke out like no popular British performer before or since. Only at a moment when musical legitimacy was defined *entirely* by the authenticity of the re/presentative voice could that quavering, stripped-bare Dagenham voice ever have been taken seriously.

In 1988, a number of things happened. The advent of Acid House marked the emergence for the first time of a popular music which did not focus on the singing voice, and given the significance of the voice in the discourses of western culture the importance of this development can hardly be overestimated.[34] While Disco and Northern Soul had shifted the consumption of music away from the concert and back to the dance-floor, they had retained the singing voice as a central point of musical identification and representation, and a notion of dance as a mode of competitive performance. The emergence of rave displaced those terms and left in their place a radical deconstruction of the status of audience, artist music and dance (and it is quite possible that such a non-competitive mode of dance had *never* before been known in the West). Making no claim to musical integrity, Acid House offered pleasure - as much as possible - *entirely* for pleasure's sake; where even disco had sometimes promised that a successful performance on the dance floor would be rewarded one way or another at the end of an evening, Acid House (which had more-or-less detached itself from its origins on the Chicago gay scene by the time it reached the UK) offered only itself.[35] This valorisation of the moment is, I suggest, the organising logic of rave culture and of the various political movements which have come to be associated with it in recent years.

AFTER THE FUTURE

The Criminal Justice Act has done more than anything to highlight the connections between rave culture (specifically the free rave movement) and the resurgence of direct-action politics. What I think is important to understand is that a particular if ambiguous logic does underlie all of these

33. It might well be pointed out that this wasn't exactly new; The Beatles spawned look-a-likes and were supposed to represent the spirit of their age. But it is important to understand that the Beatles and their contemporaries were different because, they legitimated themselves variously according to their ability to offer a good time or to the authority with which they claimed to *lead* their culture (being presented as in tune with rather than in opposition to the political culture of their day), representing the highest possible point of fulfilment of their audiences' aspirations (rather than representing the truth of their audiences' situations). Likewise the Bowie fans of the early 1970s who dressed up to look like Ziggy Stardust were self-consciously participating in a *critique* of authentic identity. A proper consideration of these issues might lead us to Borch-Jacobsen's notion of mimetic identification on the one hand, to Judith Butler's model of phantasmatic identification on the other.

34. I should be borne in mind that the transformation of jazz from a popular to an 'intellectual' music coincided with the decline in importance of the song form to jazz composition.

35. The emergence of Acid house and its significance is usefully discussed by various writers (with varying degrees of hyperbole, inaccuracy and theoretical inconsistency) in Redhead (ed), *Rave Off*, London, Avebury, 1993.

36. Laclau, *op. cit.* pxv.

related politico-cultural developments. In a certain sense these developments might be said to take part in 'Radical Democracy's abandonment of revolutionary politics (predicated as it was on a historical teleology and a simplistic model of power) for a politics concerned with 'the multiplication of 'public spaces' [36]. But they are also in danger of collapsing into what we might term a radical *spatialization* of politics; a search for immediacy and an abandonment of any real orientation to the future. Where the politics of representation is about speaking vicariously - through a singer, through an MP - the new politics of the present is about trying to make something happen *now*. Get a house *now* (by squatting), stop the road *now*, dance *now*, rush your little head off *now*. The future, as an abstract point to be waited on and hoped for, has no purchase here; this is a politics which occurs in space - the space of raves, of squats, of roads - but which doesn't have time to occupy itself *with* time. We hear this in the music; techno, trance, jungle and garage are all about creating a pleasurable moment rather than telling a story. They are not, like rock songs, about creating a space for fantasy, for identification or catharsis. They are not to make us feel that we are like (or different from) the performer, or to give us hope, or to make us angry. They are to be used rather than to be *understood*. They are about collapsing the future into the present. One of the most vivid illustrations of this phenomenon lies in the fact that the core group who have made up the 'crusty' culture which has been central to the development of the free-rave movement, was in fact drawn from the remnants of the Anarcho-punk culture of the 1980s. A culture whose politics and aesthetics were more radically determined by an anti-hedonist revolutionary fatalism (until the revolution, the only legitimate form of music would be a painful, noisy, repetitive background to didactic political sloganising) than any other, gave way to one centred on immediate sensory pleasure almost overnight.[37] What do we make of this spatialization of politics and culture?

37. I should point out that this assertion - and indeed, much of the latter part of this paper - is based on no more or less reliable source than my own participation in these cultures over the past few years.

38. The role of figures like John Peel in this process can't be ignored; it was specifically the Smiths' singularity and originality which Peel always claimed to be impressed by.

On the one hand this is a realistic and fairly effective response to political and cultural situation of the past decade. A consideration of other events of 1988 can certainly give rise to such a reading. This was the moment when the Labour Party Policy Review first signalled to the world that the British labour movement was abandoning any vision of a future that would be radically different from the present. 1988 also marked a profound break in the critical discourses of rock culture itself. With the departure of The Smiths, the search for a band to take their place quickly came to be couched in terms of a need to *maintain a tradition*. Whereas The Smiths (who, in remaining the hegemonic artists of British rock culture for five years, had served as an unprecedented point of consolidation and sedimentation for a particular set of values) had initially been legitimated in terms of their originality, the whole series of bands who were heavily promoted as their successors were discussed in terms of the authenticity and sincerity not with which they represented a unique and historically specific present but with which they reproduced rock's past.[38] The Stone Roses were the first (but not the last) band to whom the music press attached the term 'retro', not as a term of abuse, but as a badge of authenticity. Rock culture had declared itself explicitly conservative.

So from one perspective, what began to happen in the most radical areas of popular culture in 1988 - and has continued since - was the only thing left that could happen. To put it very simply, we - the radical youth - stopped waiting for things to improve and started to try to make life bearable for ourselves. We had given the mainstream political culture (or its revolutionary doubles), and the Labour Party which was part of it, a decade to get itself together. We had gone out and voted for it, we had joined the young socialists and CND, marched, stayed at peace camps. We had bought Billy Bragg records (or hand-pressed Crass albums), and we had gotten nowhere. Our voices were just not being heard. If life could not be made tolerable by the welfare state, if the crying of voices was not going to make our lives worth living, then it would have to be made so by means which the poor and disenfranchised had always used; drugs, dancing and sporadic physical resistance.

Rave music and direct-action politics threatens a whole set of values which underpin not just the culture of the home counties, but of the Labour Party and *Melody Maker* as well; the reaction to this threat is coming from a number of not unrelated areas. The post-1988 generation's abstention from a certain political culture involved a wholesale rejection of that metaphysics which underpinned it; that same metaphysics which had guaranteed the authenticity and representativeness of the rock voice, so that at the same moment; traditional politics *and* rock culture began to lose their youth constituency. We've all gasped in horror at the social conservatism of Jack Straw and Tony Blair, but we should also consider the hysterical efforts of the music press in 1995 in insisting that good old-fashioned pop songs with proper choruses and well-written lyrics was what good music is all about. No-one who reads the British music press regularly can fail to have noticed that the critics and hype-merchants who invented 'Britpop' have been acutely aware of the need to declare over and over and over again that rock'n'roll isn't dead - *honest!* - as if Blur and Oasis would slip down the plug hole of history if they let them out of their sight for a moment. Well, they're probably right, but the guardians of this culture of the voice are not going to allow their last white hopes to peter out, because Britpop is nothing more and nothing less than the organised cultural reaction to all that is most threatening about rave. As young people started to dance to music without words - made originally for black queens - the boys in the indie press began their desperate rearguard action, and it isn't yet over. We've seen it every time a pallid vocalist backed by a conventional four-piece has been heralded as the second-coming of those great saviours, The Smiths (who appeared at just the moment when, faced with post-punk experimentation, New Pop and the first stirrings of electronic dance, British Rock last looked in danger of collapsing), and we'll see it again.[39]

39. The Stone Roses, The Happy Mondays, James, Suede, Blur, Echobelly are just a few of the bands to have been touted explicitly as 'The New Smiths' - for at least a week - over the past six years.

Even the name 'Britpop', makes clear what it is that this reaction offers as an alternative. It offers a coherent, inclusive yet restricted sense of community. This is specifically British music; not American, not European (and therefore not black, not queer, not experimental, not dangerous), not even aware that anywhere else exists. Perhaps this is one reason for the fierce rivalry between Blur and Oasis; the need for a coherent sense of community ('communion', even), for a unified and univocal culture, cannot tolerate competing visions of what that culture should look or sound like. And here we can see Britpop's close affinity to Blairism.[40] Rather than offer any radical solution to the collapse of their respective traditions, both projects seek to re-imagine a lost coherence, a moment when we all spoke with one voice, and one voice spoke for all of us.[41] It's hardly surprising that the most radical elements of British popular culture have looked to musical and political forms which refuse utterly the terms shared by Britpop and the new communitarianism.

And yet, while recognising the real possibility of it's articulation with radical democratic agendas, we can hardly endorse uncritically the nature and shape of this refusal. I borrowed the term 'spatialization' which I used to describe this new tendency from Ernesto Laclau, and his deployment of that term makes it quite clear that such a process is far from being progressive. Laclau writes:

> The 'spatialization' of an event consists of eliminating its temporality.[42]

The failure to conceive of power and causality in temporal and historical terms is the overriding weakness of the emergent political culture, which so far has had little success in defending itself from the Criminal Justice Act. Its enacted deconstruction of the politics of representation and the culture of the voice, is largely being conducted in terms which perpetuate an equally powerful metaphysics of presence, a metaphysics of the immediate and a metaphysics of the *deed*. A faith in representative politics is being replaced not so much by a constructive critique of that politics but by a faith in the consoling virtues of 'direct action' as a *replacement for* engagement in forms of politics which - although failing to offer the unmediated experience of physically stopping someone from tearing down a house at just that moment - actually have any hope of achieving their stated goals.[43] It is important to understand that a real and effective materialist pragmatism is also part of the discourse of the new direct action movements, but it is a part which is often rhetorically submerged by millenarianism and an explicit metaphysics of presence; *being here now* is often given as the ultimate and only legitimate mode of political expression. What we must recognise, from a deconstructive and radical democratic perspective, is that while the Criminal Justice Act and Blairism and Britpop manifest a particular and conservative politics of modernity, a politics which simply constitutes itself as the polar opposite of this tendency is no solution. What all of these positions share is that in a

40. A friend of mine recently started work as a research assistant for a Labour MP. He was saddened, if unsurprised, to discover on one of his first days at work that Jack Straw's office is staffed entirely by Oasis fans.

41. For a discussion of communitarianism with which I am entirely in sympathy see Beatrix Campbell 'Old Fogeys and Angry Young Men' in *Soundings*, Autumn 1995.

42. Laclau, *op. cit.*, p41.

43. For some interesting observations on these new and not-so-new political forms, see Doreen Massey's interview with Heather Hunt in *Soundings, op. cit.*

certain sense their responses to the dislocations and disruptions of (late?) modernity and industrialisation are all in danger of collapsing into mere reaction, seeking to preserve something rather than re-imagine it. We can also see the de-historicising and reifying tendencies at work in rave culture when we consider that the most powerful political discourse of that culture defines its resistance to existing modernity, not in terms of a deconstructive critique of Enlightenment reason or phallogocentrism, but in terms of the definitively teleological models of New Age. The belief in a pre-ordained 'evolutionary leap' as the source of our salvation, the belief that 'By changing ourselves we can change the world', serve to contain any radical possibilities that this culture may have. [44] This is *not*, I want to emphasise, because this 'alternative' culture is failing to constitute itself as sufficiently 'oppositional', but because in replicating these terms it is constituting itself as no alternative at all to the culture it claims to critique.[45] For New Age is, if nothing else, the ultimate politics of the proper. Individualising all problems and all solutions, it offers a protection against the world, a picket-fence around your subjectivity, and (in its millenarian forms) a salvation without the difficulty of social action. Let us return to Nancy's comment on ecstasy :

> 'Ecstasy...defines the impossibility, both ontological and gnostological, of absolute immanence...and consequently the impossibility either of an individuality, in the precise sense of the term, or of a pure collective totality'[46]

Immanence is precisely what the currently hegemonic discourses of rave culture (and - in certain ways - the direct-action movement) seek to define as its central experiences. The ecstatic experience of raving is taken in all of its radical alterity and defined as on the one hand a cosy buffer against the presence of others, on the other as the point at which all identity collapses into an atemporal (therefore undifferentiated, therefore meaningless) unity. The historicity and politicality of this experience are defined entirely in terms of an evolutionary (and technological determinist) teleology[47]. Drugs in themselves, outside of social relationships and situations, are thought of sources of pleasure and enlightenment. Digital technology is thought of as liberating in itself. 'The Earth' is thought of as an independent organism with an implacable and unitary will. All of these developments are explained according to a scheme which seems uncannily like the Hegelian model of human consciousness moving towards the Absolute, which Marx critiqued so very long ago. And as Laclau writes, 'Any teleological conception of change is...essentially spatialist', and therefore reifying, de-historicising, mystificatory.[48]

If the opportunities which rave culture has to engage in and articulate with democratic struggles are to be realised, then it is as much the discourses of New Age as those of Communitarianism, Back-to-Basics and the communitarian back-to-basics of Britpop which need to be

44. This was the launch slogan of the New Age trance club, Megatripolis in 1994.

45. I'm referring to the distinction (no longer sustainable, I would suggest) drawn by Raymond Williams between 'oppositional' and 'alternative' cultures in his essay on the Base/Superstructure question.

46. Nancy, *op. cit*. p6.

47. See, for instance , the writings of the 'rave guru' Terrence Mckenna, such as his *Food of the Gods*, in which he argues that the collective ingestion of pscilosybin is both the source and the key to the future of human evolution.

48. Laclau op. cit. p42

deconstructed. The deconstruction of that metaphysics of presence which governs the thinking of many involved in the new direct action movements (including those committed to the defence of rave culture) is a task imperative to the possible realisation of their goals as much as anything else. Without some engagement with the politics of representation, with parliamentary politics, the CJA is never going to be repealed, and it still seems unlikely that a single road-building plan will be shelved. Without a politics of the future as well as of the present, the day after the E wears off will always be a nightmare. And we shouldn't blindly condemn the aspirations which rock culture's defence of the communal song embodies; the culture of the voice may often have suppressed the pleasures of the dance, but it has also made possible the invention of democracy, and the very discourse of human and civil rights according to which the CJA is now being resisted. It isn't even as if this has not been recognised. Various developments, from the involvement of rave groups in voter-registration campaigns to the quite remarkable form of community politics being pioneered by the Exodus collective in Luton demonstrate, as vividly as any philosophical analogy, that rave culture has the potential to offer models of democratic participation which can manifest simultaneous commitments to collective action and to the passionate defence of plurality and individuality in ways which few other cultural formations can.

The points which I want to emphasise are therefore only small and cautionary. On the one hand, those on the Left who (as most seem to) wish to maintain a principled and well-intentioned opposition to the Criminal Justice Act might have to be prepared to challenge some the most fundamental common-sense notions of self, of rationality and identity which underlie our political culture.[49] That might mean, for instance, not just supporting the legalisation of raves, or of cannabis, or of ecstasy, but of taking the far more radical step of being prepared to ditch the whole idea that drugs and their attendant pleasures are a *problem*, and to realise just how much is shared by the Left and the Right, and even by the dominant strands of 'youth culture' (so often thought as inherently 'oppositional', or at least 'alternative'). On the other hand, and given the current wave of enthusiasm for movements such as the anti-roads movement on the independent left we must avoid falling into an uncritical irrationalism or a naive endorsement of cultural tendencies whose meaning is still being contested. These interrelated movements do not constitute a homogenous phenomenon, and the possibility of a radical rave culture is still only one possibility among many, dependant as it is in large part on a certain resistance to the hegemonic discourses of New Age individualism. Whatever forms our support may take, we need to think carefully about where we lend it.

Thanks to Rachel Bowlby, Anne Coddington, James Donald, John Gladney, Anthony Hewitt, Emma Mulvey, Judith Squires and Mark Perryman for direct and indirect help and encouragement.

49. It might be said that this is no new comment, that people have been saying this for decades. True enough, but it needs saying again at this moment as it perhaps never has before, if the failure of the Left to maintain any sizeable youth constituency is ever going to be addressed.

e IS FOR *EKSTASIS*

Drew Hemment

Dance culture is interesting for its journeys through sound and explorations into bodily expression, but also for the numerous sites of cultural activity that have paralleled its growth or been inspired by its example. However, debate all too often focuses on the question of its association with the drug 'ecstasy'. In what follows I seek to shift the terrain away from pharmacology by investigating ecstatic dimensions that do not come in tablet form. This has required an extensive philosophical discussion to develop terms adequate to the task, although I try to balance this with a consideration of actual sounds and concrete events, wherever possible discussing events that I have experienced at first hand.

Traditional cultural critique has drawn on the notion of *authenticity* to oppose the tendency of capitalism to reduce all social interaction to commodity relations of universal equivalence. This, it is claimed, drives all experience towards the meaningless exchange of commodities, and renders the genuine expression of the actors' social conditions impossible. Any attempt to subvert is short-lived, serving only to strengthen the capitalist machine.

This strategy then would have us *protect* culture from capitalism's tendency to subvert its codes and undermine its points of reference. But in doing so it only serves to provide the support that capitalism needs to progress. Capitalism needs a continual supply of new markets, and it is through developing new sites of cultural meaning that new markets are opened up. No-one does this so well as those academics and journalists who build careers out of searching out and labelling new sites of resistance or authentic culture in the name of a politics of liberation.

An alternative strategy that is perhaps more appropriate to an age of nihilism is to work from within so as to 'push that which wants to fall'. Rather than clutch at the elusive straws offered by a past we never had, seek points of departure within the potentials of the present. Instead of placing hope in a future liberation, exploit folds or fissures within the machine where new autonomies can flourish today.

A term that may be articulated against the technologies of the present without drawing us into a dialectical, and so ultimately self-defeating, opposition is *ekstasis*. This is the original Greek word for 'ecstasy'. It was reanimated by Martin Heidegger, in whose philosophy it stands for a difference or a standing out from the surface of life's contingencies that allows a more profound contemplation of Being. Heidegger considered this to be the fundamental ontological principle of human Being, the most essential dimension or dynamic of human existence, yet it could be compromised by the technologised existence of modern life, which does not give people the chance to stand apart from the discourses and practices in which they are ensnared.

In this paper I shall be using 'house' as an inclusive term for what has come to be termed 'dance music' and 'dance culture'. In doing so I am following the use of the term prevalent in the UK between roughly 1988 and 1991, the period which provides most of the inspiration to this paper. I shall thereby depart from an understanding of house as one specific genre of dance music. This creates some strain in the text when I discuss the evolution (or involution) of the various genres, but this is a strain that is already present in the cultural field.

Ektasis may seem an inappropriate term for a cultural site edified for its hermeneutic depthlessness. House is the dark side of critical theory's dystopic moon. It has flowered on the barren ground consequent upon the death of aura and authenticity: house is not art *in* the age of mechanical reproduction, it is the art *of* the age of mechanical reproduction. It is a celebration of the texture of expression, a manipulation of sounds and a soliciting of distortions: the medium is the message, and its mutation the mode. But here I want both to place under question the easy assumption of an insipid postmodernism and to depart from the heights of Heideggarian philosophy and rearticulate a theorisation of *ekstasis* in accordance with the concerns and considerations of dance culture itself.

HOUSE WITHOUT A HOME

It is revealing to consider the genealogy of the meaning of the word 'ecstasy': it has changed from denoting religious revelation to signifying a mixture of intense pleasure and loss of control (usually sexual or drug induced). What is important is not the religious aspect, but that it has degenerated from a life affirming experience fundamental to one's orientation to the world to a casual and inconsequential psychological state. Indeed, the meaning has strayed even further from that of any significant lived experience with the word coming to denote a means by which this state is achieved, namely the drug methylenedio-xymethamphetamine (MDMA). To say that this amounts to a degeneration is not to criticise a particular technology (MDMA), but to criticise the general technologisation of modern life.

Whilst we might be dissatisfied with the condition of modernity, it would be a mistake to call for a return to a pre-modern form of life. The ecstatic mode is less of a lost past than a potential which lies dormant in the present, blocked both by modernity and by the hallucinogenic visions of the good life with which modernity is opposed. To turn to *ekstasis* is to (re)turn to a mode of existence which we have forgotten - which we have written off as *mere* pleasure, not worthy to be treated as a serious concern, and as an exception or extreme, as something extraneous to day to day existence.

But a turn to *ekstasis* is not intended to rescue our humanity - quite the reverse. For it is our humanity, and specifically the puritan self, that holds our desire in suspense, and which would be undone by a resurgence of *ekstasis*. Two thousand years of Christian history has burnt DEBT into our flesh. Under capitalism this heritage is reanimated such that the same expenditure is seen not as atonement or penance for an original or prior sin, but as the price of the pleasures and securities which we naturally lack. Under the cover of the seemingly benign discourse of needs and wants, desire is driven towards a negative determination.

> The deliberate creation of lack as a function of market economy is the art of a dominant class. This involves deliberately organising wants and needs amid an abundance of production; making all of desire teeter and fall victim to the great fear of not having one's needs satisfied.[1]

1. Deleuze and Guattari, *Anti-Oedipus*, University of Minnesota, 1983, 28, p35-6

Lack actively structures the subjectivity of the modern individual, resulting in Nietzschean terms in a reactive, slave mentality, where action is guided not by its own propensities, but by a resentful reaction against its environment. This is not just a matter of individual angst, however, but of the determination of desire by social codes: blocked up and hemmed in, desire is channelled down prescribed routes, unable to follow the trajectory of its own potential.

This is a dilemma which will not be answered by political means, which operate at the level of calculative rationality. This itself drives desire towards stasis and only serves to reproduce the dominant mode of organisation and investment of desire. As opposed to introducing an extra level of codification - as a political intervention would do - it is only through scrambling the social codes that desire can be let loose.

But to say that politics is inadequate to this task and call for an intervention in the structuring of desire is not to invoke a naive politics of self-expression. It is rather to confront questions of unconscious desire that are effaced or ignored by standard modes of political action. This is thus what Foucault, Deleuze and Guattari refer to as *micropolitics*. This involves a thinking of desire as a positive and primary field of forces which underlies subjectivity and the derivative determinations of need, and which is not restricted to the internality of the human subject, but directly invests the social field. These forces are a conjunction of intensity of desire and direction of desire. The rationalist ego represents a sedimentation of these forces in which they are pinned down and secured against their own tendency to divert.

In dance the body stands forth and becomes ecstatic. If the self is a sedimentation of a certain stable alignment of forces, the ecstatic body sets those forces loose. To lose the self, then, is not just an abandonment of rational thought, but a positive freeing of the forces that traverse the body.

Ekstasis exposes the body to its own finitude, by taking emphasis away from the body as an object and placing it on the body as the unstable intersection of these forces. The ecstatic body is constantly unfolding: completed only by death, a body's inner-most nature is to differ from itself, to break with the present, to stand out from the norm.

Much is made of such a 'loss of self' on the dancefloor. But it should be noted that we are witnessing a generalised loss of self both on and *off* the dancefloor. The self that is 'lost' on the dancefloor is neither abstract nor eternal, but the historical product of a puritan heritage - and this heritage is in crisis. Amidst a generalised loss of meaning, the modern subject is cut adrift, disorientated and unsure.

But while some shift the features of the cultural landscape around in a postmodern pastiche, for others irony doesn't signal detachment. On the other side of nihilism new formations are emerging, this time exploiting the faultlines in the cultural landscape by slipping through the gaps. Ecstatic dance offers one such line of flight. Dance culture exploits the power of music to build a future on the desolate terrain of the present.

it may be that the sound molecules of pop music are at this very moment implanting here and there a people of a new type.[2]

2. Deleuze and Guattari, *A Thousand Plateaus*, Athlone, 1988, p346

This autonomy exacerbates the insecurity of traditional power centres - from international corporations to local politicians - and thus invites reprisals. Steering a course between *flight* ('dreams are not enough') and *protectionism* ('don't protect it, let it loose'), house builds a space which functions by an independent logic - and which is thus hidden by virtue of being incommensurable and protected by virtue of being unassimilable. This explains its enigmatic relation to the postmodern world of which it is a part: at the same time as being a method of escape, house has provided many with their only home, a source of meaning in a meaningless world.

Music is a powerful mobilising force. It carries an unrivalled potency for breaking the restraints imposed by an environment, of uprooting and setting things in motion. But at the same time the practices of taking up the music and making it one's own (listening, dancing, playing, producing, promoting/organising) yield a sense of belonging and a space in which to dwell. This is more than metaphorical excess when it comes to house music. The history of house can be seen as an answer to the command to *turn this house into a home*.

The present privileges enjoyed by club culture had to be fought for. It was only through the struggles of the early pioneers that a space was created within the socius for a nondenumerable cultural site: the relaxation in the licensing of night clubs took place only to 'defuse the acid bomb'. I do not wish to fetishise the efforts of any one set of 'pioneers', however. It is only retrospectively that their actions seem heroic, and the greatest pioneers are not necessarily those who act first.

In my case even the possibility of fighting these battles owed much to earlier struggles. I was the DJ at the first regular house club in Leeds, the 'acid blues' Twilight Zone.[3] This gave house the chance to establish itself and develop the strength needed to take on the establishment. But it managed this by inserting itself into the space created by the West Indian sound-system culture of all night parties ('blues'), and was wholly parasitical on the success of the West Indian community in Chapeltown in persuading the police to back off. This opening has now effectively been closed down - although this is more a result of the ravages of crack-cocaine on the inner city than of renewed police action.

Dance itself is an articulation of belonging in the sense of an existential projection; the negotiation of Being through the expression of individual style (in the sense of the playing out of one's being-in-the-world). The music is an environment, a house in which one can dwell. And it is through the dance that this house may be turned into a home:

> This mutation [of secondary production - the dance] makes the text [the music] habitable, like a rented apartment. It transforms another person's property into a space borrowed for a moment by a transient.[4]

In moving with the music the dancer becomes a transient, a *nomad*. Just as Australian aborigines sing up the ancestral territory as they travel the songlines, so ecstatic bodies create their own world through the dance. The change is from a sedentary structure of desire, determined through a negative reaction to a hostile outside, to a nomadic structure wherein desire is guided by the features of the landscape themselves. The difference is in the relation between the site of belonging ('house') and the belonging pertaining to it ('dwelling'). A nomad is never without a house - but that house is constantly on the move, never reaching the stasis of a final resting point. And this continual slippage means that the nomad is perpetually faced with the task of turning the house into a home. Only for a nomad is the question of dwelling so immediate.

Nomadic mobility cannot be taken for granted. Modernity suppresses the potential for *ekstasis* through the insistence of its time of continuity. If there is to be any actualisation of the potential for *ekstasis* in the present, the temporal structuring of experience must be contested. Walter Benjamin noted that a general prerequisite for an action-event to affect the world rather than just perpetuate its constrictions is that it must be wrested from the present of historical continuity by a 'blasting apart' of the 'empty, homogeneous time' (calendrical or clock time) that serves only to mask and prolong injustices.[5] Benjamin's primary concern was with the possibility for political action, but the same temporal considerations apply in the case of *ekstasis*. The ecstatic dance is not in itself political, but it is a *micropolitical* event - an intervention in the formation of desire. This requires that the chains of the rationalist ego be broken, and these chains are linked by time.

3. I was no pioneer, however. The credit must go to Jungle Warrior sound system and the urban warriors who provided the energy and attitude to go with it. More than anyone, Angela Cameron was responsible for teaching Leeds how to let it loose.

4. Michel De Certeau, *The Practice of Everyday Life*, University of California Press, 1988, p.xxi

5. See 'Theses on the Philosophy of History', in Walter Benjamin, *Illuminations*, Schocken, New York, 1968. This text has been referred to as 'a handbook for urban guerrillas.'

It is in the resolute encounter of entering the dance that the individual is blasted apart and given anew. Time is given a shock, shattering the coincidence of past-present-future and opening up the fissure from which dancing bodies issue forth. This is the moment of the present's differentiation from itself, the fracture between past and future that is the condition of creativity and change.

The disappearance into the singular field of the music is articulated within a general becoming-unlimited, by which the identities and hierarchies of the ego are abandoned as the dancer confronts the limits of pure possibility. At this point both self and others disappear together. Indeed, the categorical distinction between Self and Other itself disappears, releasing a profound sense of unity.[6]

In entering the dance bodies are lifted out of themselves and onto a plateau at which they confront the externality of the potentials and directionalities of the music. In this collective moment bodies become one with the music, each distinct gesture the fractal-expression of the singular sonic algorithm. This convergence is not-yet an identity; it is rather that music and body enter into a zone of proximity with each other, such that each term becomes indiscernible from the other. This is a reciprocal relation wherein the musical flow is actualised as body-music: music becoming embodied in dance, dancers becoming disembodied as music. These are the two sides of a singular symbiotic relation or block of becoming: 'block is formed, essentially mobile, never in equilibrium'.[7] This dual structure of becoming ensures that this is an *unnatural participation* rather than a return to either a primitive-tribal or natural-infantile state. The externality of the field of music opens up experience to the contingency of the world, thus supplying a vehicle for a becoming-other of the body.

House functions by taking a simple melody or unit of sound (a refrain), setting it in motion, weaving it through a rhythm: 'what is necessary is a simple figure in motion and a plane that is itself mobile'.[8] This mobility ensures that the refrain is always in excess of the structure, able to stand out from its environment. It is out of this ecstatic distance that its affects are produced: set loose from any determining context, the refrain is able to assert itself all the more forcefully in the instant of its recurrence, its power amplified by its simplicity and space. It draws a zone of consistency, a territory, but only in the ambiguity of a territory unsure of itself, perpetually in motion. It is a nomadic block of space-time, a house without a home (HWH).

Swept up and carried off, dancing bodies move with the drift, across peaks and plateaus, in a journey with no destination, just the intensity of the musical moment. The musical energy solicits a flotation of the senses: all determination, 'everything that roots each of us in ourselves, in our morality' is abandoned as the body enters this zone of proximity with the music.[9] 'By process of elimination one is no longer anything more than an abstract line, or a piece in a puzzle that is itself abstract.'[10]

House music has no 'message' and does not 'represent' the social

6. We must be wary when talking of unity, in case this is taken to imply a reduction to the Same, in the same way that the Nazi's channelled the 'collective fascination' of music towards the affirmation of the race at the Nuremberg rallies. Hitler was well aware of the power of amplified noise: 'Without the loudspeaker, we would never have conquered Germany.' Adolph Hitler, *Manual of German Radio*, 1938. Quoted in Jacques Attali, *Noise: The Political Economy of Music*, Minnesota, 1985. What distinguishes ecstatic dance from the Nuremberg shuffle is that the former constructs a unity only through an affirmation of the difference of the body: it is a unity which does not add up.

7. Deleuze & Guattari, 1988, p.305.

8. *Ibid.*, p.344.

9. *Ibid.*, p.279.

10. *Ibid.*, p.279.

conditions of the participants. Words do not feature in house - or, at least, not as themselves. What lyrics there are have invariably been converted into musical elements which carry no epistemological content. In general we may say 'house music makes no sense'. And yet that does not mean that it is *meaningless*. If we challenge the view which sees meaning as exclusively propositional and accept a wider definition of meaning as 'a relationality between subtle patterns of matter ... and the faculties of constitution,'[11] we see that the dancefloor is a space filled with meaning:

11. Justin Barton, *Immanence, Will to Power, Eternal Recurrence,* unpublished doctoral research, University of Warwick, 1995, p.5.

> The different processes of perception and interpretation that go into hearing music generate an experience which repeatedly must be seen as one of meaning - as more than just raw gusts of emotion - even though the meaning is not capable of being translated into propositions.[12]

12. *Ibid.,* p.5.

On the dancefloor there is a disappearance of language, and a disappearance from language: the subject of enunciation becomes inoperative, and hence so does the force of objectification that it carries. Neither subject nor object exist in music. This adds to music's effect of displacing the primacy of vision and rendering the objectifying gaze redundant. This is not to deny that the floors of many night clubs are filled with spectacular glamour. But this usually represents a recolonisation of the dancefloor by the male gaze and is not an inherent tendency of acoustic space, itself 'boundless, directionless, horizonless, the dark side of the mind'.[13]

13. Marshall Mcluhan, *Counter Blast,* (Rapp & Whiting, 1970), p.13.

The unnatural participations are intensified by the inhuman sounds of electronic music. The tonalities and structures of traditional music are limited by the parameters of the instruments on which they are played. Electronic music on the other hand sets tonality loose (releasing creativity from the *discipline* - and exclusivity - of musicianship). The alien aesthetic of techno in particular operates explicitly through the deterritorialisation of sonic matter, creating unsettling sonic profiles that defy any easy emotional response. And, pushing contemporary sound technologies to their extremes, drum'n'bass predicates its aesthetic upon the infinite extension, decomposition and recontextualisation of the sonic instant. A sample is 'time-stretched' (lengthened without change in pitch, robbed of its temperality) and then broken down into the sonic shards from which the rhythmic shapes and proliferating textures are built.

Here music is an *environment*. Form and content implode to leave a flat intensive surface, with musicality more a matter of texture (the *grain of the machine*) than of progression or tonal harmonics. In a similar way to which Brian Eno's ambient music presents compositions which work on and with a particular location, musicianship becomes a craft of sculpting sounds to engage with the energetic surface of the crowd - the aim not intellectual refinement, so much as bodily mobility. Under the impersonal address of the PA it is no longer necessary to strain the ears and focus the mind. Instead one can feel the musical energy traverse the body, and surrender to its flow.

As architecture is 'frozen music' (Schelling), so the soundscape is *fluid*. Though house is an affirmation of the instant, it is not a collection of separate moments but a continuous flow. Whilst many affects result directly from the intensities and textures of the sounds, others follow from the dynamics of the overlapping and intertwined plateaus, which are placed one over the other *in the mix* to create a singular dynamic field. In the studio different elements are layered and juxtaposed, whilst the basic frontline unit of two record decks and a mixer allows the DJ to seamlessly blend sounds in a running mix, or contrast and disrupt in a cut and paste pastiche - refusing the art work any unity or completion, submerging the art 'object' within the *process* of 'working' the floor (DJ terminology).

Since the first time Kraftwerk left the stage and let the drum machine do its thing, repetition has been central to electronic music. Building on the minimalist beats aesthetic developed by the early deck pioneers (who played drum breaks back to back using two copies of the same record), machines which failed in their representational function of simulating real instruments were used to construct a new paradigm characterised by intensive, insistent rhythms.[14] This has resonated with a beats philosophy that traces its origin to tribal ritual and which has marked both the cultural impact and aesthetic of dance music. In this, rhythm is not restricted to a descrete realm of aesthetic contemplation or pleasure, but directly invests the field of lived experience.[15] All action-events have rhythm, a 'way of flowing', just as the body has its own ingrained, 'natural' rhythms (breathing, walking). By creating a sphere of play and experimentation that is fundamentally rhythmic, the music can set up interference patterns that excite the body at the same time as instilling a *zen*-receptivity free from the inhibition of the mind.

With relentless machinic repetition, what used to imply a lack of change becomes the very condition of change, as innovation enters between the beats. Each beat is a sonic missile which cuts into the fabric of narrative continuity, punctuating time and soliciting change. In the continuous 4/4 time of house the main beat propels you forward while cross rhythms pull at you from the sides, distortions and contrasting rhythmic motions toying with your expectations by creating tension and strain.[16] This regular structure can inhibit sonic expression (as is all too often the case), but can also supply a platform from which to depart - both in dance and through disruptions of its rigidly quantised structure in syncopation and swing. Whilst the time structure maintains the regular flow, the spaces between the beats can trip you up and undermine the security of a regular pulse.

These are general points, although their specificity varies across domains. Whilst house and techno play with continuity, drum'n'bass is a play on continuity, picking you up just to drop you down, haunted by the reverb, and then catching you with another break before you can fall back to earth. Building on jungle's fusion of the hyperintensity of hardcore with a ragga bassline playing at half the speed, drum'n'bass raises rhythmic complexity

14. A special case is the Roland TB-303 which functioned by breaking down: notoriously bad at what it was designed for (simulating bass-guitar lines), it was very good at making mistakes. Its programming procedures were so complex that the operator's intentions would become lost and unexpected results appear out of the confusion - with the mistakes proving more interesting than what was intended. Soon the misuse became the norm, as the unique squelching sounds produced by its filters came to define a whole genre of music - acid house. Like the drum-machine which kick-started the house revolution, the Roland TR-808, it was bought cheap on the second hand market following its premature discontinuation because of its failure to emulate real instruments.

15. Art and artist are modern inventions.

16. Not to be confused with the dramatic tension aiming at resolution that is common in Western music.

to a new plane, cultivating chaos in its disjointed exploration into the genetics of the percussive code.[17] From the dancefloor pragmatics of DJ Hype to the erudite musings of Squarepusher, jungle's broken beats and fractured soundscapes refuse any moment of harmony or resolution, demanding a very different kind of attention to that of the disco trance. In contrast, a tune like Lil Louis' *French Kiss* (Diamond Records, 1989) is an endlessly repeated loop with only minor modulations in texture and tone. This simplicity greatly enhances the potential of the running mix: less determined by the structure of the record, the refrain is able to drift in and out, such that its point of entry is forgotten, its direction lost.

After catching the critics off-guard, drum'n'bass has since found favour with the music intelligencia. But it is not its 'sophistication' which is radical, but the fact that it took the body poetics of house and the raw energy of hardcore - fused with influences from black musical traditions - into new zones of (musical and cultural) experimentation. Just as hardcore took dance music beyond itself towards a limit of sheer intensity,[18] and ambient has floated away from the dancefloor towards more abstract, 'musical' zones of expression, drum'n'bass has exceeded dance music's determination (fracturing house music's claim to inclusivity), at times even abandoning all pretence of being 'dance' music at all (Squarepusher). But whilst sometimes unmoored from the demands of the dancefloor, these lines of flight are not yet (decapitated) 'head' music. Rather than dance music maturing and returning to a traditional register of musicality, these initiatives demonstrate how the dance virus has mutated while spreading and impacting on a wider musical sphere.

FROM REPETITIVE BEATS TO REPEATED BEATINGS

The ecstasy of the body has invigorated electronic music - heightening an *ekstatic* standing-out within the music itself - as well as in the world beyond with its influence felt in fields as diverse as the visual arts, multimedia and the internet. And just as the determination of art extends beyond the record onto the dancefloor, so the dance crowd extends its affect beyond the intimate space of the discotheque. The crowd's disruptive unity is a chaotic mass that knows no bounds: neither internal regulation nor external boundary. *Ekstasis* upsets modern individualism on two fronts: as we have seen, the codes of proper conduct that striate and compose the internality of the modern self are disrupted. But there is also a corresponding disturbance of the social codes that govern the privacy of space and property.

A nomadic structuring of space was thrust upon the early dance scene. Driven underground by its criminalisation, it was forced to situate itself outside of the established framework by which space is divided up and parcelled out. It became impervious to the distinctions of property relations, and seeped and flowed into whichever place presented itself. In the 'warehouse parties', the abandoned spaces of the industrial age were reclaimed and turned to a new purpose - a saprogenic flowering on the

17. Rather than programming just synthesised drum sounds, samples of drum patterns are used, each one a window onto a different temperality. Just as the genealogy of house is intimately related to the accessibility of synthesisers and drum-machines, so is the development of jungle intimately related to the availability and creative application of digital sampling technology.

18. A limit at which noise and speed operate as cultural weapons.

corpse of industrial decline. The inner-city breakout was not enclosed by any boundaries or channelled along any established route. It was thus hydraulic, posing a challenge to everywhere and everybody simultaneously. Its proper place is on the dancefloor, but in HWH the dancefloor is not tied to any one place, but is a space which follows the dancer wherever he goes. The nomad carries his house on his back. In HWH the dancefloor is not *in* space but *of* space. The refrain is a way of thinking the occupation of space: it fills it as it goes; smooth space is simultaneously filled and composed.

House was already an affront due to its amoral excess; but it was in this conflict over the structuring of space - between the open plain and the fenced and patrolled enclosure - that house became an intolerable menace. And this isn't a question of possession or even of occupation. The conflict over space marks the conflictual liminality or margin of modernity, at which the hegemony of its disciplining mechanisms is contested and enforced. In this conflict we see the disproportionate dread inspired by an unbounded unknown, and the consequent paranoiac enforcement of the norm. This should not be analysed in terms of a struggle between social mores and individual desires. It was rather a struggle over (the modern form of) sociality itself.

This conflict may be traced in one of the most intense and sustained periods of disco debauchery in the history of house. Over a two year period (1989-1990), Blackburn, a small town in the north of England that 1980s economics forgot, became the focus for a series of weekly acid house parties involving up to 12,000 people. What was remarkable about this was that the actions of so many individuals could be covertly co-ordinated without an institutional framework and without any clear leaders. After a decade of Thatcher and economic decline, the parties provided a source of hope and an outlet for the immense amount of energy released by the breaking down of the social codes of a bankrupt reality. An anecdotal testament to this was the renaming of the city 'Boomtown' - paying homage to the anti-Thatcher dream at the same time as marking its emergent illicit economic power. The area was declared an Autonomous Zone: the alternative road signs were still in place three years later.[19]

19. Compare Hakim Bey, *The Temporary Autonomous Zone*, Autonomedia, 1991.

It was a continual struggle between party-goers and police, each side trying to outwit the other. A different location would be used each week. And new equipment would have to be constructed or acquired to replace that confiscated the week before. There was a need for a continual mobilisation of resources, which interrupted the sedimentation of control around any particular group or individual. And the close attention of the police meant that no stars or personalities could emerge.

Boomtown was only visible once a week, surviving the rest of the time as an underground network of roots that had no leader but constituted a flat rhizomatic meshwork that linked at every point. It was continuously evolving, and so police action against a single point meant nothing as the flow simply redirected itself and swept on, forever in excess of its own achievements.

You can't arrest what you can't see.

Confronted with this profusive excess, the authorities responded by attempts at restratification. The first major intervention was at a warehouse near Nelson in Lancashire, when a solid line of blue marched into the party zone, batons hitting linked riot shields in time with the beat of their hob-nailed boots. A pure line of control stamping order upon the chaotic mass. Blue lines operate by dissection and 'sterilisation' (police jargon). The chaotic mass is first blocked and hemmed in, then divided and striated, and finally annihilated in the reclaiming of the contested space.

The events at Nelson changed the nature of the situation altogether. The incident entered the collective memory not only of the people there, but of everyone involved in the northern rave scene. It welded people together as a community more determined than ever not to lose their way of life. It gave rise to the imagined community (*halluci-Nation?*) of *House Nation*. An entertainment had become a movement, for which people were willing to break the law. In the resulting climate, new people were attracted to the parties who went only to fight with the police. Months of violent confrontation were to follow: 'repetitive beats' met with repeated beatings. This situation reached a climax on the 21st July 1990 in the mass arrest of 836 people at a single party at Gildersome near Leeds. This was one of the biggest peace-time arrests in Europe this century, and yet virtually no charges were brought. I had my records confiscated at this event, and the only other DJ - Rob 'parasite-electric' Tissera - was sent to prison for inciting a riot (Section 2 Public Order) and 'Dishonest Abstraction of Electricity'.[20]

House was a flow of the unnameable that was intrinsically non-oppositional, and yet which found itself in direct opposition to the striated space of property relations. It is revealing that the primary justification for closing down the warehouse parties was not illegality or danger, but *the lack of a clear regulative framework*. Even in the health and safety debate what is usually at issue is not the concrete risk of fire or injury, but the presence of recognised procedures of safety.[21] The parties were closed down *for administrative reasons!* For the dance scene to be permitted in the eyes of the law, it was sufficient that it be brought back from the unknown, and placed within the blue lines of a bureaucratic and legalistic structure. The club replaced the warehouse: a nomad no more, house had come home. Hermetically sealed within a private space, lured by the promise of individual freedom, then policed to extinction.

In 1997 the situation is more stark and more desperate than ever. Following the Increased Penalties Act in 1990, and the notorious Criminal Justice and Public Order Act (the Drug Misuse Bill) in 1994, the latest piece of legislation under review is intended to make it easier for clubs to be closed down, and, ludicrously, to enforce intermittent periods of silence during all-night parties.[22] Here the specifics of the measures are less important than the fact that they will give local authorities massively increased leverage. Indicative of the trend to come, clubs are being coerced

20. These events occurred long before the days of the CJA, demonstrating that it is not the law that matters so much as the way that it is enforced.

21. These insights are based on an interview with Chief Inspector Beaty, the officer in charge of policing the Blackburn parties (although not responsible for Nelson or Gildersome), at Lancashire Police Force Headquarters, Preston, 15 July 1995.

22. The Increased Penalties Act introduced a £20,000 fine for organisers of paying parties. The CJA introduced draconian new legislation (which includes the prohibition of 'repetitive beats') directed against travellers, protesters, and squatters, as well as festivals and free-parties. The Drug Misuse Bill was instigated by the Conservative MP Barry Legg.

into installing close circuit television cameras (CCTV) to spy on the proceedings within, turning zones of autonomous expression into panopticons of visibility and control. HMP Clubland.[23]

23. 'What have you got to hide?!!', 'Her Majesty's Prison'

DEALING ECSTASY

The demands of regulation presented 'planet tune' with two choices: swallow the poisoned pill of respectability or disappear from view. The current cultural landscape has been split from itself by the binary logic of the law, with the 'free parties' opting to stay outside of the legal framework and the commercialism which it bred. Whilst they are not a movement in the sense of a conscious and explicit project with dischargeable goals of social and political transformation, the free parties are a movement in the sense of a shift away from commercial exchange and towards an unmediated experience of the music. They have maintained the radicalised mode of organisation of the warehouse parties, whilst simultaneously supporting transverse connections with festival and traveller culture (Castlemorton), international political conflict (Desert Storm in Bosnia), and emergent modes of political contestation such as eco-politics and road protest (Reclaim the Streets).

Jealously guarding its supposed 'artistic autonomy', club culture, on the other hand, gives the impression of an idealised sphere of maximised expression and release. But this comes at the price of an ever tightening enforcement of the code. Whereas partying was a total social fact - everyone used to do and be everything - privatisation splits the participants into producers and consumers, and places them within a strict hierarchy. Similarly, professionalisation confers on everyone involved a role and a proper place. Capitalism striates the chaotic mass, inhibiting the potential for revolutionary connections. And whereas the warehouse parties produced a strongly inclusive sense of identity, commercialisation yields a reactive identity constructed in opposition to other clubs and other sociocultural forms. The club scene differentiates itself through group fantasies around 'institutional objects': 'name DJs', established clubs and record labels, classic tunes, legendary parties. This is in sharp contrast to the flat plane of autopoesis of HWH and the crowd open to its own finitude and individuated by group affects.

Nevertheless, whilst the demands of regulation and visibility suffocate clubland, this is only a relative homecoming. Beyond the statistical reductions of the door and cash register, the crowd retains a certain opacity, providing a site beneath the threshold of visibility of the bouncers, undercover cops and licensing committees from which a thousand becomings and atypical expressions can issue forth.[24] Where this does risk stasis is when it degenerates to repetition of the Same, with abstract images towering over the dancers, separating them from their potential, reestablishing them as coherent individuals defined and delimited by their relative inadequacy and lack.

24. This of course is threatened by the penetrating gaze of CCTV and the consequent visual structuring of space it brings.

Further, it would be wrong to conclude that 'buying in' automatically entails 'selling out'. This would be to remain trapped within outmoded oppositions. Naked simulation and the dilution and compromise that that entails is a tendency and a limit which both club promotion and musical production constantly face. The situation is only distorted, however, when viewed in terms of a simple opposition between original authenticity and vampiric commercialism. A more constructive approach is to look to the folds and fractures that house opens up *within* capitalism.

A concept which can help us both identify ecstatic dimensions within these two spheres and specify their connection is that of a 'minor music'.[25] A minor music is a standing out from the accepted norm or established canon. It is not so much an alternative musical system so much as an alternative *usage* of music, one which sets the musical terms and co-ordinates in motion and extracts from them unexpected results.

25. Compare the discussion of a 'minor literature' in Deleuze and Guattari, 1988, *op. cit.*, pp101-106.

A minor music isn't something set over and against a people, but is something that is essential to their collective existence and public life. It is not that music is tied to a specific community or group so much as that it itself can create (articulate, unite) a community or group: it is through a minor usage that the house is turned into a home. But neither is it about building a wall round a certain location and declaring it your own. A minor music can come from the ghetto, but it is not about reproducing or creating ghettos within music - which would just be to instantiate a major music on a smaller scale. It is rather to subvert the major music from within by making it a stranger to itself. A minor usage is like the secret strategies used by a foreigner, who uses linguistic terms for purposes for which they were not designed. A foreigner does not create a separate domain or dialect within language, but turns all language into something secret and strange.

The concept of a minor music thus theorises simultaneously the operationality of the club and the singularity of the music. Clubs are communities of strangers, whose only common point of reference is a *directed alienation*. This is articulated in the music: the music is not the *expression* of the alien-ation, but rather the medium in which it is played out. Clubs run in such a 'minor' key are thus intimately related to the genealogy of a specific form of music. Whilst there is an increasing tendency towards proto-corporate 'supermarkets of style' (complete with their own marketing and merchandising divisions), there is also a trend towards greater differentiation as the club concept is reinvented and reapplied, with a plethora of clubs now providing a specialist experience to a specialist crowd.

But whilst clubs offer an *unheimlich* home to the music, the fact that the music is tied to specific forms of practice does not mean that it is imprisoned within the club walls. The clubs are specific instantiations of a musical tradition which has its own momentum and its own multiple trajectories.

Whilst 'house' music used to be an eclectic fusion of many styles into a singular aesthetic, since roughly 1990 dance music has fragmented and shot off down numerous trajectories (some of which may be accounted for in terms of colour, class and sexuality). The initial sense of unlimited potential started to run up against its own limits, and explorations of disparate frontiers separated out to form distinct styles. This has resulted in proliferating folds of sonic involution, but also in a parallel multiplication of names, as artists and journalists stick a flag in a piece of sonic territory and call it home. Hi energy, nu energy, electro, trip hop, garage, gabber, techstep, hardstep, hardcore, happy hardcore, speedcore, artcore, darkcore, breakcore, breakbeat, industrial breakbeat, drum'n'bass, jungle, darkside jungle, trance, goa trance, psychedelic trance, techno, house, acid house, amyl house, dream house, deep house, progressive house, softhouse, hardhouse, hardbag, handbag, ambient, illbient ... to name a few.

As the 'loose ends' of the sonic web are reterritorialised, the arteries harden and creativity congeals. A zone of exploration establishes its patent, becoming itself a norm with an official history and a clearly marked set of official co-ordinates - classic tunes, prime movers, seminal times.[26] This is most visible at the centre - in the determination of 'house' and 'techno', which distinguish their lineages with the mythology of their respective origins in Chicago and Detroit in the mid-80s.[27] Seeking to produce 'true' techno, European artists attempt to emulate the 'Detroit' sound, whilst those who made the original grooves emulate simulacra of themselves. This leads some to devise sophisticated strategies to elude the legacy of their own success (such as Underground Resistance's masked faces, long silences and pointed communiqués), while others get trapped within a backward looking self-referentiality. This can be seen in the recent release (by a major label) of the compilation *True People: The Detroit Techno Album*: 'indeed an apt title for this album ... Techno belongs in Detroit.'[28] Whilst the record contains much diverse and innovative music, the sense of self-referentiality, of toying with its own inheritance, is clear.

The specificity of distinct genres should not be lost amongst rhetoric of autonomy and diffusion, and yet nomadism isn't about building cities in the desert. The proliferation of coherent market categories indicates only the pluralisation of the major usage. Minor music operates along more diverse routes, preferring secrecy to the false unity of the name. Never closed or finished, genres are not formulae to copy, but points of reference from which to depart.

The primary issue with commercialisation and so called 'reincorporation' by the major record labels is neither the profit motive as such nor the scale of production, but the fact that business considerations and commercial technologies come before the music. The music is suffocated, forced to fit the contours of marketing strategies and advertising campaigns. Risks are avoided, and a conformity to representational categories is sought. Fundamental to major music is the unity of the name and the refusal of undecidability.

Capital seeks and procures difference; but only so that it may be sold as a dead artefact. Difference is objectified such that it can be infinitely reproduced in the naked simulation of a preformed model. And in this neutered form the cultural object is then circulated and distributed in a

26. In the phenomenon of 'trainspotting' we see an obsession with the original dressed as musical education.

27. What has been referred to as 'house' above emerged from the interstice of these two traditions.

28. Colin Dale, quoted on album insert, *True People*, React, 1996.

system of equivalence. The difference between minor and major music is the difference between positive and negative production - which are the two opposing tendencies of capitalism. Capitalism operates by exploiting minor musics so as to open up new markets. But once a new market has been opened, it seeks to solidify it so that it may be mined for all it is worth. In the pursuit of the maximum return minor music is turned into major music. It is only when the market is flooded or the vein expended that it is ready to move on. In moving on (the positive production) it is indistinguishable from the productivity of HWH, the minor musical production which follows a nomadic line of exploration and innovation. But in HWH this exploration is no longer subordinated to a future stasis. A minor music can upset capitalism because it is perpetually in excess of the attempts to pin it down. House always risks being brought home, its floating domain objectified and pinned down by concerns extrinsic to the music. But HWH anticipates and prevents the realisation of this limit. Its first term is a destruction that subverts its own inherent tendencies towards identity. The production of rhythm is itself rhythmic, a matter of differential return, a power of discontinuity and transformation that induces a spasm or a strain in the music, and so breaks down the 'clichés' of our musical habits.

Dance music has proven resistant to the effects of capital because of its mediation by club and DJ, but also because of its disruption of the logic of identity. Produced by anonymous engineers and prioritising the record over the stage performance, electronic music is marked by a 'facelessness' that distinguishes it from the phallic posturing of rock.[29] And prevalent naming strategies favour a dispersal of identity, with artists operating under different names and in a variety of styles, and multiple, shifting allegiances replacing the stable 'group'. This tendency is accentuated by the material conditions of production and distribution. Disseminated through specialist shops and local distribution networks, house music is dominated by a mixture of anonymous one-off 'white labels' and the products of 'small labels': a system of minor musical production flourishing beneath the threshold of visibility of the majors.[30]

This autonomous zone is threatened by the increasing influence of the media. Magazine record reviews (conveniently organised into market categories) now offer a guide through the morass of weekly record releases. This increases the availability of information, but at the cost of objectifying the sonic domain and taking the process of education out of the participatory contexts of the club and specialist record shop, rendering the addressee a passive consumer.

The scene of house was always partially conditioned by the media. But there was a qualitative change in the media's affectivity that went along with the increase in both scale and specificity of its coverage. It is the technologies of visibility of the media that have replaced the anonymous DJ with the 'name DJ', reintroduced sexual hierarchies and stereotypes, and even made an abstract image of excess itself by reporting incidents

29. Increased access to cheap technology and a pervading ethos of do-it-yourself have given birth to a new generation of sonic artists. For a discussion of the extent to which the record had already attained ontological priority in rock, see Theodore Gracyk, *Rhythm & Noise: an Aesthetics of Rock*, I.B. Tauris & Co, 1996.

30. This is helped by the fact that the major corporations have consigned vinyl to history. Notwithstanding the music industry's recent trend towards fine focusing their investment strategies, the DJ record market constitutes a backwater resistant to the march of corporate thinking, a fold in the unbroken surface of capital.

31. In a sense the CCTV debate was prefigured in the intrusion of 'journalistic vision' into club culture. The former is far more dangerous, however, because it is not a part of the culture which it exposes.

such as club personalities 'biting peoples' legs'.[31] This disseminates and cultivates house as much as it inhibits it. The startled rabbit stands up on its rear two legs and starts doing the can-can in the glare of the oncoming headlights.

But at the same time the two dimensional mediascape is disrupted by small-scale and minor media - fanzines, flyers given to clubbers, and posters lining the city streets. These are no longer the accessible, autonomous communication they once were (comparable to the punk small-press ethos): a minimum standard of design and production is often expected, and even the one-on-one interaction of handing-out flyers is being challenged by companies such as Renamo who offer a distribution service which collects different flyers together in a single, advertisement-adorned plastic bag. But nevertheless minor media offer dispersed and open channels of communication resistant to control and regulation.

At the close of the twentieth century even the major corporations are beginning to realise that talk of the 'mass market' is increasingly anachronistic, and that real economic growth lies in niche markets. Capitalism is becoming increasingly insidious, creeping into every corner as the corporate device is 'down-sized' almost to the point of being indistinguishable from local or 'street' culture. The question this raises is whether the fragmentation and miniaturisation represents a disruption or an extension of the logic of the commodity. Does it allow cultural practitioners to stand out from it, or does it pin them down even more firmly than before? Is it a decentralisation, or an intensification of control? This is not a question that can be answered once and for all, but is rather the nature of the enigmatic state of affairs that dance culture must confront if it is to keep the music on the move.

Recent developments - particularly the growth of corporate clubs, corporate magazines, and corporate in-house dance labels - might make us pessimistic about the future. But there are reasons to believe that it will take more than economics to put out the fire. At the *In The City 95* music industry conference, a business consultant specialising in corporate culture who had been shown round the 'superclub' Cream in Liverpool was invited to give his opinion on dance culture. But all he could report was that the people he saw seemed very passive and weren't interacting with each other. The corporate man could not see what was happening even when it was thrust in his face: the dancers' intimate relation with the music proved invisible to the corporate gaze. No instrument can as yet measure *ekstasis*. And you can't sell what you can't see.

32. Quoted in Dean & Massumi, *First and Last Emperors*, Autonomedia, 1992, p.123. 'This was Bush's rallying cry in his first campaign swing around New Hampshire in 1992 *Montreal Gazette*, 20 Jan 1992, B3.' (*ibid.* p.187, note 18)

So long as the ecstatic mode proves to be opaque, there will always be lines of flight away from the cultural death we have been prescribed. To sample George Bush,

'Gonna be alot of wierd dancin' goin' on.'[32]

THE RACE OF SPACE

Richard Cavell

If the emergence of a field of discussion is historically linked to the development of cities this is because the concentration of different ethnic and/or professional groups in the same space, with in particular the overthrow of spatial and temporal frameworks, favours the confrontation of different cultural traditions, which tends to expose their arbitrariness practically, through first-hand experience, in the very heart of the routine of the everyday order, of the possibility of doing the same things differently.

P. Bourdieu, *Outline of a Theory of Practice*

I

A 'raced' discourse of *monstrosity* has emerged since the 1980s with reference to domestic architecture in Vancouver, Canada. Couched in terms of 'design', 'heritage', 'character', 'standards', and, increasingly, of 'race', this discourse of the 'monster house' has become one of the most controversial public issues in Vancouver's postwar history. The debate has particularly (though not exclusively) concerned the most prestigious address in the city, First Shaughnessy (so-designated to distinguish it from later and lesser accretions), many of whose mansions were built in the first two decades of this century to house the city's elite in a style redolent of Tudor England.

In 1982, fearing that this heavily-treed haven of larger than average lots was threatened by redevelopment, Vancouver city council (the majority of whose members have traditionally dwelt on that side of the city which includes Shaughnessy among its enclaves) enacted a bylaw restricting changes that could be made to houses built in the Shaughnessy area before 1940 and requiring new houses to conform to design standards. This prompted one local architect to comment that he would no longer accept commissions to design houses in Shaughnessy, since the design guidelines encouraged 'terrible pseudo architectural styles'.[1]

By the end of the 1980s, the issue had become one not simply of 'design' or 'heritage' but also of size. The term 'monster house' entered into the arena of debate, which began to be coded with phrases such as 'single family' (the neighborhood profile which the bylaws sought to preserve) and to make reference to the owners' countries of origin. Because these houses were technically within the law, which governed house size for the entire city, a group of property owners combined to draft a bylaw affecting their own particular area of the city. With the Mayor publicly supporting them, their

1. Dan White, quoted by Elizabeth Godley in 'Shaughnessy sets a stern design challenge', *The Vancouver Sun*, 19 November 1988, p2.

2. Paul Ohannesian, 'How we saved Shaughnessy from monsters', *The Vancouver Sun*, 23 June 1990, pp10-11.

3. Pamela Fayerman, 'It looks like a condo, but it's just one big house', *The Vancouver Sun* 2 March 1991, p5.

4. Isabel Minty, 'Let's fight these monsters', *The Vancouver Sun*, 16 January 1992, p15.

5. Daphne Bramham, 'Vancouver council unsure if new house bylaw will tame the monsters', *The Vancouver Sun*, 11 April 1990, p1.

6. Kevin Griffin, 'A monster problem in Shaughnessy', *The Vancouver Sun*, 17 November 1992, pp1; 4.

7. Elizabeth Aird, 'There's a "monster problem" on the street where they live', *The Vancouver Sun*, 2 October 1993, p3.

bylaw was passed on 14 June 1990; the newspaper story detailing the history of the bylaw was headed 'How we saved Shaughnessy from monsters'.[2]

The issue, however, refused to go away. *The Vancouver Sun* reported on 2 March 1991 that a 'huge' house costing $3 million was being constructed on the fringe of Shaughnessy by an individual 'involved in the real-estate development business in Asia'.[3] The owner 'was amused by a rumor going around the neighborhood that the house would be occupied by 15 people. He says only his wife, ... three children and their nanny will live in the five-bedroom home.' The house was described by one resident as looking monstrous 'from the front' only. On 16 January 1992, the same house (photographed from the front) was discussed in a personal opinion piece which the newspaper headlined 'Let's fight these monsters'.[4] 'Do we want to "Soweto-ize" our city?' asked the author, at the same time invoking the privately-authored bylaw which was now being looked upon as the model for success in what another critic had dubbed 'the monster mash'.[5] In one of many attempts in the controversy to elide race by class, a local 'heritage' expert explained that the issues complexly concerned what he called 'the cultural landscape', which in this case meant 'old money, settled, prestige, not nouveau riche'.[6] 'What's happening', he explained, 'is that the whole baggage that goes along with the cultural landscape, the births and deaths in a community, the changes in gardening fashions - the whole history of community is being negated. This effectively is brand-new Vancouver because it has wiped out the history of Shaughnessy'. The article went on to point out that 'One view of the Shaughnessy rezoning controversy is that all Asian-Canadians want and like the monster houses; the resident Anglos just want to keep the tasteful Tudor and Colonial homes the way they are.'

By autumn 1993, the discourse surrounding the monster house debate had become fully racialized. In an article titled 'There's a "monster problem" on the street where they live', Elizabeth Aird interviewed a Vancouver resident who described what Aird called 'a godawful heap' as 'our Chinese-Greco-Tudor'.[7] Aird went on to note that the house 'was built by a Chinese contractor, and was later sold in a secret Hong Kong sale'. This 'Chinese' thing comes up again and again in our conversations about the new house[s]' Aird wrote. While no one she interviewed would admit to racism 'because no one wants to risk being called a racist ... there's no denying that an awful lot of people - read Caucasians - are struggling to come to terms with change that goes well beyond a bunch of new houses.' Aird quoted one of the residents as stating that the new houses undermined the 'basic values' of 'our fathers and grandfathers', among them a love of 'old English gardens and our love of beautiful trees.' The resident concluded with the comment that 'I think it's time that people who want to live in newer houses ... go off to another area.'

In reply to this article, Rosa Ho wrote a letter to the Editor in which she stated that 'The quotes Ms Aird uses ... feed the sentiments of others who also equate the monster house blight with Chinese purchasers, and who have been feeling self-righteously that the basic values of their neighborhoods have been transgressed. But these sentiments also vilify, stereotype and make scapegoats of the Chinese. ... Whether the feelings of residents ... are justified or not by what is happening on their street, it is nevertheless a "racist" thing to name and blame only one identifiable group as the culprits.'[8] That same year, the term 'monster house' was given the imprimatur of *Exploring Vancouver*, the definitive academic guide to Vancouver architecture. While virtually every entry in the guide is headed by the name of the person it was built for or by its public designation, one entry is simply designated 'Monster Houses': '[a] kind of large house built to maximize floor space and site coverage and ... characterized by a pastiche of "period" detailing (often featuring an overblown double-height entry). The "monster house" has been sharply criticized for its intrusion into the fabric of existing neighbourhoods. The banality of its design is probably its worst feature'.[9]

The debate over monster houses also spread to suburban areas of the city, including North Vancouver and West Vancouver (which has the highest per capita income bracket in Canada), where councils likewise enacted bylaws to change zoning regulations, thereby preventing large houses from being built. In West Vancouver, the monster house problem was felt most acutely in the British Properties area of the municipality. According to *Exploring Vancouver*, '"Monster houses" proliferate in the [area], adding to the pot-pourri of styles ... but ignoring the "garden city" ethos by which the neighbourhood was originally planned.' The guide goes on to state that one such house 'pretentiously attempts to play the correct tune but manages, through overemphasis, to strike all the wrong notes in an enjoyably kitsch performance.'[10]

The British Properties is a 4700 acre area which the Guinness family, of brewing fame, purchased in 1932 for upscale real estate speculation. To link West Vancouver with the city proper, a bridge was built with financing from the British government; the 'Canadian government agreed to allow its construction providing Chinese labourers were not used'.[11] Writing in June 1994 for the Toronto based *Globe and Mail* (an indication of the national attention now being accorded the controversy), Robert Matas noted how the area was meant to reflect British values (its ratepayers' newsletter is called *Tally Ho*), and how it restricted what could be built there and who could build it. 'Restriction No. 7 ... states that "no person of Asiatic or African race or of African or Asiatic descent (except servants of the occupier of the premises in residence) shall reside or be allowed to remain on the premises"'.[12] While Canadian law does not permit such discrimination, Restriction No. 7 has never been rescinded: 'It can't be enforced, so what's the difference' asks an official. In 1994, 'residents born in Asia account[ed] for almost 20 per cent of the British Properties population, which puts them only slightly behind those of British origin', Matas noted, adding that 'a company spokesman contends that most Asian buyers "have a sense of humour" about the

8. Rosa Ho, 'Don't sidestep issue of neighborhood racism', *The Vancouver Sun*, 'Letters', 6 October 1993, p16.

9. Harold Kalman et al, *Exploring Vancouver: The Essential Architectural Guide*, University of British Columbia Press, Vancouver, 1993, p154.

10. *Ibid.*, p239.

11. Robert Matas, 'When cultural worlds collide', *The Globe and Mail*, 18 June 1994, pp1; 6.

12. The controversy gained international recognition with the publication of Jeffrey Gilliard and Murray Whyte's article, 'The House that Ate the Neighborhood' in the New York-based *Metropolis*, July/August 1995, pp12;16-17, which repeats rather than critiques the terms of the debate. See also Matas, *op.cit.*, p6.

fact that "in the early days the clause was intended to exclude them but the Asians are now the ones that can best afford" to buy in the neighbourhood.'

Despite the various bylaws enacted to eliminate monster houses, or at least to modify their appearance (by enforcing, for example, the number of bay windows allowed, in order to eliminate 'bug-eyed houses'), these houses continued to provide the locus of a discourse whose components were consistently race and space.[13] At the same time, observers of the scene sought to use class to elide the issue of race (rather than complicate it), as in a letter published on the subject in a 1995 issue of the *Globe and Mail*: 'What's monstrous about the so-called monster homes to people who use the term is often that they can't afford to buy one'.[14] The debate was also characterized by gestures of dislocation and dehistoricization. In a 1995 article called 'Building a better big house', Frances Bula wrote that, 'While Vancouverites tend to believe the so-called "monster-house" problem is unique to their city and a product of Asian-Caucasian cultural differences, that isn't so. The "teardown" phenomenon, as it's known in the United States, has affected every North American city where land values in older neighborhoods have risen sharply.'[15] Monster houses, in fact, 'will always be with us', wrote Bula, quoting a Canadian professor of urban and regional planning at the University of Waterloo (Ontario) who told her that 'economics and specialized zonings like the one Vancouver is introducing create and perpetuate the big-house pattern'. David Ley, who teaches in the Geography Department at the University of British Columbia, is quoted as saying that 'although the debate over new housing in Vancouver has a racial dimension now, it's wrong to locate it entirely in race. Neighborhoods are always concerned about a symbolic investment that they've made. If it's threatened, then you resist it.'[16] Bula also referred to a thesis on monster houses written in 1993 by Barbara Pettit, who argued that 'it's difficult to tell how much of the trend in new-house design is truly caused by cultural differences in taste and how much is a product of builders convincing naive buyers that this is what is considered attractive in Vancouver. ... Because builders build what they think is attractive to the majority, all new houses have the same look and are bought by those who haven't yet been educated about local taste.'[17]

A year after its article on monster houses in the British Properties, *The Globe and Mail* rejoined the issue with 'Alas, poor Kerrisdale, and those who loved it', by Karen Krucik. The tone of her opinion piece, about an area of Vancouver adjacent to Shaughnessy, is set by an epigraph from *Paradise Lost*. 'I was raised in that stodgy bastion of Anglo-Saxon virtue', wrote Krucik.[18] 'Vancouver has changed a lot since I was a child. ... When my brother graduated from [highschool] in 1984, there were just a few Asians in his graduating class. When I graduated ... in 1989, they made up approximately 50 per cent of the class. Now ... I would place the

13. 'What RS 6 means', *The Vancouver Sun*, 10 November 1995, p2; the title of the article refers to a type of zoning.

14. Margery Fee, 'Kerrisdale' ['Letters to the Editor'], *The Globe and Mail*, 30 June 1995, p10. Fee's letter is in response to Karen Krucik's article, noted below.

15. Frances Bula, 'Building a better big house', *The Vancouver Sun*, 10 November 1995, p1-2.

16. Frances Bula, 'How design affects taste: Don't blame race entirely for housing disputes, expert says', *The Vancouver Sun*, 10 November 1995, p2.

17. *Ibid.*, p2

18. Karen Krucik, 'Alas, poor Kerrisdale, and those who loved it', *The Globe and Mail*, 14 June 1995, p16.

percentage as high as 75 per cent. The comfortable little exclusive Anglo-Saxon world is gone forever, replaced by a thriving Chinese community from Hong Kong.' As a result of this influx, 'Old houses were torn down at an unprecendented rate to be replaced by "monster houses", huge, three-level brick mansions with brick fences that now tower over hollows of older, smaller, one- or two-level Tudor-style houses and one-level cottages.' Krucik's article was accompanied by a drawing showing an enormous rectangular building shingled in Canadian currency, set against an etiolated Vancouver skyline over which flies a plane with 'Hong Kong' writ large on its side. In the foreground stands a blonde-haired woman who looks appalled and downcast.

Krucik's article occasioned a response from Chung Wong, who wrote in an opinion piece titled 'Paradise lost - or found?' that 'The Chinese issue just won't disappear.'[19] To Krucik's evocation of 'a dream of what once was Kerrisdale', Wong replied that 'the Chinese, who helped to build the country's unifying railway, did not even have the right to acquire that same dream until recently. If one examines old deeds in Kerry's Dale, one will find that "Orientals" were banned from owning property there. ... They also could not become engineers like her father until recent decades because they were banned from many professions in Canada. Barriers did not break overnight, even after the Chinese gained the right to vote in 1947. This is why many politicians reading Ms Krucik's article are not Chinese.' As Wong noted, 'It is doubly ironic that Hong Kong is often singled out as a main cause behind the loss of this residential paradise. Let us not forget how Hong Kong came to be. What Ms Krucik calls Anglo-Saxon virtue created Hong Kong as it is today. The British are also known for bringing dramatic changes to various landscapes around the world. In fact, much of their wealth or "commonwealth" is derived from these exploits. ... Ms Krucik should not find it difficult to see how this translates into the history of her paradise.'

19. Chung Wong, 'Paradise lost - or found?', *The Globe and Mail*, 29 June 1995, p18.

II

In origin, Socrates belonged to the lowest class: Socrates was plebs. We know, we can still see for ourselves, how ugly he was. But ugliness, in itself an objection, is among the Greeks almost a refutation. Was Socrates a Greek at all? Ugliness is often enough the expression of a development that has been crossed, thwarted by crossing. Or it appears as declining development. The anthropologists among the criminologists tell us that the typical criminal is ugly: monstrum in fronte, monstrum in animo. But the criminal is a decadent. Was Socrates a typical criminal? At least that would not be contradicted by the famous judgment of the physiognomist which sounded so offensive to the friends of Socrates. A foreigner who knew about faces once passed through Athens and told Socrates to his face that he was a monstrum - that he harbored in himself all the bad vices and appetites. And Socrates merely answered: 'You know me, sir!'

Nietzsche, *Twilight of the Idols*

20. Kay J. Anderson, 'The Idea of Chinatown: The Power of Place and Institutional Practice in the Making of a Racial Category', *Annals of the Association of American Geographers* 77(4), 1987, p584.

In an article on 'The Power of Place and Institutional Practice in the Making of a Racial Category', Kay Anderson has written that 'Almost no attention has been given to the process by which racial categories are themselves constructed, institutionalised, and transmitted over time and space. ... Racial ideology has been materially embedded in space ... and it is through "place" that it has been given a local referent, become a social fact, and aided its own reproduction.'[20] 'Monster house' is one such racial category; it poses the question of how space gets 'raced', and the related one of how monstrosity emerges as a sign of race. To ask these questions is to seek the epistemology of the monster house.

The association between house and monster is well-established in film, where it has become a Hollywood cliché: House of Dark Shadows; House of Evil; House of Exorcism; House of Freaks; House of the Damned; House of Fear; House of Frankenstein; House of Dracula, and so on. The psychoanalytical implications of this association have been worked out in some detail by Barbara Creed in *The Monstrous-Feminine*. Creed begins by rehearsing the Freudian *unheimlich*, usually translated as the 'uncanny', but literally the 'unhoused' or 'unhomely.' As Creed goes on to note, it is the memory of the womb which is repressed in experiences deemed uncanny, such that the house becomes a figure of the womb, the place which we all know yet which none of us can ever really know. 'The symbolization of the womb', writes Creed, 'as house/room/cellar or any other enclosed space is central to the iconography of the horror film. Representation of the womb as a place that is familiar and unfamiliar is acted out in the horror film through the presentation of monstrous acts which are only half glimpsed or initially hidden from sight until revealed in their full horror.'[21] What is particularly productive in Creed's reading is the association between the (monster) house and the womb *as place of origin*. Noting Freud's comment that 'in some languages the German term an *unheimlich* house is only translatable as a *haunted* house,' Creed continues: 'The house is haunted by the ghost or trace of a memory which takes the individual back to the early, perhaps foetal, relation with the mother', what Freud terms in his essay a 'phantasy ... of intra-uterine existence.'[22] It is thus possible to develop Creed's gender-based analysis in the direction of race by focusing on the activity of positing origin/ origins/ originality (and the power positions which accompany that activity) as a major component within the production of a racist discourse. For it is precisely through the imposition of a discourse of origins that the monstrous emerges as a sign of 'race'.

21. Barbara Creed, *The Monstrous-Feminine: Film, Feminism, Psychoanalysis*, Routledge, London 1993, p55.

22. *Ibid.*, p54. Creed quotes from Freud, 'The Uncanny'. S.Freud, 'The "Uncanny"', *Standard Edition* XVII, Hogarth Press, London 1955, p244.

The notion of the uncanny - *unheimlich* - has, as Freud notes at the beginning of his essay, a somewhat wider application than that discussed by Creed; in addition to meaning the opposite of 'homely' it also opposes itself to '*heimisch*', meaning 'native.'[23] For what Freud seeks to demonstrate in his essay is that the uncanny feeling is produced not only by the unfamiliar, but by the *familiar* as well. In his etymological and linguistic examination of the term *heimlich*, Freud finds that the usages of the word consistently turn upon aspects of the familiarity of the home and of the neighbourhood, with the *unheimlich* constituted by that which comes from afar, as in the following example: 'That which comes from afar ... assuredly does not live quite *heimelig* (*heimatlich* [at home]), *freundnachbarlich* ([in a neighbourly way]) among the people.'[24] Freud further links this element with the idea of the double - 'Thus we have characters who are to be considered identical because they look alike.'[25] In one particularly telling example, Freud recounts the story of a 'couple who move into a furnished house in which there is a curiously shaped table with carvings of crocodiles on it. ... [W]e are given to understand that ... the wooden monsters come to life in the dark.'[26]

David T. Goldberg writes in *Racist Culture* that the 'category of space is discursively produced and ordered. Just as spatial distinctions like 'West' and 'East' are racialized in their conception and application, so racial categories have been variously spatialized more or less since their inception into continental divides, national localities, and geographic regions. Racisms become institutionally normalized in and through spatial configuration, *just as social space is made to seem natural, a given, by being conceived and defined in racial terms*'.[27] In Vancouver's Shaughnessy district, the naturalization of social space takes the form of positing the architecture of the English Tudor period as the 'originary' style of domestic architecture.[28] *Exploring Vancouver* tells us that 'Tudor revival was the favoured style in Shaughnessy, evoking visions of the English country manor and its attendant culture, gentility, and wealth'.[29] In addition to being the symbolic repository of 'gentility' and an icon of Englishness (which already invokes the question of race), the Tudor period was historically the one in which Europe embarked on its great cosmographical and exploratory colonisation of the New World. What is first of all being 'naturalised' in the appropriation of Tudor architectural style, then, is colonisation itself, the European attempt to declare itself 'original' in the place where it can only be secondary.[30]

Rudolf Wittkower has demonstrated in his essay 'Marvels of the East' that the history of the monster has been inseparable from issues of race and 'ethnography'. Beginning with Greek texts, and particularly those by Megasthenes and Pliny, Wittkower examines how India becomes in these texts the 'land of marvels' where such creatures as the acephali are found.[31] Wittkower goes on to state that the 'classical conception of India as the land of fabulous races and marvels kept its hold on Europe right into the 15th and 16th centuries. At that time the outlook began to change; the Indian marvels were by no means discarded, but they lost their connection with India and were located in other parts of the world.'[32] A constant in these stories of monsters is the distance at which they are placed from the writer, such that the 'other' and the 'foreign' become synonymous.

23. *Ibid.*,p220.

24. *Ibid.*,p223. The cognate term *Heimat* is capable of containing similar ambiguities; see Celia Applegate, 'The Question of Heimat in the Weimar Republic', *New Formations*, No.17, Summer 1992, pp64-74.

25. *Ibid.*,p234.

26. *Ibid.*,p244-5.

27. David T. Goldberg, *Racist Culture: Philosophy and the Politics of Meaning*, Blackwell Oxford 1993, p185, my emphasis.

28. Compare Krucik's reference *op.cit.* to the 'older, smaller, one- or two-level Tudor-style houses, that are being replaced by monster houses.'

29. *op.cit.*, p150.

30. These activities might be said to double themselves. Ashis Nandy has remarked that 'Modern colonialism won its great victories not so much through its military and technological prowess as through its ability to create secular hierarchies incompatible with the traditional order.' See *The Intimate Enemy: Loss and Recovery of Self under Colonialism*, Oxford University Press, Delhi, 1988, px.

31. Rudolf Wittkower, 'Marvels of the East: A Study in the History of Monsters', *JWCI* 5, 1942, pp.159-97, p160.

32. *Ibid.*,p194.

33. Bernard McGrane, *Beyond Anthropology: Society and the Other*, Columbia, New York 1989, pp9-10.

34. Donna Haraway, *Simians, Cyborgs and Women*, Routledge, New York 1991, p180.

35. Joseph-François Lafitau, *Customs of the American Indians Compared with the Customs of Primitive Times*, ed. and trans. W.N. Fenton and E.L. More, 2 vols., Champlain Society, Toronto 1974, vol. 1, plate 3.

36. *Ibid.*,p xvii.

37. Anthony Vidler,

The Writing of the Walls: Architectural Theory in the Late Enlightenment, Architectural Press, Princeton 1987, p10.

Transposing these tropes to the New World, Hartmann Schedel's *Liber chronicarum* (1493) displays its inhabitants as monsters. The deformed figures, as Wittkower suggests, go back to descriptions in Pliny which in turn drew on Greek writings about barbarians, part of a long chain of texts which sought to situate cultural origins along racial lines, as Martin Bernal has demonstrated in *Black Athena*. By the sixteenth century, however, as Bernard McGrane notes in *Beyond Anthropology*:

> cosmography does not experience itself as progressing beyond the limited cosmography of the ancients, but rather as breaking with this tradition, a past, that it now experiences not so much as false, ... but rather as fabulous and fantastic. ... The geographical imagination has been permanently altered; the nature of geographical space has been permanently transformed, and with that transformation the nature of the possible objects that can be discovered, located and deployed in that space undergo an equally deep transformation.'[33]

This is to say that the 'monstrous' continued to undergo discursive transformations long after it ceased to be figured exclusively in monstrous beings, these transformations defining, as Donna Haraway puts it, 'the limits of community in Western imaginations.'[34] This process is figured in a plate from Joseph-François Lafitau's 1724 *Moeurs des sauvages amériquains, comparées aux moeurs des premiers temps*, which is based on Lafitau's stay as a missionary to the Iroquois at Khanawaga (now in the province of Québec) from 1712 to 1717. The plate shows a headless monster whose type is recognisable from the *Liber chronicarum*; it is inserted, without any sense of discontinuity, among the more 'realistic' representations of the natives encountered by Lafitau.[35]

What is most striking about Lafitau's study is its obsession with origins. The editors of the Champlain edition of Lafitau's *Moeurs* state that 'in his researches on the Indians [Lafitau] was constantly on the prowl for evidences of similarities that would link them with the 'First Times', though, they continue, 'this kind of thinking was already two centuries old when Lafitau published in 1724'.[36] Lafitau's comparative methodology was linked to a degenerative model, whereby differences represented aberrations from original perfection, which, for Lafitau, was embodied paradigmatically in Adam and Eve (and thus the trope of 'paradise lost'). Based on an impossible similarity to an absolute original, Lafitau's comparative ethnography - his writing of race - was in fact constructed to deny difference.

Lafitau applies this degenerative hypothesis to the architecture of the *amériquains* as well, thereby establishing what Anthony Vidler calls 'a spatial phenomenology of dwelling that corresponded to his understanding of the mores and customs of different peoples'.[37] Of the American Indians Lafitau writes: 'Laziness, indolence, inactivity are to their taste and form the basis of their character so that, having neither learning nor duties, having no longer or scarcely having, the regulated exercises of past times which might hold them in check, they are the idlest people in the world'; this is reflected in their 'miserable hovels or thatched huts.'[38]

The 'spatial phenomenology of dwelling' evident in the architecture of the period immediately following the French Revolution is of particular interest from the point of view of the establishment of 'origins', for in architecture as in other areas the revolutionaries sought to make a new order. As becomes clear in James A. Leith's copiously illustrated study, *Space and Revolution*,[39] this involved the revival of classical architecture, invoked according to its place within the 'originary' polis of European civilization - although, as Martin Bernal has demonstrated in *Black Athena*, this status was itself an eighteenth-century construct which had racialist overtones.[40] The work of Jean-Jacques Lequeu stands out from these neoclassical efforts because of the bizarre form a number of his architectural renderings took in their attempt to establish an originality *outside* of architectural convention, and thereby to parody the highly conventional 'originality' of the designs which consistently were awarded the commissions his own work failed to attract.[41] In his monumental *Cowshed*, the attempt to impose a post-revolutionary architectural origin aligns itself with an extreme naturalisation. What is 'monstrous' in Lequeu's work is the 'failure' to conform to an architectural convention, thereby exposing the convention as such, and denaturalising it in the process.

By the nineteenth century, the racialisation of space which had been evident in the great cosmographic and exploratory projects underway since the fourteenth century had given way to a science of morphology, as Thomas Richards demonstrates in *The Imperial Archive*.[42] Here the discourse of monstrosity undergoes yet another transformation, though, once again, we find this discourse involved in an attempt to posit origin, namely Charles Darwin's *The Origin of Species*. Thomas Richards sees Darwin's book, and the science of morphology which it promulgated, as an attempt to eradicate the category of the monstrous precisely through the universalising domains of scientific inquiry. To posit an origin of the species, thus, becomes a way once again of eradicating difference. As Richards writes:

'Morphology put all beings on the same imperial family tree. ... The order of things went from being the order of ordered things to being the order of all things that had ever existed. Thus did the one characteristic move of all formal explanation in the nineteenth century - the ranking of all species by historical descent and modification - wipe out in one broad stroke the conditions of possibility for the stories of monsters that had once abounded in texts of literature, travel, natural history, and natural philosophy. Henceforth the forces of monstrosity would have to be located outside the Darwinian world-view.'[43]

38. *op.cit.*, vol.2, pp15,17.

39. James A. Leith, *Space and Revolution: Projects for Monuments, Squares, and Public Buildings in France 1789-1799*, McGill-Queen's, Montreal 1991, pp22-5.

40. Martin Bernal, *Black Athena*, Rutgers, New Brunswick 1987, *passim*.

41. See Vidler, *op.cit.*, 114-24.

42. Thomas Richards, *The Imperial Archive: Knowledge and the Fantasy of Empire*, Verso, London 1993, pp46-48. Compare Haraway's comment *op.cit.*: 'Unseparated twins and hermaphrodites were the confused human material in early modern France who grounded discourse on the natural and supernatural, medical and legal, portents and diseases - all crucial to establishing modern identity', p180.

43. *Ibid.*

III

> Haven't ... multicultural and intercultural radicals begun to convince us that nature is precisely not to be seen in the guise of the Eurocentric productionism and anthropocentrism that have threatened to reproduce ... all the world in the deadly image of the Same? ... The commonplace nature I seek, a public culture, has many houses with many inhabitants which/who can refigure the earth.
>
> Donna Haraway, *The Promises of Monsters*

And it was precisely outside the Darwinian world view that monsters *were* found. Darwin's world view was specific to its own place and time to the extent that it coincided with the high point of British imperialism; his scientific system was likewise a form of colonisation. And (as with imperialism) there was resistance to this colonisation which, in the Darwinian schema, was represented as the biological mutant. What is important to note here, in this conflation of colonisation and schematization, is precisely the *elision* of biology and race. As Edward Said writes in *Culture and Imperialism*, 'even as European power grew disproportionately with that of the enormous non-European *imperium*, so too grew the power of schemata that assured the white race its unchallenged authority.'[44] Thus to find something, such as the biological mutant, which *did* resist that authority, threatened (in the words of Thomas Richards) 'to bring about the end of Empire'.[45] To put it another way, for those in power the very idea of resistance was monstrous.[46]

According to Richards, one of the sites of such resistance is Bram Stoker's 1897 novel *Dracula*, which 'makes it clear that there are some species whose origins cannot be understood using the Darwinian model, and that these originless species, impossible according to Darwin, had become the archetypal monsters of the twentieth century'.[47] This lack of origin is displaced onto the diaspora: Dracula is unambiguously an immigrant, one whose aristocratic status is overwritten by race, and one whose Balkan realms are consistently orientalised by Stoker (as Richards notes): the entry into Budapest is described as 'leaving the West and entering the East'; the trains run as late as 'in China'; the people remind the British narrator of 'some old Oriental band of brigands.'[48] And the Balkans (again, as Richards notes) were the place where the colonial empires began to break up, and where some of the great diasporic movements of the twentieth-century began.[49] Judith Halberstam has linked Dracula specifically with the fear of the diaspora by identifying him with the figure of the Wandering Jew. 'As the prototype of the wanderer, the "stranger in a strange land", Dracula also exhibits the way that homelessness or rootlessness was seen to undermine the nation.'[50] Halberstam goes on to note that '"home" in the 1890s was precisely an issue resonating with cultural and political implications. Coming or going home, finding a home, was not simply a compulsive return to the womb; it involved nationalist, imperialist, and colonialist enterprises.'[51] And

44. Edward Said, *Culture and Imperialism*, Knopf, N.Y. 1993, p101.

45. *Ibid.*, p49.

46. As Franco Moretti has suggested in 'Dialectic of Fear', *Signs Taken for Wonders*, Verso, London 1988, pp83-108 esp. 107.

47. *Richards, op.cit.*, p49.

48. Bram Stoker, *Dracula*, Oxford 1983, pp1-3; quoted by Richards *op.cit.*, p64.

49. Freud's theorization of the uncanny also coincided with the breakup of empires heralded by the first world war.

50. Judith Halberstam, 'Technologies of Monstrosity: Bram Stoker's *Dracula*, *Victorian Studies*, vol 36 no3, 1993, p343.

51. *Ibid.*

John Stevenson has noted how, in *Dracula*, 'foreigness merges with monstrosity', and identifies Dracula with the fear of exogamy.[52]

The displacement of the racial onto the spatial in the twentieth century was perhaps most powerfully encoded in film, as (paradigmatically) in the 1933 Cooper and Schoedsack film *King Kong*. Kong is associated with prehistoric animals on his native Skull Island, as well as with the islanders themselves, and at one point in the film is described as being 'big as a house'. Among the crew of the expedition that sets out to capture him is the stereotyped Asian, Charlie the Cook, the only person of colour among Kong's captors and the one who is associated with the guilt of allowing the Fay Wray character to be abducted by the black islanders from the expedition's ship. When Kong goes on the rampage in New York, he is explicitly shown violating Fay Wray's highrise apartment, reaching in to pluck her out, and thereby enacting the fear of 'social climbing', as Meaghan Morris has put it. Morris adds that 'Kong was a force of mystery, terror, and above all, monstrous uncertainty. Neither man nor beast, he *was* the ambivalence of the border between Past and Present, Nature and Culture.'[53] In the publicity shot for the movie, Kong's 'monstrosity' is doubled by New York's skyscrapers, on the tallest of which Kong will meet his death, the uncanny embodiment of what Mike Davis has called 'urban gigantism'.[54]

There is a similar doubling in Hitchcock's *Psycho*, in which Norman Bates's Gothic mansion looms over the modernist motel where Marion is murdered. As Slavoj Zizek notes, this doubling figures the binary of tradition and modernity, as well as locating Norman spatially as 'a kind of impossible "mediator"... condemned to circulate endlessly between the two locales'.[55] Zizek goes on to suggest that 'Norman's split... epitomizes the incapacity of American ideology to locate the experience of the present, actual society into a context of historical tradition, to effectuate a symbolic mediation between the two levels.'[56] This is so because that context of historical tradition is itself a simulacrum, like Norman's *pseudo*-Gothic mansion (out of time and out of place), and like the 'Tudor' mansions of Shaughnessy. David Ley reads this doubling in terms of its colonialist implications: 'the nostalgic myth of a nurturing English tradition, transposed to a Vancouver of leafy streetscapes and Tudor mansions, is disrupted by "a hybrid national narrative" which presents the double of Anglophilia, its *own other* history of economic liberalism, the chainsaw, and dispossesion. As elsewhere, the "legacy of colonialism negates the possiblility of a unitary, stable English identity".'[57]

The simulacral status of these Tudor mansions - this 'architectural uncanny' - is othered *as* the 'monster house' precisely to preserve the 'originary' status of the 'Tudor' mansions. To explore the implications of these *revenants* one can follow the critique of the Freudian 'uncanny' made by Hélène Cixous, who argues that Freud fails to problematize sufficiently the boundary lines between the *heimlich* and the *unheimlich*.[58] Not to do so is

52. John Stevenson, 'A Vampire in the Mirror: The Sexuality of Dracula', *PMLA* 103, 1988, p143.

53. Meaghan Morris, 'Great Moments in Social Climbing: King Kong and the Human Fly', *Sexuality and Space*, ed. Beatriz Colomina, Architectural Press, Princeton 1992, p23.

54. This cityscape reappears in the illustration to the Globe article on monster houses, *op.cit.* Mike Davis, *Beyond Blade Runner: Urban Control - The Ecology of Fear*, Open Magazine, Westfield N.J. 1994, p2.

55. Slavoj Zizek, '"In His bold Gaze My Ruin is Writ Large"', *Everything You Always Wanted to Know About Lacan (But Were Afraid to Ask Hitchcock)*, Verso, London 1992, p232.

56. *Ibid.*

57. David Ley, 'Between Europe and Asia: The Case of the Missing Sequoias', *Ecumene* 2.2, 1995, p204; Ley quotes Joanne Sharp, 'A Topology of "post" nationality', *Ecumene* 1, 1994, pp65-76.

58. Anthony Vidler, *The Architectural Uncanny: Essays in the Modern Unhomely*, MIT, Cambridge Mass. 1992.

59. Ken Gelder,
Reading the Vampire,
Routledge, London
1994, p43.

60. On the
relationship of the
originary and the
Real see Gelder's
discussion of Freud's
dream of Irma, p49.

61. Joan Copjec,
'Vampires, Breast-
Feeding, and
Anxiety,' *October* 58,
1991, p28. See also
Gelder pp48-55,
from whose
discussion I have
profited here.

62. Kalman, *Op.cit.*,
p239.

63. Doreen Massey,
'A Global Sense of
Place', as quoted by
Angelika Banmer,
'Editorial', *New
Formations*; no.17,
1992, p viii.

64. Compare Ashis
Nandy *op.cit.* that
'What looks like
Westernization is
often only a means
of domesticating the
West, sometimes by
reducing the West to
the level of the
comic and the trivial'
(p108).

65. I am grateful to
Gillian Creese and
Sneja Gunew for
reading and
commenting on
drafts of this article,
to Jeff Miller for his
knowledge of
Nietzsche, to
Margery Fee for
sourcing the *Globe*,
to Graeme Wynn,
Derek Gregory and
David Ley of UBC's
Geography
Department, and to
Peter Dickinson for
his help throughout.

to remain precisely within a discursive practice of 'origins.' As Ken Gelder argues;

> 'it is ... possible to read the vampire [or monster, in general] as a Self-image, a means of figuring socio-political-sexual excesses which, although represented as foreign, actually lie much closer to home. "The fantastic" in fact draws Self and Other together, showing the boundaries between them to be fragile and easily traversed. In "the fantastic", the Self is thus ontologically destabilised by an Other which, far from being different, turns out instead to be disconcertingly familiar.'[59]

Adopting a Lacanian discourse of the Real and the symbolic, it is possible to argue that the Real in the architectural discourse of Shaughnessy houses has been posited in Tudor revival architecture.[60] The anxiety provoked by the Real is evident in the attempt of the symbolic to negate it. As Joan Copjec has argued, this negation takes place through repetition, 'through the signifier's repeated attempt - and failure - to designate itself'.[61] These are precisely the terms in which *Exploring Vancouver* discusses the monster house, 'which pretentiously attempts to play the correct tune but manages, through overemphasis, to strike all the wrong notes'.[62] It is here precisely that the monstrous emerges - in the repetition of the 'original', such that the 'original' can no longer be seen as *originary*.

As Doreen Massey has argued, the global village has necessitated the rethinking of the concept of home:

> not, as some lament, "home" itself, but rather the aura of its uniqueness, the notion that its special meaning derives from the fact that it is "singular and bounded". Instead of lamenting the loss of *this* concept of home (which has largely been a tenuous, if not mythic, concept anyway), she suggests, we might reconceptualize home in relational terms as the place(s) we inhabit with others in the shifting geography of social relations.[63]

By repeating the 'originary' architectural discourse of Vancouver's Tudor architecture, the 'monster house' denaturalises it, showing those origins to be a construct at once of space and of race.[64] The threat of the monster house is thus not its size but in the way in which its representation of space displaces the discourse of origins, which the 'original' houses sought to establish, with the differences that discourse sought to elide.[65]

THE SINGAPORE WAY OF MULTICULTURALISM:
WESTERN CONCEPTS/ASIAN CULTURES

Ien Ang and Jon Stratton

Like the other successful 'dragons' of East Asia, Singapore has become interesting for the West (and here we do not have the time to nuance and qualify our use of the term 'West') mainly for reasons of economic self-interest. As the Asia-Pacific region is set to become the main site of global economic activity and wealth in the next century, the old, Western heartlands of modern capitalism are now eager to do business in this region and to exploit its booming markets. This shift in relations of economic power is being accompanied by a shift in geo-cultural relations. The impressive economic ascendancy of the nation-states of East and Southeast Asia, the most successful of which has been Japan, has led to a growing cultural self-confidence within these nations, which, Samuel Huntington warns us, 'increasingly have the desire, the will and the resources to shape the world in non-Western ways'.[1]

This situation marks a transformation, but not a cancellation, of the parameters of the discourse of 'the West versus the Rest'.[2] While in the past the West could luxuriate in speaking about the Rest as a passive, silent Other, as in the discourse of Orientalism, the Rest is now talking back and interpellating the West on its own terms. In the process, the binary divide between West and non-West is reproduced at the same time that it is updated and, for lack of a better word, 'postmodernised'. Perhaps the most important site of this talking back at present is 'Asia', a term which becomes more problematic as the talking back becomes more loquacious and more assertive. What is increasingly often called the 'Asianization of Asia' is a signal of an ever more self-conscious 'East' or 'Orient' wishing to define itself by relegating 'the West' to the realm of the Other.[3] Of course,we must remember that this restructuring is taking place within the pre-existing, modern representational structure of 'West' and 'Other' which is itself a part of the colonial thrust of Western epistemology.

Singapore has developed a particularly strong voice in this new Asian self-identification by 'cast[ing] itself as Asia's ideological champion'.[4] For example, former Prime Minister Lee Kuan Yew, generally touted as the architect of independent modern Singapore, can now visit Australia, a nation located on the geographic if not the cultural periphery of 'the West' - and lecture with authority that Australians should learn more about hard work and discipline in order to compete with Asia. Another recent example was the caning sentence in Singapore for an American teenager convicted of vandalism, Michael Fay. While President Clinton officially protested against

1. Samuel Huntington, 'The Clash of Civilizations?', in: *Foreign Affairs*, Vol 72 No 3 (1993), p26.

2. For a discussion of 'the West' as an idea, see Stuart Hall, 'The West and the Rest: Discourse and Power', in: Stuart Hall & Bram Gieben (eds.), *Formations of Modernity*, Cambridge: Polity Press, 1992, pp275-320.

3. See for two Japanese perspectives on this trend, Yoichi Funabashi, 'The Asianization of Asia', in: *Foreign Affairs*, Vol 72, No 5, 1993, pp75-85, and Ogura Kazuo, 'A Call for a New Concept of Asia', in: *Japan Echo*, Vol 20, No 2, Summer 1993, pp37-44.

4. Edward Mortimer, 'New world order, but struggles will not end', in: *The Straits Times*, January 10, 1994, p29.

this form of punishment which he considered 'inhumane', the Singaporean government defended the sentence first by referring to the need to maintain law and order in Singapore, but also, more agressively, by pointing to the *breakdown* of law and order in the US, suggesting that, clearly, Singaporean methods were more effective.

Such incidents suggest that Singapore, one of the powerhouses of what has come to be known as 'Asian capitalism', is now a prime site for the contemporary rearticulation of the Orientalist master-narrative of West versus East, where an empowered East, having appropriated and reconstituted Western modernity, now unsettles the established hegemony of the West by questioning its moral worth. What we have here is a clash between an *imagined* West and an *imagined* East. From a Western point of view, the clash is between a West representing itself as 'free and democratic' against an East imagined as 'authoritarian and despotic', while from an Asian point of view, the same clash is constructed as one between an East representing itself as 'ordered and harmonious' against a West constructed as 'decadent and selfish'. Both 'West' and 'East' here are imaginary entities constructed through a mutual symbolic mirroring, in a battle of overlapping, interested Self/Other (mis)representations.

In this paper, we want to show how the discursive construction of 'Singapore' both unsettles and reinforces the narrative legacy of Orientalism which underpins this renewed ideological investment in the binary oppositioning of 'East' and 'West'. The discourse of the East/West divide is essential for an understanding of Singapore not only because it lies at the very historical origin of Singapore as a colonial construct, but also because, as we will show, it is structurally constitutive of Singapore as a modern national cultural entity. Furthermore, we want to suggest that many aspects of Singapore's social and political reality have been shaped precisely by the ambivalent cultural status of the Singaporean nation-state within the modern world-system of nation-states, an ambivalence emanating from its positioning as a country which, in a fundamental way, is both non-Western and always-already Westernised. The contemporary staging of the representational divide between 'East' and 'West', played out at the level of ideology and rhetoric, is both an articulation of, and an attempt to provide a solution for, this ambivalence. It is an imagined and imaginary divide in the formation of an always-already problematic global modernity which nevertheless has very real effects.

As Chua Beng Huat has remarked, in Singaporean political discourse there is a great concern for the morality of the people, in which 'the battle [is] always one of the moral East fighting hard to slow down the penetration of the moral decay of the West'.[5] In other words, the discursive construction of an East/West divide is continually mobilised by the Singaporean political leadership in its attempts to control the population through mechanisms of moralisation. In saying this, however, we do not want to reiterate uncritically all-too-easy liberal Western accusations of Singapore which denounce it for

5. Chua Beng Huat, 'Confucianization in Modernizing Singapore', paper presented at 'Beyond the Culture?' conference, Loccum, West Germany, October 1990, p17. See also Beng-Huat Chua, *Communitarian Ideology and Democracy in Singapore*, London: Routledge, 1995.

its allegedly '1984-like atmosphere'.[6] Many Western commentators see the intense preoccupation with moral education and discipline in Singapore, which is an instance of a sustained policy of moulding the people into law-abiding national citizens (the most widely ridiculed examples of which have been the banning of chewing gum and the imposition of fines for not flushing the toilet), as a sign of Singapore's non-Western otherness. But we should remember that the concept of social engineering as a task of the national state is in fact a very Western preoccupation. It is a European idea which has been part and parcel of the construction of the modern nation-state, as indicated by the many debates in Western nation-states over the purpose of state-based mass education from the mid-nineteenth century onwards. Thus, Singapore's appropriation of this concern should not be seen as essentially 'Western' or 'Eastern', but must be regarded as a result of the *translation* of a Western idea in a Westernised non-Western context. At the same time we must also recognise that the Singapore government is keen to present its own policies as faithful to Asian traditions and values. In other words, while the East/West divide is a discursive construction which has its origins in Western thought that enabled and legitimated European colonialism and imperialism, it now circulates among elites in the East as well, where it is inflected and articulated in ways suitable for their own purposes. As Edward Said has observed, 'the modern Orient ... participates in its own Orientalizing'. We would add that this modern Orient uses its new 'Oriental' or, in the context we are discussing, 'Asian' identity, built out of aspects of Western Orientalist discourse and pre-existing cultural forms, as a stage for critiquing, othering, and finally, reconstituting the 'West' or at least the identity presented by it.

To put it simply, Singapore is a contradiction in terms: on the one hand its very existence as a modern administrative unit is a thoroughly Western occasion, originating in British colonialism; on the other hand the Republic of Singapore now tries to represent itself as resolutely non-Western by emphasizing its Asianness. The irony is, of course, that the practice of caning - to mention but one example - is actually a British inheritance, not an indigenous Asian form of punishment.[8] (Even in the US caning was legal until it was ruled unconstitutional in 1948.)[9] The fact that it can now be represented in the arena of global geocultural struggle as a signifier for Asian superiority over the West, at least when law and order is your highest aim, evidences that what is accepted as 'Asian' today is the product of discursive work, of a concerted effort to *reproduce* an absolute binary opposition between East and West. In short, the work of discursive demarcation is carried out on both sides of the divide: there is a complicity between Western neo-Orientalist discourses which continue to construct Singapore as an alien Other to the West, and Singaporean discourses of self-representation which, as we further discuss below, rely heavily on the twin strategies of Occidentalism and self-Orientalization.[10]

If, as Edward Said has theorised, nineteenth century Orientalism was a

6. Jean-Louis Margolin, 'Foreign Models in Singapore's Development and the Idea of a Singaporean Model', in: Garry Rodan (ed), *Singapore Changes Guard*, Melbourne: Longman Cheshire, 1993, p86.

7. Edward Said, *Orientalism*, London: Penguin, 1985, p325.

8. In this respect, it is interesting to point to the complex cultural semiotics of power involved in caning. The transportation of this practice, common in English public schools, to the colonies overlaid the patriarchal state/disciplined child binary with an infantilization of the colonized peoples. Where in the context of the public school caning was a part of a disciplinary system which was assumed to produce moral rectitude and personal control, introduced in a governmental judicial system it tended to become viewed commonsensically more as a form of punishment, as Americans generally viewed it in the Fay case. Furthermore, the Fay case represented an interesting reworking of the colonial structure. Here, a youth from the West was caned by the assertively patriarchal Singaporean state whose disciplinary regime was originally framed by

British colonial administrators. Hence the official American sense of horror over Fay's caning can be understood to have two sources. First, a misrecognition of discipline for punishment, and second, the interpellation of Fay, a youth from the USA, the leader of the supposedly dominant West, in a situation where the semiotics of colonial relations are inverted.

9. This information was provided in Ed Koch, 'Bring Back Caning in US', in: *The Straits Times*, April 21, 1994, p26. Interestingly, Koch, former Mayor of New York, argued in favour of caning as a way of restoring law and order in the streets of American cities.

10. *Cf.* Chua, 1990, *op cit.*

11. Said, *op. cit.*

12. Chua, 1990, *op. cit.*, p8.

13. Ezra Vogel, *Japan as Number One: Lessons for America*, Tokyo: Charles E. Tuttle Co., 1979; Steven Schlossstein, *The End of the American Century*, Chicago: Congdon & Weed, Inc., 1989.

14. David Morley and Kevin Robins, 'Techno-Orientalism: Futures, Foreigners and Phobias', in: *New Formations*, No. 16 (Spring 1992):136-156.

discourse fashioned by the West in order to rationalise its colonial domination of the East, contemporary neo-Orientalism is equally governed by Eurocentric motives and biases.[11] As Chua observes: 'the way the issue of ascendancy of Asian capitalism is posed by some western intellectuals tells us more about ... their desire to revitalize the superiority of the West than about the nature of the Asian societies as such'.[12] This is evidenced, for example, in books such as Ezra Vogel's *Japan as Number One: Lessons for America* and Steven Schlossstein's *The End of the American Century*, which both discuss the nature of Japanese competition (and that of the other Newly Industrialised Economies of East Asia) in order to find recipes for the reinvigoration of American global hegemony.[13]

Not surprisingly, Japan has been the most sought-after target in the new Orientalism. Not only its economic superpower status, but its high-tech futuristic cultural image combined with the exotic mysteriousness which has traditionally been the orientalist perception of Japanese culture, has awed many Western observers. David Morley and Kevin Robins have described the late-twentieth century Western reworking of this orientalist construction of Japan as Techno-Orientalism.[14] This new Orientalism is no longer enunciated from a position of self-assured superiority but from a position of insecure defensiveness. Japan is the first non-Western country to have assimilated modernity and to have productively reconstituted it on its own terms, allowing it to challenge both the economic and cultural hegemony of the modern West. As a consequence, it manifests a cultural difference which cannot be absorbed into a wholesale westernisation. What Japan has invented for itself is a non-Western, Japanese modernity which now forms a powerful centrepiece of the 'new Asia'.[15]

But while Japan has received the (dubious) honour of being the object of both fear and admiration from a 'West' increasingly forced to examine its own claims of modernity, Singapore does not seem to be given such respect. Unlike Japan, Singapore is a small country which will never acquire superpower status, no matter how successful it is. More importantly, also unlike Japan, which has traditionally been a fantasmatic anchor point for classic Orientalist discourse, Singapore has not become for the West the symbolic site of a primordial, mysterious, and resolutely *other* culture. Unlike the intricate images popularly associated with Japanese culture, such as tea ceremonies or divine Imperial grace, as well as samurais and the practice of hara kiri, which the West considers the signs of a high (if sometimes barbaric) civilization singularly different from its own, Singapore's 'exotic Asianness' has been associated more with lowly images of coolies and rickshaws, generally signifying the mundane and pedestrian, rather than practices of cultural worth.[16] While Japanese modernity is feared but respected by the West, Singaporean modernity is generally derided and dismissed as inauthentic, synthetic, derivative. For example, a recent Australian TV documentary referred to the urban modernisation of Singapore in the last twenty-five years in the following scathing tone:

A wonderfully chaotic, Asian place was turned into an ordered, user-friendly metropolis. ... The old Singapore was full of character... Singapore these days is architecturally so sanitized, you need reminding you are in Asia.[17]

What Singapore is accused of here is that it no longer fits the old Orientalist image of colonial 'Asia'. Singapore is a non-Western Other which does not know its place: in becoming modern, it has lost its innocuous exotic charms, while it will simultaneously never match up to the standards of western modernity. Singapore's economic success may be recognised, but Singaporean cultural modernity is jeered at. Western tourists find Singapore 'too Westernised', while Western social scientists find Singapore wanting for failing to live up to Western definitions of a truly modern society (generally defined politically in terms of reified Enlightenment notions of freedom and democracy). Here we see, in a nutshell, the quandary of Singapore's place on the Western-dominated international stage: it finds itself positioned between two competing systems of representation; it is neither in the West, nor properly in the Asia constructed by the West.

Singapore's history as a colonial trade entrepot has left it not only with a deeply embedded Western legacy, but also with a very ethnically mixed population, most of whom were recruited as labourers by the British from China, India and Malaya. Thus, the city-state is an historical construct steeped in hybridity. Yet it is precisely this reality of hybridity, with its related dynamics of cultural impurity, mixture and fusion, which presents a problem in the dominant global cultural order, where nation-states are supposed to have pure and unified, if not homogeneous national cultures. In the cultural logic of the East/West divide, Singapore cannot be represented: the problematic positioning of Singapore exemplifies, perhaps more than any other nation-state, the exclusionary effects of the binary logic of the East/West discursive dichotomy. Here, a blurring of the boundary between East and West can only be signified negatively, as a lack, a deficiency, which excludes a country from either the 'East' or the 'West'. A short historical overview of the creation of modern Singapore enables us to understand the historical determinants of this predicament. Singapore is caught in an irresolvable dilemma: it owes its very existence to the West, and its 'Asianness' can never be defined externally to the West. Singapore, a product of Western colonial practice, entered the modern world through the direct intervention of the West.

TO CONSTRUCT A NATION WHERE THERE WAS NOT ONE

In 1819, Sir Stamford Raffles was given the task by the Governor-General of India to establish a trading station at the southern tip of the Malay Peninsula. He landed on the island of Singapore after having surveyed other nearby islands, and turned it into one of the Straits Settlements under the control of British India. Raffles is still routinely commemorised as the

15. For an examination of Japan's active role in its own Orientalization, see Koichi Iwabuchi, 'Complicit Exoticism: Japan and its Other', in: *Continuum: The Australian Journal of Media and Culture*, Vol 8, No 2 (1994): 49-82.

16. This image is mirrored in the title of James F. Warren's *Rickshaw Coolie. A People's History of Colonial Singapore*. Kuala Lumpur: Oxford University Press, 1986.

17. *Mini Dragons on Singapore*, ABC Television, 1991.

founder of modern Singapore - a clear sign of Singapore's intrinsically Western parentage. Singapore's success as a trading entrepot was remarkable and rapid. When Raffles arrived, there was a small indigenous population of about 1000 people, mostly Malays. By 1821 there were around 5000 people on the island, with roughly three times the number of Malays to Chinese immigrants. By 1860 the population had increased to 80,000 and in 1975 it stood at two million. From 1827 onwards immigrants from diverse parts of China made up the dominant group. Of the present day population 77.6 per cent are described in official census data as ethnic Chinese, 14.2 per cent as Malays and, 7.1 per cent as Indian. This plural pattern of immigration and settlement provides the background for Singapore's state policy of multiracialism, about which more later.

Singapore remained under British administration until 1959, when self-government was attained. The first general election was held in that year, which implemented the new Legislative Assembly and swept the People's Action Party under the leadership of Lee Kuan Yew to power. The party has retained power ever since. Apprehensive that 'an independent Singapore would be viewed by the neighbouring Malay countries as a Chinese city-state living off their wealth and raw produce', the PAP fought hard for a merger of Singapore within an independent Federation of Malaysia.[18] Though this was achieved in 1963, Singapore's membership of the new federal state only lasted until 1965. This history is usually taken as a straightforward explanation as to why a permanent sense of crisis pervades the Singaporean state's experience of itself. It is said that this sense of crisis erupted from the very moment that Singapore was catapulted into the status of a fully independent nation-state after it was forced to leave the Malaysian Federation. The connotations here are, in the first instance, familial: Singapore as the bastard child forced out of the Malaysian family and forced to fend for itself. Now that the British had gone home, Singapore, which could lay no claim to indigenous authenticity, was ostracised by its neighbours, Malaysia and Indonesia, who defined *their* postcolonial national identities precisely on the basis of discursive claims to territorial belonging. Mary Turnbull has described the moment of Singapore's independence in this way:

> Singapore's expulsion from Malaysia destroyed the basis on which responsible Singapore politicians had considered the state viable. She was unique among colonial countries in having independence thrust upon her unilaterally, her prime minister publicly lamenting in tears this 'moment of agony.' [19]

National independence, then, has been constructed in Singapore's official discourse as a deeply involuntary historical moment. It is important to gauge properly the symbolic significance of this involuntariness. It provides an historical explanation and legitimation for why the national narrative is

18. Raj K. Vasil, *Governing Singapore*, Singapore: Singapore National Printers, 1984, p91.

19. M. Turnbull, *A History of Singapore*, Kuala Lumpur: Oxford University Press, 1987, p297.

suffused with the felt urgent need to struggle for Singapore's survival.

To illustrate how this rhetoric has been developed, we can quote from a recent fact sheet published by the Ministry of Information and the Arts. It describes what happened after the separation from Malaysia in the following way:

> Thereafter commenced the struggle to survive and prosper on its own and to build a national identity and consciousness among a disparate population of immigrants. Its strategy for survival and development was essentially to take advantage of its strategic location and favourable world economy.[20]

20. Singapore Fact Sheet Series, No 3, History, published by Resource Centre, Ministry of Information and the Arts, November 1993.

Here the main themes of official Singaporean history are clearly reiterated: Singapore only reluctantly became an independent nation-state. Against its own free will, it was launched into a 'struggle for survival' which it subsequently carried out through determined, rapid economic growth. Where many nation-states commonly use external threats to bind their people together, Singapore also makes much use of the fear that it is not a properly constituted nation-state (defined, of course, in the modern Western sense). The state's drive for economic success on Western terms is, then, legitimated by the rhetorical claim that it has had to struggle to become a viable independent nation-state. Economic viability has always been seen as the *sine qua non* for Singapore's survival. And to a large extent, economic success has become the ideological benchmark for Singapore's *raison d'etre*.

However, economic success alone is not enough to provide Singapore with the sense of identity which every modern nation-state requires as a vehicle for self-representation. As Stuart Hall has remarked:

> a nation is not only a political entity but something which produces meanings, *a system of cultural representation*. People are not only legal citizens of a nation; they participate in the *idea* of the nation as represented in its national culture.[21]

21. Stuart Hall, 'The Question of Cultural Identity', in: Stuart Hall, David Held and Tony McGrew (eds), *Modernity and Its Futures*, Cambridge: Polity Press, 1992, p292.

In other words, what the new nation-state needed to develop was a system of cultural representation which gave meaning to Singaporeanness, and which enabled the population of the city-state to identify with being Singaporean, to be Singaporean citizens not only by law, but also, more importantly, in their hearts. The state's preoccupation with the construction of a national identity is rhetorically legitimated by the official history of Singapore's untimely birth as a nation-state. Its struggle to exist, previously used to justify Singapore's drive to develop its economy, is now reformulated as a struggle to develop a distinctive Singaporean identity. But Singapore lacks the conventional resources for the construction of a national imagined community, to use Benedict Anderson's term: the people's deep connection with the territory and with each other through a common, primordial

22. Benedict
Anderson, *Imagined
Communities*,
London: Verso,
1983.

ancestry.[22] Singapore has no precolonial past which could give ready meaning
and justification to its postcolonial, newly achieved nationhood. It is
impossible for Singapore to erase its derivative and artificial existence as a
Western colonial construct: more than any other nation in the region,
Western colonialism is inscribed in Singapore's very ontology, and in the
very composition of its predominantly immigrant population.

SYNTHETIC ASIANNESS AND THE MULTIRACIAL NATION

This genealogy, of which we have presented a brief summary, is a crucial
factor in shaping the peculiarity of Singapore as a nation. Bearing in mind
Singapore's divided heritage between 'Asia' and the 'West', it is a genealogy
which marks the *necessary impurity* of Singapore's origins. There is a strong
concern with 'purity' in Singaporean rhetoric on 'race' and 'culture' which,
as we will discuss shortly, is allied with an official policy of multiracialism.
The discourse of racial and ethnic homogeneity has been central to the
Western conception of the nation-state, as was the presumption that the
more homogeneous the people, the more legitimate the nation-state. One
of the most important subtexts of the Western infatuation with, and fear of
Japan has been the perception, produced and reinforced by Japan itself,
that it is a racially and ethnically homogeneous nation-state. However, since
before independence Singapore has always had to perceive itself as racially
and ethnically heterogeneous. As a result, the idea of homogeneity is an
impossible one in the Singaporean context. Furthermore, given the fact
that modern Singapore is generally conceived as a nation of immigrants,
what Rey Chow observes as 'the inevitable tendency towards nativism as a
form of resistance against the dominance of western colonial culture', and
which so often forms the basis for a postcolonial legitimation of the nation-

23. Rey Chow,
'Between Colonizers:
Hong Kong's
Postcolonial Self-
Writing in the
1990s', in: *Diaspora*,
Vol 2, No 2 (1992):
p154.

state, would appear to have been an unfeasable trajectory for Singapore to
take.[23] However, what is remarkable about Singapore's search for national
identity after 1965 is precisely its nativist tendency, a nativism which is
necessarily fraught with contradiction. In the absence of a pure, native
tradition, the PAP embarked on a large-scale program of *inventing* nativity.
In a context which was inevitably always-already Westernised, Singapore
was determined to turn itself into an authentically Asian nation by celebrating
the native origins of the different migrant groups which together make up
the population of the city-state.

24. Yong Mun
Cheong, 'Some
Thoughts on
Modernization and
Race Relations in
the Political History
of Singapore', in:
Yong Mun Cheong
(ed), *Asian Traditions
and Modernization:
Perspectives from
Singapore*, Singapore:
Times Academic
Press, 1992, p57.

At this point, we can begin to understand the complex centrality of the
policy of multiracialism for Singapore's project of producing a distinctive
national identity. Singaporean multiracialism is a population policy which
is not only aimed, in the absence of racial homogeneity, at creating inter-
racial harmony (which is a key myth in modern Singapore and deemed
essential to its national identity), but also, in a more fundamental sense, at
enhancing, if not producing, authentic Asianness.[24] The very idea of
producing authenticity may sound paradoxical, but it is precisely this

paradox which marks Singapore's desparate attempt to escape, at least at the official level, its hybrid fate, the perceived curse of its impurity.

Singapore's ability to construct itself as a national imagined community suffers from an originary identity deficit. It cannot lay claim to a myth of indigenous origin (which is the case for Malaysia), nor to a history of heroic struggle for independence against colonial oppression (as is the case with Indonesia), which in these two (and in many other) contexts have provided the basis for a transcendental legitimation of the postcolonial nation-state.[25] Due to a lack of these kinds of mythic resources on which to base its national identity, the Singaporean state has sought to assemble such an identity from the discursively distinguished racial and ethnic elements available. As Jacqueline Lo has put it:

> The official approach to nation-building is aimed at the creation of a synthetic Singaporean identity composed of the 'traditional' elements of all the major communities.[26]

This project is overdetermined by a dualistic system of representation: national/ethnic; synthetic/organic; modern/traditional. On top of all these we can put the master-binary of 'Western' versus 'Asian', which is thus inscribed at the very core of Singaporean national identity. In other words, in its very conception Singapore's national Self cannot escape the tension created by this master-binary. It is a tension which cannot be resolved *precisely because Singapore's national identity depends on it.* As John Clammer puts it, Singaporean modernity is characterised by 'the tendency to oscillate uncomfortably between a desire for modernisation at all costs, and an equally strong desire to build a unique, but distinctively Asian culture, a culture which is strong, but always precarious'.[27] The policy of multiracialism provides the state with the tools with which it seeks to counter the precariousness of Singapore's 'Asianness' - indeed, to strengthen and reinforce it.

In view of our earlier observation that Singaporean reality is intimately bound up with Singapore's status as a Western construct, it is important to note here that the policy of multiracialism is a postcolonial appropriation of the system of ethnic separateness which had developed in Singapore under British rule. Modern Singapore's official construction of itself as having a multiracial make-up, consisting of an enshrined Chinese-Malay-Indian trichotomy, is thus the result of a crystallisation of colonial practice. As Geoffrey Benjamin has observed, British colonialism maintained control over the colony through:

> the institution of 'indirect rule,' which was based on the assumption that each 'race' had distinctive propensities that were best developed by setting up a political structure which maintained things at the stage they appeared to have reached when colonisation started. ... [As a result] ...

25. For a general discussion of mythic origins for the nation-state, see e.g. Ernest Gellner, *Nations and Nationalism*, Oxford: Basil Blackwell, 1983.

26. Jacqueline Lo, 'Myths of Nationalism and Cultural Purity in Singapore', in: *The Indian Ocean Review*, September 1992, p5.

27. John Clammer, *Singapore: Ideology, Society, Culture*, Singapore: Chopmen Publishers, 1985, p29.

racial stereotypes came to provide both the informal and formal bases for social interaction.[28]

28. Geoffrey Benjamin, 'The Cultural Logic of Singapore's "Multiracialism",' in Riaz Hassan (ed), *Singapore: Society in Transition*, Kuala Lumpur: Oxford University Press, 1976, p118.

29. *Ibid.*, p120.

30. The 'Other' category, comprising less than 2 per cent of the population, consists mostly of those designated as 'Eurasian'.

Ironically, then, multiracial Singapore has perpetuated the ethnic absolutism contained in this colonial 'divide-and-rule' politics. In this policy, as Benjamin puts it, '"race" is the macro-divisive base of cleavage'.[29] Singapore citizens must carry an identity card which identifies the 'race' to which the holder claims (or is asserted) to belong. In national censuses, in government reports, and in the schools, there is a constant reiteration of the Chinese-Malay-Indian-Other categorisation.[30]

Needless to say that the categories of 'Chinese', 'Malay' and 'Indian' are in themselves by no means homogeneous and internally cohesive categories. Their racialisation was achieved through a suppression of internal ethnic differences within each category. The 'Indians' for example consist of various ethnic groups such as Tamils, Punjabis, Gujaratis, and so on; the 'Chinese' category encompasses distinct linguistic and cultural groupings such as Hokkien, Cantonese, Teochew and Hakka. Thus the three key so-called 'races' in Singaporean discourse, which all come within the more general discursive descriptions of 'Asian', are not 'identities' which evolved spontaneously from lived cultures of particular ethnic groups; rather they are categorical classifications, developed and imposed during the British colonial period, which have now been naturalised in government policy. The 'cultures' of the different 'races' are seen as the major building blocks of an integrated Asian national Singaporean culture. Inevitably there are tensions between and within the various cultural groupings of 'Indians', 'Chinese' and 'Malays' who are reduced to these officially sanctioned categories, and the state, which attempts this reduction. These tensions, born of the state's efforts to homogenise highly disparate groupings, are compounded by the state's intervention to extinguish perceived cultural traits (such as lack of enterpreneurial ambition among the Malays) thought to be undesirable in the new Singaporean identity. As David Brown argues:

> the national community is portrayed as a multi-cellular organism which derives its character, identity and values from those of its component cells, specifically denoted in ethnic terms. The Singaporean national identity and values are thus seen as developing out of the component Malay, Chinese, Indian and Eurasian cultures. Since not all aspects of the original ethnic cultures were perceived by the state elites to be both admirable in themselves and fully compatible with each other, the state has made considerable effort to depoliticise the cultures and to engineer them so as to eradicate the undesirable elements, while fostering those aspects which could constitute building-blocks for the national identity.[31]

31. David Brown, 'The Corporatist Management of Ethnicity in Contemporary Singapore', in: Rodan (ed), *op. cit*, p. 21.

Here, Brown clearly suggests the functionalist nature of the government's interest in the validation of race/ethnicity. The effort is to 'engineer' racially distinctive ethnic cultures in such a way that they fit into their proper and harmonious place in the larger 'national culture'. In Benjamin's words, '"[c]ulture" as an object of public discussion in Singapore almost always means a traditional, ethnically delimited culture, a Golden Age to which each "race" can look back separately for inspiration'.[32] A 'culture', then, is what a racial group is imputed to bring with it from its 'homeland'. It is thought of not so much as a living, mutating and diversifying concatenation of relatively shared practices, but as a fixed system of claimed traditional elements often exemplified by customs and rituals to justify the predetermined cultural categorisation of people as members of a particular race.

Singapore invests enormously in the official validation of the three separate reified Chinese, Malay and Indian cultures (the Other category, often designated as 'Eurasian', is generally ignored), as it is through these three 'Asian high cultures' that Singapore aims to forge its unique and quintessential multiracial Asianness. As a result, ethnicity has been lifted out of the realm of unselfconscious, lived culture and into the sphere of ideology. Chineseness, Malayness, and Indianness, in the Singaporean context, are constructed as sites of authentic Asianness designed to provide the national culture with substance and originary solidity, what in Singaporean discourse is called 'cultural ballast'. As Benjamin astutely puts it, 'Singapore's Multiracialism puts Chinese people under pressure to become more Chinese, Indians more Indian, and Malays more Malay, in their behaviour.'[33] The paradoxical consequence of this is that just as Singaporean national identity is to be an avowedly synthetic construction, so Chineseness, Malayness and Indianness are also becoming synthetic cultural formations in the modern Singaporean context, fabricated rather than 'natural', and designed to represent a 'planned Asian authenticity' produced in order to fit the national order.

THE RETURN OF THE HYBRID REPRESSED

It should be clear by now that a fundamental contradiction lies at the heart of the Singaporean state's attempt to construct a national identity. On the one hand, Singapore is looking for a unitary identity which can, in a general sense, be described as 'Asian' rather than 'Western'. In order to reach this, the state has identified, and seeks to build on, the 'cultures' of three 'Asian' 'races'. On the other hand, setting aside the problems of equating 'culture' with 'race', we can now see why, from the state's point of view, the project of generating a unified Singaporean identity must always be seen as something in process, a utopian dream which mobilises 'crisis' and 'struggle' as prime rhetorical terms. As Lo has put it:

The contradiction inherent in the multicultural model [i.e. the assertion of ethnic culture as the basis for a national culture] is partly the reason why public discussion about the distinctive "Singaporean Culture" is

32. Benjamin, *op. cit*, p120.

33. *Ibid.*, p122.

34. Lo, *op. cit.*, p6

35. Lee Kuan Yew, in *The Straits Times*, 26 November 1986, quoted here from Lo, *op. cit.*, p5.

36. See the *White Paper on Shared Values*, Singapore: Singapore National Printers, 1991. For a critical analysis of this White Paper, see John Clammer, 'Deconstructing Values: the Establishment of a National Ideology and Its Implications for Singapore's Political Future', in: Rodan (ed), *op. cit.*, pp34-51.

37. Chua Beng Huat, 'The Concept of "Rights" in Non-Liberal, Democratic Singapore', in: *Trends*, July 30, No. 23, 1992.

38. It should be noted that this recognition of 'Asian values' is not confined to Singapore. For example, according to Ogura Kazuo, Malaysia's Prime Minister Mahathir Mohammed has suggested that 'diligence, courtesy and discipline (...) are universal values that Asia can proclaim' (*op. cit.*, p40).

39. See for example Etienne Balibar, 'The Nation Form: History and Ideology', in: Etienne Balibar and Immanuel Wallerstein, *Race, Nation, Class: Ambiguous Identities*. London and New York: Verso, 1991, pp86-106.

always projected into the future. It is envisaged that only when the people see themselves as Singaporeans first and foremost, before claiming ethnic membership, can a truly "Singaporean Culture" exist.[34]

In other words, while each 'race' is defined by its idealized and reified traditional 'culture', something needs to be installed which can function as a centripetal unifying force. Lee Kuan Yew himself drew upon the language of functionalist sociology when he asserted that it was not the government's policy to 'assimilate' but to 'integrate our different communities', that is,

> to build up common attributes, such as one common working language, same loyalties, similar values and attitudes, so as to make the different communities a more cohesive nation.[35]

The state's concern with the need to actively bring about national cohesion is reflected in the establishment of a government policy on Shared Values, which locates the source of national unity not at the level of 'culture', but that of 'ideology'.[36] In this logic, what is believed to bind the Chinese, Indians, and Malay together is a shared value system. The *White Paper on Shared Values*, released in 1991, lists five such presumably shared values: (1) nation before community and society above self; (2) family as basic unit of society; (3) regard and community support for the individual; (4) consensus instead of contention and (5) racial and religious harmony. What is most important in the context of our argument is that these shared values are defined as quintessentially 'Asian'. Discussing the affirmation of these 'Asian values' in Singapore and their use in the ideological construction of an 'Asian culture' which is independent of, and opposed to, 'Western values', Chua has argued that '[t]he intensity of criticism of the West as essentially individualistic is matched by the vehemence of the insistence that Singapore, or Asia, is essentially collectivist in cultural tradition'.[37] The state believes that there is a need to refine and inculcate these 'Asian values' in the population so that they can become the basis for a common Asian Singaporean national identity.[38] The paradox is, then, that while the 'Asian' heritage of each 'race' is located in the past, Singapore's national 'Asianness' is projected into the future, something which in the present needs to be constantly struggled for.

A well-known example of the problems posed by the policy of multi-racialism is to do with language. Language has always occupied a special place of importance in the politics of national homogenisation in the modern nation-state.[39] There are four official languages in Singapore: Malay, Chinese, Tamil and English. While Malay, for astute geopolitical reasons, is the national language, used, for example, in the national anthem, English is the language of business and administration. However, while English is widely spoken among all ethnic groups, it is not officially considered one of the so-called 'mother tongues'.[40] English, after all, is the language of the coloniser, its prominence symbolises the hegemony of the West, although it is also acknowledged by the leadership, somewhat ruefully, that English is the language of science and technology, so necessary for Singapore's modernisation. For pragmatic reasons related to Singapore's colonial heritage and to do with its importance as the international language of global capitalist modernity, English has been declared the sole medium of instruction in all schools.[41] In addition, however, the Singaporean education system has a rigorous policy of bilingualism in place which requires each child to study their ethnic 'mother tongue' - a policy designed to counter the 'negative' effects of English (ie Westernisation) and to inculcate the children with the cultural heritage of their 'race'. The policy of bilingualism, then, is a concrete outcome of Singapore's desire to become modern without becoming Western, to have access to Western science and technology while cultivating 'Asian values'. 'Asian' and 'Western' cultures are portrayed as 'primordial opposites' which are permanently in tension with one another.[42] Teaching all Singaporeans their 'mother tongue' is seen as a way of strengthening 'Asian values' in a condition where 'Western' influences are perceived as a 'necessary evil', of ensuring the perpetuity of 'Asian' authenticity in the face of 'Western' inauthenticity.

However, the contradictory nature of this binary oppositioning between authentic Asianness and inauthentic Westernness is revealed in the way 'mother tongue' is officially defined. One's 'mother tongue' in Singapore is not the language actually spoken with one's mother in childhood, but the language that belongs criterially to the 'race' to which one claims membership, regardless of fluency or usage.[43] Consequently, only three languages have the formal status of Singaporean mother tongues, corresponding to the three 'races', they are Malay, Tamil (for the Indians), and Mandarin (for the Chinese). In line with the classificatory logic of multiracialism, all Singaporeans get *assigned* one of these 'mother tongues'.[44] This is a formalist and essentialist definition of the 'mother tongue' which not only articulates and reinforces the ethnic absolutism inscribed in Singapore's multiracialism, but also highlights the synthetic, artificial nature of Singaporean Asianness: while it is presented as a validation of cultural heritage, a nativist recovery of 'roots', and a celebration of authenticity, it actually operates as a thoroughly inauthentic, planned construct, on which Singapore's desired cultural future is projected.

This can be most clearly illustrated through the case of Mandarin, the assigned 'mother tongue' of all ethnic Chinese in Singapore. The artificiality of this assignment is highlighted by the long-term 'Speak Mandarin Campaign', launched by the government in 1979, in which all ethnic Chinese were urged to speak less dialects and more Mandarin. The ethnic Chinese in Singapore are a linguistically heterogeneous group; Clammer cites a survey from 1980 according to which as many as 30 per cent of the total population were Hokkien speakers, 17 per cent Teochew, 15 per cent Cantonese, 5 per cent Hainanese and also 5 per cent Hakka. Less than 1 per cent were native Mandarin speakers.[45] The Speak Mandarin Campaign

40. This official exclusion of English as a mother tongue is not uncontested, but is subject of considerable debate. See for example Koh Buck Song, 'English: A Mother Tongue Too?', *The Straits Times*, June 14, 1994, pp4-5.

41. Vasil, *op. cit.*, p103.

42. Lo, *op. cit.*, p7.

43. Benjamin, *op. cit.*, p123.

44. Mixed blood children get assigned the ethnic 'mother tongue' of their father; Eurasians can choose between one of the three Singaporean 'mother tongues'.

45. Clammer, Singapore, *op. cit.*, p91-2.

is a concerted effort to eradicate the use of dialects in order to homogenise the Chinese: an attempt to impose order on a heterogeneity perceived by the state as threatening because it operates below the level of 'race', as it has been officially articulated, in other words, out of sight of the administrative structure of the state. As a result, Singaporean Chineseness is an engineered discursive construct portrayed essentialistically as a traditional culture encapsulated in Confucian values and the Mandarin language which is often at odds with the wide range of concrete cultural and linguistic practices of ethnic Chinese people, many of whom use dialects, or English, despite the government's insistent promotion of Mandarin.[46]

46. Cf. Brown, *op. cit.*, p24.

What drives Singaporean national cultural policy, then, is the desire to eradicate 'cultural contamination' which is seen as a key threat to the creation of a viable national identity. This represents a fear of the processes of hybridisation which expose and emphasise the necessarily impure, unoriginal, mixed, and provisional nature of all identities emerging and proliferating within the boundaries of Singaporean national space. It is to counter this perceived danger that official discourse reifies the East/West divide, which in turn becomes a self-perpetuating, self-legitimising system of representation which informs the symbolic construction of the national culture. David Birch dismisses the fear of over-Westernisation in Singapore as 'really more an expression of a deep distrust of the effects of international modernisation'.[47] However, this underestimates the pressure placed on any nation-state in the modern world-system to foster a distinctive national culture and identity which validates its own status as a sovereign entity. For a nation-state obsessed with its own survival and legitimacy, hybridity is anathema because it signals a lack of identity: this is the significance of Clammer's observation that 'the activity of demarcating, the importance of boundaries and the significance of ideas of pollution are all widespread in the Singapore classificatory system'.[48]

47. David Birch, *Singapore Media*. Melbourne: Longman Cheshire, 1992, p4.

48. Clammer, *op. cit.*, pp24-5.

It is important to stress, finally, that if this concern for clear and clean boundaries appears pathological, it also needs to be understood, within the present geocultural organisation of the world, as a defence mechanism which is a response to the West's continuing refusal to recognise the consequences of its own hegemony, and continuing insistence on the non-Western world's cultural otherness. This is the case, for example, when Westerners express surprise to hear Singaporeans speak English so well. George Yeo, the current Minister for Information and the Arts, remembers exactly such an incident when studying in Britain as a much younger man with a group of other Singaporeans. A British Army major who had over-heard them speak English at dinner had remarked that they were 'a well-colonised people'. Yeo recalls, speaking at the official opening of a secondary school:

49. Quoted in 'Singaporeans should have new Asian spirit, says BG Yeo', *The Straits Times Weekly*, 29 August 1993, p6.

It was an acid remark and I do not think I will ever forget what he said for the rest of my life, not because it was an insult, but because it came so close to a very painful truth.[49]

This incident, and Yeo's response, illuminates the postcolonial intercultural dynamic which has motivated the sentiment governing the Singaporean elite's concern with cultural identity. Of course the major's remark *was* an insult, in so far as it affirms the sense of superiority and arrogance which gave him the entitlement to make the Orientalist remark in the first place. It is along these kinds of cultural faultlines where the mutual complicity of Western Orientalism and Asian self-Orientalising, and the intimate connection between Asian self-Orientalising and Occidentalism becomes evident. It is because Singapore, just like Japan, is not allowed into the exclusive inner circle of 'the West' that it now capitalises on its idealised 'Asianness'. Indeed, as Funabachi has observed, Yeo himself believes that 'a distinctively Asian civilization, which carries on the traditions not only of Confucianism, but Taoism and Mahayana Buddhism, is being born' in Singapore.[50] Here we can see the wishful construction of a generalised Asianness formed as a syncretic system of values.

50. Funabachi, *op. cit.*, p78.

How then to disentangle this complicated web of mutual otherings and challenge their continuation? Clearly, it has to be emphasised that Orientalism in the West is not dead; on the contrary, as we have seen, classical Orientalism has now been transformed into a neo-Orientalism, where it is no longer a powerless, colonised Asia which is subjected to othering, but an empowered and, to a certain extent, threatening *modern* Asia. Struggle against this neo-Orientalist discourse remains urgent and necessary. On the other hand, in Asia itself a different politics is at stake.

In the Singaporean context, one site of struggle and negotiation is around the emergent notion of the 'new Asian', and the complex and contradictory ways in which this figure is represented and imagined. The idea of the 'new Asian' is being increasingly brought into circulation as a way of describing the ideal of the proposed new synthetic Singaporean identity. Minister Yeo for example has suggested that Singaporeans should embody a 'new Asian spirit' precisely to overcome their abject status as 'a well-colonised people'. Yeo puts it this way, echoing the importance of multi-racialism for safeguarding Singapore's Asianness:

> I like the term 'new Asian' because it expresses both the past and the future ... However much we may be influenced by the West, we will remain Asian at our very core because as Chinese, Indians, Malays and Eurasians we are derived from civilizations with long historical memories and deep traditions.[51]

51. *Ibid.*

The rhetoric is clear. What is promoted here is an idea of 'Asianness' which is both flexible and particularist: flexible in that it can accommodate the consequences of modernisation and modernity, but particularist in that this concept of the 'new Asian' defines its boundaries through a categorical repression and supression of the encroachments of Western universalism. Singapore is presented as representative *par excellence* of this 'new Asia', precisely because it harbours within its borders three ancient Asian civilizations, museumised, memorialised and memorised for their contributions to human greatness independent of European civilization. It is in this way that the Singaporean state mobilises the figure of the 'new Asian' to legitimise and strengthen its cultural nationalist agenda: a new, modern 'Asianness' is promoted through the construction of the 'West' as Other, and which, in its self-Orientalising, Occidentalist opposition to Westernness, mirrors the West's persistent neo-Orientalist othering of modern Asia.

To conclude, it should be clear that our critical discussion of Singapore's attempt to produce a national identity, leads to a problematisation of the discourses of the 'West' and of 'Asia'. Situated between the historically privileged discourse of the 'West' and the newly powerful and vocal discourse of 'Asia', the Singaporean context provides the opportunity for a deconstruction of both these discourses. If the state's construct of the 'new Asian' is motivated by the quest for a sovereign national identity, characterised by notions of cultural purity and authenticity, then it is the idea of hybridity, with its notions of mixture and fusion, which enables us to understand contemporary Singaporean reality. Ordinary Singaporeans testify to this in the practice of their everyday lives. As Geraldine Heng remarks, '[t]he Singaporean is a hybrid being ... springing forth from accidental circumstances, and held together by the beauty and majesty of an act of will that is constantly and collectively renewed.'[52] Thus, despite the massive promotion of the 'mother tongues', more and more Singaporeans of all 'races' now speak English at home.[53] However, lest Westerners rush to the chauvinistic and reassuring, but misleading conclusion that Singaporeans are therefore becoming 'more like them', ie more 'westernised', it should be added that the most popular Singaporean vernacular is Singlish, a creatively hybrid and uniquely Singaporean version of English which is laced with Chinese, Malay and Tamil expressions. While the government has banned Singlish from official use (e.g. on radio and television), this informal, impure, and thoroughly heteroglossic language thrives on the streets, among friends, and in popular culture.

This paper was first presented in the public lecture series 'Multiculturalism in a Global Context' at the East-West Center, Honolulu, Hawaii, in August 1994. An earlier version was published in the Singaporean journal Sojourn. *We dedicate this article to all our Singaporean students at Murdoch and Curtin Universities who provided us with invaluable insights into what it means to be Singaporean.*

52. Geraldine Heng, 'Hybridity, Identity and the Modern Singaporean', in: *Trends*, No 27, November 26, 1992.

53. 'More use English and Mandarin in their homes', *The Straits Times Weekly*, May 1, 1993.

CIVIL WAR, IDENTITY AND GLOBALISATION

Michael Humphrey

CONTEMPORARY CIVIL WARS

The outbreak of civil wars in states of the periphery has become increasingly commonplace. Generally they are formulated as 'ethnic' conflicts, conflicts between groups based on solidarity and identity located in 'imagined past communities' and unaccommodated in the nation-states that enclosed them. They are seen as the historical product of decolonisation which mismatched territory (national space) and people (national community). Consequently in the process of decolonisation - national self-determination, the principle upon which claims of national autonomy are made - was realised only for a portion of the people enclosed within the boundaries of nation-states.

Genocide in Rwanda is accounted for by Belgium's colonial practice of recruiting Tutsi tribespeople into positions of command and control over the majority Hutu; the disintegration of Yugoslavia is seen as the product of dormant or repressed national aspirations which re-emerged with the collapse of the Socialist Bloc rupturing the fabric of the state; the Lebanese civil war was seen as the product of colonial misadventure, with the French acting as colonial midwife to create a Christian majority state. According to the decolonisation 'mismatch' theory these ethnic conflicts and new demands for self-determination have occurred because of political change in the interstate system - the end of the Cold War and the retreat of superpower hegemony. Hence these new demands for national self-determination are simply the surfacing of long denied aspirations.

The nation-state, however, is not a natural form of community with a finite number of global aspirants but a 'naturalised' one with invented traditions and attachments and a potentially proliferating number of aspirants. Historically, social membership in nation-states could not precede their formation - the nation-state had to be invented before people could think in terms of the nation. Anderson's description of the nation-state becoming 'available for export' makes this point.[1] The ethnic nationalisms that are today asserting themselves are not only predicated upon the availability of the nation-state model but their own experience of nation-states. They are not realising their destinies because the lid has been taken off their forced enclosure in other nationalisms so much as being shaped by the experience of the nation-state and the larger processes of change in the global system.

The characterisation of contemporary civil wars as 'ethnic conflicts' is in fact historically contingent and needs explanation. Their characterisation as 'ethnic' points to the internal fragmentation of national society, the failure of the national story. These conflicts are indicative of the demise of national

1. Benedict Anderson, *Imagined Communities*, London, Verso, 1982.

sovereignty, the decline in a state's ability to regulate its borders and to prevent interventions by outside states, corporations or political movements. Moreover despite their popular representation as internal conflicts they are in fact international (cross border) wars which can usually only be sustained because the state can no longer regulate its borders.

Contemporary 'civil wars' correspond to what Said calls 'border wars', new forms of totalising space through the technology of mass culture and violence. Border wars are the unwelcome extension of earlier nationalist projects which created many new categories of people, including the wanted (citizens) as well as the unwanted (subordinate minorities, exiles and refugees). Contemporary civil wars are in part the consequence of creating boundaries and failing to include as equals the unwanted, the '...discontented, challenging urban mobs and the floods of semi-forgotten, uncared for people'.[2] Instead border wars have sought to essentialise an exclusive national identity.

The focus of this paper is the idea that violence can create a safe social space and reconstitute identity. Violence has become integral to the fragmentation and reterritorialisation of identity in civil wars. The now familiar (and awful) phrase 'ethnic cleansing' which came out of the writing on the disintegration of Yugoslavia is extremely evocative of notions of primordial attachment to a purified social body located within homogeneous social space. 'Cleansing' has been characteristic of contemporary civil wars, each conflict generating its own litany of 'massacres' for all sides in these conflicts. Moreover the retention of the social memory of massacre is made the basis of rekindling conflicts generations later.

The phrase 'ethnic cleansing' suggests a particular relationship between social space, identity and violence. The homogenisation of place is the basis for the construction of a new social body through elimination or expulsion of those deemed to be out of place. But the relationship between identity and acts of violence is more fundamentally a question of sociality. What kind of social relationships are possible in the context of national disintegration? In this case identity is constructed around 'community' - social belonging - not simply difference. The 'imagined ethnic community' is generally constructed as a subset of the national community that had previously enclosed them. The term 'ethnic nationalism' best describes this construction of a new 'imagined community' since it emphasises descent as the essential defining element for social membership.

Violence is integral to the definition of identity in civil war because it ruthlessly promotes the territorialisation of identity. Its potency derives from the fact that collective violence - massacre - is simultaneously an act of social death and social birth. The spatial delineation of community is written on the social body.

Massacre rids the 'community' of the external contamination of the 'other' and uses the 'space of death' to exclude other constructions of

2. Edward Said, *Culture and Imperialism*, Chattus & Windus, London, 1993, p396.

the 'social' or other possible political action.[3]

Violence constructs identity and sociality through spatial separation, by making sociality contingent on sameness.

However, violence extends the fragmentation of identity rather than creating the fissures in the first place. The fragmentation of civil war occurs in the context of the fracturing of an homogenising identity space of modernity - in particular that of the nation-state. The declining hegemony of the global system has generated a '... proliferation of new identities, new social categories, and often political groups'.[4] The pluralisation of identity as ethnicity and increased levels of ethnic conflict are expressions of this decline in hegemony and homogenising identity spaces.

VIOLENCE AND IDENTITY

One of the disturbing aspects of contemporary civil wars is the dependence on identity as a source of redemption, of the subordination of the self to '...a greater social project'.[5] This stands in opposition to the emergence of selfhood in modernity as 'alterity', the idea that the self is always becoming, fulfilling other possibilities of identity and existence. In modernity the self is achieved and is not natural or ascribed.[6]

However it is not violence itself which is constitutive of the collapse of 'modernity as an identity space' but the projects which deploy it. Violence has not intruded upon the ordered and homogeneous space of the nation-state but has been integral to its very constitution in the first place. In the European experience war-making was an integral part of state making. States eliminated or neutralised their opponents, offered protection, extracted rent and, in the process, enhanced their war-making capacities.[7] However a corollary to the development of state power and war-making were the constraints imposed by their own populations. Internal struggles against great regional lords and the taxation of peasant villages shaped the state in particular ways. Military power was gradually subordinated to civilian control, the economy to bureaucratic regulation, and individuals gained the right to address their wronged interests to parliament and petition. The realisation of citizenship rights paralleled the enhanced capacity of the state to make war.[8]

Violence has been even more central to the formation of the colonial and post-colonial state. The military was developed as a central institution of colonial power to pacify subject populations unconstrained by internal struggles between the 'rulers and ruled'. The European model of external war-making and counterbalance of citizenship rights was not 'available for export' to the colonial, and subsequently, post-colonial state (to use Anderson's formulation of the cultural dispersion of the nation-state). No other institutions rivalled the military in organisational and coercive power and in the post-colonial state no such counterweight emerged to state military power. Thus while war-making was important in the formation of European

3. Michael Humphrey, 'Civil Wars: between communalism and globalism', *Communal/Plural*, No 1, 1993, pp105-128.

4. Jonathan Friedman, 'Order and Disorder in Global Systems: A Sketch', *Social research*, Vol 60 No 2, 1993, pp205-234, 207.

5. Friedman, *op.cit.*, p223.

6. *Ibid.*, p217.

7. Charles Tilly, 'Warmaking and Statemaking as Organised Crime', in P. Evans, D. Rueschemeyer and T. Skopcol (eds), *Bringing the State Back*, Cambridge University Press, Cambridge, 1985, p181.

8. Michael Mann, 'Ruling Class Strategies and Citizenship' *Sociology*, No 21, 1987, pp339-354.

9. Charles Tilly, *Coercion, Capital, and European States*, AD 990-1990, Basil Blackwell, Oxford, 1990, p186.

states they '...almost never experienced the great disproportion between military organisation and all other forms of organisation that seems the fate of client states throughout the contemporary world'.[9]

In contrast to the European pattern of external war-making, postcolonial states have generally made war against their own populations. The consolidation of state power and the integration of diverse populations has been regularly achieved through pacification. Reliance on violence has seen many postcolonial states forge alliances with other states, rather than with their own populations, to secure state power. This has resulted in such states becoming ever more dependent on external political and military guarantees and less responsive to their populations.[10]

10. Fred Halliday, 'State and Society in International Relations' *Millennium*, Vol 16, No 2, Summer, 1987, pp215-229.

Historically the deployment of violence as a strategy in nation-state formation has produced different outcomes. As a container of cultural identity nation-states became a global phenomenon but they were never equivalent in the level of institutionalisation, centralisation, democratisation or cultural standardisation they achieved. Their institutional variability was noted by Wallerstein's classification of states as belonging to the core, semi-periphery or periphery. States are said to be weak or strong according to the extent to which they are able to regulate the flow of capital, commodities and people across their boundaries and influence events in other states.[11]

11. Immanuel Wallerstein, *Geopolitics and geoculture*, Cambridge University Press, Cambridge, 1991.

In both the core and periphery, the North and the South, the homogenising space of the nation-state is fragmenting. Pluralism is no longer an issue of modernity, of the possibility of exchangeable lifestyles for the self. It is now an expression of the search for new social identities which are subordinated to larger social projects which have religious qualities.[12] Meaning is being found in subordination of the ego to the group project. In the North this is usually expressed in identity politics, and in the South in the chauvinistic rhetoric and militancy of ethnic nationalisms.

12. Friedman, *op.cit.*, p223.

The repositioning of the self in the social body is often experienced as 'rebirth'. When combined with acts of violence this sense of rebirth is reinforced. Violence becomes a vehicle for separation and making the new social body or community. One's messy biographical entanglement in history can be severed through acts of violence.

Ethnic cleansing is a radical strategy of separation in the name of the new community and its historical project. 'Ethnic cleansing', the idea that through cultural homogeneity the moral community (in the Durkheimian sense) can be realised, is more than just an instrumental action. It is also a consummatory rite exercising the creation of community by massacre. There are two sides to violence, one is physical destruction, the other metaphysical desecration. Violent acts are as likely to be '...followed by purification as much as direct retribution'.[13] Hence a common feature of civil war, massacre (collective killing), is simultaneously an act of destruction and creation. Massacre purifies the 'community' by eliminating the other. This violence is deployed to redefine the social and the moral community and make other mobilisations and conceptions of social identity almost impossible. Violence

13. David Parkin, 'Violence and Will' in David Riches (ed), *The Anthropology of Violence*, Basil Blackwell, Oxford, 1986, p206.

underwrites the essentialising character of the politics of cultural identity, reinforcing fragmentation and difference.

DISCOURSE ON DEATH

If violence in civil wars essentialises identity it must also engage the meaning of death. The discourse on death, however, even in the 'identity space of modernity', has been problematic. The massive scale of military violence and destruction of human life this century has been difficult to assimilate culturally. In modernity individual death became constructed in relation to the 'progress' of one's life as a biography of achievement. The obituaries of significant persons still record the progress of exemplary lives in our daily press. However the emergence of mass war made death anonymous. The 'Great War' marked the beginning of mass war and mass carnage, even the destruction of entire cities, amongst working class conscript armies only recently educated into the possibilities of self-advancement.[14]

A literate and literary English infantry symbolised the optimism of modernity as they went to their slaughter with a belief in the educative powers of the classics and English literature and self-improvement through popular education.[15] Individual identity was lost in the face of mass death. The 'Field Service Postcard', used as an official standardised form of communication to convey minimal information, encapsulates the interchangeability of the self.[16]

However in the mass trench warfare of the Great War death still had its place - the Front. It consisted of three zones:

> the line where there were only fighting men; the next zone that was semi-immune to shellfire, where there were ancillary services, Army Service Corps, casualty clearing stations, horse lines, and possibly heavy guns. There were also some civilians and one could buy food, wine and women ...; finally the back areas peopled by old men, cripples, children and virtuous women.[17]

Between the living and the dead there were also three states of existence. 'First man; then, when hit, animal, writhing and thrashing in articulate agony or making horrible snoring noises; then a "thing"'.[18]

In contemporary civil wars the victims (if not the object) of violence are overwhelmingly civilians, not soldiers. War enters into peoples' homes and lives uninvited. All social space is potentially a zone of war and every place the site of potential invasion, destruction and death. There is no inside and outside, home and not home. In this context death itself can act as the basis of a discourse on the amoral and anarchic. The 'space of death', as Taussig puts it, can be constitutive of order through terror. Order and chaos are symbiotic: '...that great stemming morass of chaos that lies on the underside of order and without which order could not exist'.[19]

14. Fussell, Paul, *The Great War and Modern Memory*, Oxford University Press, Oxford, 1975, p40.

15. *Ibid.*, p157.16. *Ibid.*, p186.

16. *Ibid.*, p186.

17. *Ibid.*, p125.

18. *Ibid.*, p126.

19. Michael Tausigg, *Shamanism: A Study in Colonialism and Terror and the Wild Man and Healing*, University of Chicago Press, Chicago, 1987, p4.

The particular terror of civil wars is the idea of total destruction of community and place. The 'space of death' is everywhere, even the most familiar spaces. It is not a void, however, but a site for the cultural elaboration of fear in which meaning and consciousness are created. It is where '...the social imagination has populated its metamorphosing images of evil and the underworld'.[20] It is where evil resides, the thing one needs protection against. The culture of terror is nourished in the silence and myth of this space. Politically it is where fears are elaborated, crowding out other possible meanings, and used to control communities. The

20. *Ibid.*, p5.

> ...torturer's desire is prosaic: to acquire information, to act in concert on a large scale economic strategies elaborated by the masters of finance and exigencies of production. Yet there is also the need to control massive populations, entire social classes, and even nations through the cultural elaboration of fear.[21]

21. *Ibid.*, p8.

22. *Ibid.*, p9.

The culture of terror creates '...the need for a hated object and the simultaneous fear of that object'.[22] In the process boundaries are defined and victim and victimiser are terrorised alike. The Other is made the source of evil who must be destroyed. Safety can only be had with us, the 'community' through which you can also be reborn. The community's rebirth is enacted by the death and mutilation of the body of the Other.

In civil war the discourse of death is located in the survival of the group. The death of the individual is significant only in sacrifice for the group. Massacre is the centrepiece of violence in civil wars because massacre, more than any other act, defines these wars as communal. The memory of massacre creates history, identity and the focus for future mobilisations. The political significance of massacres is that they continue as a defining moment beyond the event and become part of historical collective memory reference point in the past. Or, as in the collapsing Yugoslavia, repressed events are invoked to mobilise and define new struggles.[23] Victims of earlier massacres are exhumed, made heroes, and reburied.[24]

For the participants, massacre is an act of solidarity and protection through terror. Massacres shape communal identity (e.g. sectarian, tribal, city quarter) out of social cleavages, or even loose categories, by encouraging people to 'imagine' themselves as separate and different. In this sense massacres engender, through fear, the 'imagining' of a potential 'ideal' community to be arrived at through the standardisation of culture in nation-state formation. The historicity they invoke merely reinforces cleavages increasingly etched in collective memory. This is why civil wars have an unstoppable quality and why peace cannot be achieved simply by stopping the war.[25]

Through the medium of television, massacre reaches well beyond its immediate victims and addresses a global audience. War in Bosnia, for example, was the most monitored conflict ever.[26] UN observers actually witnessed and recorded in detail the day to day slaughter. The message

23. Mark Thompson, *A Paper House: the Ending of Yugoslavia*, Vintage, London, 1992, p.108.

24. Vease B. Lincoln, 'Revolutionary Exhumations in Spain, July 1936', *Comparative Studies in Society and History*, vol 27, 1985, pp241-260.

25. Ahmad Beydoun, *Le Liban: Itineraires dan une guerre civile*, Karthla-CERMOC, Paris & Amman, 1993, p181.

26. 'Bosnia is the classic case of using humanitarian aid as a smokescreen to hide political failure' An interview with Mark Duffield, *Middle East Report*, No187-8 1994, pp18-23.

conveyed to the global TV audience by the official reluctance to act to prevent the massacres and mass displacement, was that civil war was a form of 'self-determination', unacceptable perhaps, but ultimately aimed at realising the 'natural' community of nationhood. Only by allowing the process of the 'naturalisation' of community to take its course could people achieve their self-determination and peace be restored. The destruction of one nation was, afterall, being replaced by several nations!

FRAGMENTED IDENTITIES IN THE CITY

If the violence of civil war engenders the fragmentation of identities they are located in processes which are already part of the social experience of people. The place where the fragmentation of identities and civil war collide is in the city. What has made the city the site of fragmentation and the central battleground of civil wars?

Historically national space and urban space were the two sites of social transformation in modernity. National space territorialised identity and incorporated people through a narrative of cultural unity of imagined community. Urban space socialised people into new forms of consciousness and ways of living. The intensification of economic and social life in industrial cities promoted individualism over social reciprocity and the commodificiation of all relations. In practice the industrial city was always a highly differentiated space and a site for intense regulation by the state in the contest of interests between capital and labour. However recent changes in forms of capital accumulation from intensification and stability focused on urban growth to flexibility and inter-urban mobility have emphasised the fragmented character of urban space and the increasing insecurity of urban social life.

In the immediate post Second World War period urban development had focused strongly on the intensification of investment in the built environment. Urban growth was premised upon the consolidation of investment and inflow of people. This strategy was referred to as 'demand-side-urbanisation'. Manufacturing, construction and consumption organised social space in terms of the signs and symbols of prestige, status and power.

However by the 1970s economic crisis undermined the apparent stability of the city and brought disinvestment and deindustrialisation. Demand-side-urbanisation collapsed bringing high unemployment, capital flight, factory closures and the threat of devaluation of fixed capital investments and physical infrastructures. In its place emerged a decentralised and flexible pattern of capital accumulation which intensified inter-urban competition for investment in the new economies based on high technology industries, financial services, leisure and entertainment industries.

The threat of disinvestment in urban economies has been accompanied by a reorientation in the state's role in managing the city. Previously the Fordist welfare state had supplemented wage incomes by guaranteeing a social wage - spending on public education, health and welfare. In order to retain or attract investment the state has shifted from subsidising the poor to subsidising the rich through direct concessions - eg reduced corporate taxes - or indirect subsidies such as reduction of labour costs through labour market deregulation and informalisation.

The social impact of disinvestement and the subsidising of the rich has been an increasing number of impoverished people fending for themselves in unregulated urban spaces.[27] Informalisation, the growth of marginal and illegal economic activities, relies upon the dependence of most urban households on monetary income. Consequently the urban landscape is increasingly polarised between households with high wages who can afford to buy services on the private market and households forced to survive on low (or diminished) wage incomes and made increasingly dependent on social reciprocity (self-provisioning).

The social impact of impoverishment through flexible accumulation and informalisation has been the emergence of 'urban subsistence'.[28] Urban households are forced into patterns of social reciprocity through the collapse of their capacity to receive either employment or adequate incomes. Urban subsistence strategies are more than the resurrection of older ways of community living in the city, they involve new patterns of social dependence. For example, the 'feminisation of poverty' has made female-headed households much more common and placed women '...at the heart of reciprocal strategies'.[29]

Urban subsistence strategies fragment urban space through the intensification of social relations and the way poor households live in urban space. Increased reliance on social reciprocity involves the 'continuous appropriation' of urban space, the only means the poor have to occupy urban space.[30] By living close together, socialising, caring for each other and using community networks to find employment and gain access to wider social and economic resources, people generate community and cultural identity through shared experience. Urban subsistence is about establishing a secure urban space. However the autonomy achieved through this 'urban' community is limited. In fact the very notion of community becomes integral to restrictions on choice which have helped engender the '... homogenisation of life experience' in a fragment of urban space. Urban subsistence represents an intensification and contraction of the social in increasingly unregulated urban space.

The resort to urban subsistence strategies coincides with the shift of the contest between capital and labour from the national to the international arena. The community of urban place is restricted, with little capacity to influence alliances forged at the international level. The cultural capital of 'community' and 'identity' can only be deployed collectively in a contest to secure a greater share of state redistribution of resources - multicultural politics - or individually to facilitate geographical mobility between different urban 'communities'.

Urban subsistence strategies generate community as a mode of self-

27. David Harvey, *The Urban Experience*, Basil Blackwell, Oxford, 1989, p267.

28. Enzo Mingione, *Fragmented Societies: A Sociology of Economic Life Beyond the Market Paradigm*, Basil Blackwell, Oxford, 1991, p189.

29. *Ibid.*, p295.

30. Harvey, *op.cit.*, p256.

reliance which is often culturally expressed in ethnic, racial and status distinctions. Conflict between groups can occur precisely over the attempt to preserve domains of social autonomy. The state, however, is ambivalent towards these new urban communities which it has helped create, through either its retreat from support for a social wage or, in the case of states in the periphery, winding down the much more limited support of food subsidies for the urban poor at the insistence of their international creditors. These new urban subsistence communities reduce the cost of social reproduction to the state but also become politically dangerous because they are increasingly outside the normal channels of social incorporation.

The fragmentation of cultural identity must be understood as continuous with the impact of globalisation of capital and mobility of people, particularly in the city. The proliferation of identities is part of the collapse of identity spaces of modernity, the nation and the city, expressed within specific urban histories. Identities are contingent upon the intersections of the movement of people, their continuing links with places of origin, strategies of urban subsistence and the cultural history of specific differences. In addition inter-urban competition and the success or failure in attracting different kinds of investment make social consciousness highly specific, increasingly articulated in localised identities and histories and conceived in terms of local group privilege or disadvantage.

THE CITY AS A TERRAIN OF WAR

> The war in Bosnia is obviously urbicide - cities have been relentlessly bombed into shambles. This revenge of the red-necks who have always hated the cities. The cities are where massive intermarriage and denationalisation take place, where various national groups mix and make friends, where women enter professions, where the young reject tradition. They are seats of political authority and the source of modernity. The villagers have always hated and envied the cities, and this war permits the destruction of these dangerous places.[31]

31. Bogdan Denitch, *Ethnic Nationalism: The Tragic Death of Yugoslavia*, University of Minnesota Press, Minneapolis, 1994, p185.

Urbicide, Denitch suggests here, is the destruction of the city by the countryside motivated by its resentment towards the city as modernity. The theme of the revenge of the village on the city is a common one in civil wars. In the Spanish civil war Franco mobilised the Spanish countryside against the city, and even tribal villagers from Morocco, to exact his revenge on the radical workers movements of the city. Similarly the Shi'a urban poor in the Lebanese civil war were in part responding to their historical subordination to the city from where the Sunnis and Maronites had politically and culturally dominated them.

Yet rather than being the resentment towards modernity 'urbicide' is more an expression of the crisis of modernity. It is the failure of modernity in the terms that Denitch suggests - intermarriage, denationalisation, gender liberation - that provokes the crisis. Historically the city has always been intimately connected to its hinterlands and the very identities constructed in the city expressions of the rural-urban connection. These identities, as identities of group membership, have been given salience through rural-urban migration and setting, cheek-by-jowl, social categories whose identity is reinforced by urban subsistence strategies. It is not the rage of the country against the city so much as the crisis of the city as a vehicle for socialisation into modernity. The siege and division of cities along 'green lines' is about the connection between the inside and outside, not the defence against the outside only.

However Denitch's concept of 'urbicide' does suggest two important aspects of contemporary war on cities. Firstly, that war is conducted against urban populations as an instrument of coercion, mobilisation and differentiation (border wars), and secondly, that the destruction and occupation of urban space is instrumental in the reconstruction of 'community'.

It is only since the 1930s that making war on urban populations has become commonplace. Civilians became a focus of military strategy with the emergence of mass war and the technology of distance weapons, especially the advent of air power. The use of aerial bombing of European cities began with Guernica during the Spanish Civil War - although the practice was pioneered earlier in the 1920s against recalcitrant frontier tribes on the indeterminate borders of colonial states. However it was during the Second World War that aerial bombing of cities began in earnest. These urban attacks were often called 'slum raids' because they were designed to cause maximum distress to working class districts.[32] The bombing of cities was premised upon the idea that '...the people themselves, driven by the instinct of self-preservation, would rise up and demand the end of the war'.[33] The effect of these aerial raids was 'place annihilation'. The geography of destruction included homes, families, streets, landmarks and places of congregation. Living worlds became 'dead cities' where the '...internal map no longer fits the space to which it applies'.[34]

Urbicide through mass war has different aims from that of civil war. In the former the death of cities is about dislocation, demoralisation and even total physical destruction in order to drive the state into submission; in the latter it is about the dispossession, eviction or elimination of people from urban space. Place annihilation in civil wars is more often about cultural dispossession and occupation of space rather than its absolute destruction. Ethnic cleansing is about changing the mapping of cultural worlds, through dislocation of people or erasing cultural memory attached to place/home - a house, street, or neighbourhood.

The remapping of Beirut during the Lebanese civil war is a case study in the geography of urban violence in contemporary civil wars. War came to Beirut in 1975 following the gradual political mobilisation around sectarian grievances in the confessional political system and the militarisation of the

32. Kenneth Hewitt, 'When the Great Planes Came and Made Ashes of our City... Towards an Oral Geography of the Disasters of War' *Antipode*, Vol 26, No 1, 1994, pp1-34, p18.

33. *Ibid.*, p7.

34. *Ibid.*, p20.

Palestinian Liberation Organisation in Lebanon. The city's population had grown rapidly through rural-urban migration in the 1960s and 1970s to contain around half the national population. The growth had been stimulated by Beirut's emergence as a regional financial, banking and tourist centre, a global city whose wealth depended on its service, leisure and entrepot activities. The new city populations were clustered around communities of origin creating a patchwork of regional sectarian communities which became the focus for urban political mobilisation, through clientalism. Urban subsistence, community networks and sectarian identity was the mode of integration for large numbers of unincorporated marginal proletariat whose ties to the village remained strong.

The Lebanese war began in Beirut, and most of its victims were residents from in or around the city. Moreover they were overwhelmingly civilian. It is estimated that in the Lebanese war around 75 per cent of the deaths and 86 per cent of the injured were civilians while only 15 per cent of the dead were militiamen and 10 per cent were regular soldiers.[35] Only the deaths of militiamen and their leaders were publicly celebrated, often as martyrs, in the form of black and white poster portraits plastered on walls, and sometimes painted on them, around the domain the militia controlled. The deaths of civilians were more likely to be noticed by their absence from the social landscape of a street or workplace - like the Hamra St flower-seller whose presence symbolised the continuity and even normalcy of life in West Beirut until his death in a car-bomb - than official statistics or records.

The tempo of death and destruction which remapped Beirut ebbed and flowed over 15 years as the war passed through different phases. The violence that reshaped the city covered a wide spectrum including military action by invading armies, clashes between opposing militias on the 'Green line', inter-militia violence (between groups supposedly on the same side), massacres of urban communities (especially the populations of the indistinguishable refugee camps) to provoke flight, aerial bombing by Israeli warplanes and the daily terror instilled through car-bombings, identity-card murders, kidnappings, random shelling and snipers. The responses to this violence ranged from flight, local mobilisation in self-defence and resignation.

The remapping of the city, the fighting and the dying, was carried out largely by its inhabitants rather than by invading armies. The strategic logic of urban warfare helped reinforce the solidarity of communities because in the city the military advantage lies with the resident defenders. For the attacking forces the urban terrain is costly and difficult.[36] The Syrian and Israeli military commanders recognised the advantage of the defenders and limited their direct military action in Beirut's suburbs - the Syrians only after a costly campaign in east Beirut in 1978. Instead the Syrians encouraged communal mobilisation of communities by supporting proxy militias to pursue their military interests on the streets. Not only did residents have the strategic advantage of defence but also much greater commitment to the protection of homes and families. The defenders fought as a matter of

35. Theodor Hanf, *Coexistence in Wartime Lebanon: Decline of a State and Rise of a Nation*, Centre for Lebanese Studies, I.T. Tauris, Oxford, 1993, pp339-40.

36. G.J. Ashworth, *War and the City*, Routledge, London 1991, p123.

honour, defending the integrity of the intimate space of home and their women.

The violence divided the urban landscape into three zones; 'no-man's land', 'front lines' and 'living space'. In Beirut no-man's land was called the 'Green Line'. This was the former heart of the city, the old central business and hotel district which saw massive destruction and dehabitation in the early stages of the war. The zone included important national political and cultural institutions - the parliament building and the museum. The crossing points of the zone were given such ominous names as 'snipers alley' and 'the fly way of death'.

The front lines were the inhabited districts in the line of fire. These were visually recognisable by large mounds of earth blocking streets to provide some cover for people to go about their daily lives. However front lines were often very indeterminate and shifting, especially in the area where the influence of militias overlapped and was contested. Living space encompassed the rest of the city, areas where familiarity and daily encounters were the limits of control against random violence - that comforting illusion that *wasta* (influential connections) could somehow save you from death or disappearance. However random shelling, aerial bombardment, kidnappings, carbombings and the anonymity of terror meant that nowhere was really behind the lines.

The boundaries between zones were fluid throughout the war. In part this was because violence was never consistently constructed around simple cleavages. For example, the casualty statistics of 1986 reveal that more than half the deaths occurred as a result of conflict between supposed allies while only one quarter occurred as a result of confrontations on the classic fronts.[37] The logic of political control on the streets was the 'homogenisation' of urban space, even when it involved people who were supposed to be allies. 'Homogenisation' of urban space was extensive and led to major redistributions of population. In Beirut some 40,000 Christians were forced to leave the south western suburbs (Haret Hreik, Bourj al-Barajneh and Chiyah), a further 35,000 fled from the centre of Beirut to the east. Around 115,000 Muslims fled east Beirut (mainly from the suburbs of Karantina, Nabaa and the Palestinian camp of Tel al-Za'tar which was overrun and bulldozed flat) to the West along with some 15,000 Christians who were members of Left parties or the Lebanese national movement. Moreover Beirut became the destination of many refugees, during the ebb and flow of fighting in different parts of the country.[38]

The total number of people forced into flight or expelled from local communities is estimated at around 790,000, about one third of the Lebanese population. Most of these were unable to return to their homes and many were forced to flee more than once. Flight produced a much more homogenised country. Christians are now almost totally absent from the Chouf, the Bekaa Valley and most of West Beirut and Muslims from East Beirut and most of Mount Lebanon.

37. Hanf, *op. cit.*, p341.

38. *Ibid.*, p345.

Terror facilitated homogenisation and sectarian mobilisation in a climate of fear. 'A family would man a barricade, a "village" assumed responsibility for a street, "the" Shi'is or "the" Maronites for whole quarters'.[39] Terror socialised people into the acceptance of violence as the only possible response. Civilians acquiesced in the terror of their militias, justifying it as a necessary form of deterrent. Thus they accepted kidnappings, murder, massacres and expulsions all on the basis of group survival. 'The greater the terror, the more strongly people identified with "my militia, wrong or right"'.[40]

Moreover terror could be put to the service of much grander projects; hence the kidnapping of Westerners was seen as a symbolic act in the Islamic struggle against imperialism. The total occupation of urban space through kidnappings and bombings assumed global significance through its reporting in the world media. Cleansed of Western presence neighbourhoods became the militant domains of pro-Iranian Shi'a clerics whose influence, in fact, did not extend far beyond the borders of their communities.

Although terror was a mobilising force it was also suffocating. It created dependency but did not necessarily induce solidarity and sacrifice in everyone. Only some of the young men joined militias and those who did often approached it as a job (employment was scarce) or as a neighbourhood defence group. Many demonstrated their political flexibility by even changing militia membership if their neighbourhood came under the control of a different militia. Moreover middle class families who had the means and connections to send their sons overseas, away from the fighting, did so. As the war progressed and communal fighting gave way to more intensive intra-communal fighting at the level of the street and the quarter the integrity of sectarian solidarity also appeared more shaky. It is interesting to note that during the war Lebanese historians did not subscribe to the 'communal' view of the conflict until after the Israeli invasion of 1982.[41] It was at this point that the radical Islamic movements began to gain influence amongst the Sunni and Shi'a Muslims and the reconstitution of the confessional state looked bleak.[42]

Another phenomenon which tended to limit communal mobilisation were the individual strategies of family survival, notably emigration and labour migration. The Lebanese were able to mobilise connections in an already extensive diaspora formed over a hundred years of emigration. Employment opportunities during the oil-boom years of the 1970s and early 1980s in the Gulf states also made them a major destination for labour migration. It is estimated that nearly one quarter of all Lebanese lived outside the country at some time during the war, many providing remittances for family members in Lebanon.[43] The impact of violence on social life was to parochialise communal life and identity on the one hand, and privatise and internationalise the household on the other. In order to insulate themselves from the dictates of militia power and poverty, households sought independence by securing incomes from remittances. Thus the intense

39. *Ibid.*, p331.

40. *Ibid.*, p330.

41. Beydoun, *op. cit.*, p59.

42. Michael Humphrey, *Islam, Sect and State: the Lebanese case*, Centre for Lebanese Studies, Papers on Lebanon, No 11, Oxford, 1989.

43. Hanf, *op. cit.*, *p349.*

localisation of social life -especially for men - further internationalised Lebanese life through the dispersal of some household members for incomes. Men left the country to work because of the lack of employment and because, unlike women, they were always at risk of being vicarious victims in revenge killings and kidnappings.[44] This gendered logic of civil war security was also evident in diaspora communities where generally only the women and children visited family in Lebanon. Husbands and teenage sons stayed at home for safety.[45]

44. *Ibid.*, p327.

45. Humphrey, *Islam, Multiculturalism and Transnationalism: from the Lebanese Diaspora*, I.B. Tauris, 1997.

The example of Beirut highlights the social fragmentation of civil war in the city. Firstly, the process that located people in urban space, the reliance on the cultural capital of family and community as a strategy of urban subsistence, was extended by the collapse of the state and the emergence of militia power on the streets. The politics of massacre brought about population transfers which homogenised urban space and essentialised communal identity as the natural one. A similar process occurred in the cantonisation of Bosnia leading '... in a straight line to massacres, atrocities, looting, gang rape, and concentration camps as instruments of the new demographic policy'.[46]

46. Denitch, *op. cit.*, p162.

The Lebanese civil war also witnessed the dual process of the social contraction of the local and the internationalisation of the household through labour migration. Urban subsistence, survival, was organised around participation in the international labour market, fortunately for many Lebanese at a time when the Gulf economies were booming. Labour and capital flowed out of Beirut to the new boom cities of the Gulf.

The radical reshaping of Beirut left a legacy that the assassinated former Prime Minister Rashid Karami captured in his comment in the late 1980s: 'Lebanon is a prison containing those who are unable to escape'. The destruction and homogenising of the city, the loss of communities, their cultural maps and memories irrevocably changed the city and its character. Present discussion about reconstruction always focuses on the physical landscape, not the social. That cannot be reconstructed according to the internal maps of the dispossessed.

The vulnerability of global cities as centrepieces in regional development is also highlighted in the Beirut case. War in the city led to the flight of capital and its workforce, especially skilled and professional workers. The whole basis of the economy as a service, finance and tourist centre depended on stability and confidence. It is very unlikely it will be able to regain its former role in the region. The world has moved on.

GLOBALISATION AND CIVIL WARS

The politics of identity has assumed its extreme form in contemporary civil wars. It reveals a crisis in the construction of sociality in the context of globalisation. Where massacre and ethnic cleansing become integral to identity then 'pluralism' is no longer about the possibility of 'alterity' but the subordination of the self to the group. It is an expression of not the post-modern so much as the anti-modern. The possibilities of the self are subordinated to the survival of the group through the politics of fear and radical contraction of the social world.

But the phenomenon of civil war and its characterisation as the product of 'ethnic conflict' is not an inevitable or even natural outcome of the historical unfolding of national destinies. These contemporary internal conflicts have emerged out of earlier failures of incorporation in national states and the fragmentation that has emerged from the impact of globalisation on social life. Rapid urbanisation, the inadequacy of single wage incomes and the retreat of the state from public subsidy, and protection of the poor has created new urban communities and new identities in the city. The contemporary crisis is centrally located in the city and its role as a vehicle for socialisation into modernity. The resort to identity as a source of social redemption articulates this crisis. As Said observes, it bears out Fanon's worst fear ... 'identity, always identity, over and above knowing about others'.[47] As a project it revisits an earlier period of nation-state formation where in the Middle East '...the effort to homogenise and isolate populations in the name of nationalism (not liberation) [has] led to colossal sacrifices and failures'.[48] Ethnic nationalism offers a solution of sorts for some people only and great distress, dislocation and the destruction of lives, homes and communities for many others.

The resort to identity politics expressed through local territorialisation and homogenisation is linked to the impact of globalisation on states and peoples. 'The world economy is not accessible to democratic decision making, particularly not that of a small, independent state'.[49] Moreover many states are less and less able to intervene to assure economic, political or personal security of their citizens. Understood in these terms localisation represents a strategy of control based on the idea that self-determination and peoplehood are the basis for empowerment.

But if states are losing their sovereignty, can the sovereignty of the people be the basis of empowerment in the context of globalisation? Ethnic nationalisms may represent a strategy for the sovereignty of people but they are essentially '...hostile to democracy and pluralist societies. [They represent]... a *jihad* against McWorld'.[50] Individual rights are subordinated to those of the ethnic group which is regarded as the primary reference for representation and grievances. Even where conflicts result in secession and the realisation of political sovereignty the terms of independence will still be shaped by the dictates of the market, the need to be competitive in the era of 'flexible accumulation'. Clientship will be shaped by global capital, not as before by the Cold War benefits of strategic political rent.

But perhaps the viability of the politics of identity as social exclusivity is uncertain anyway, and what we are witnessing is a phase in which internationalisation will proceed further into the level of private lives as it did in Beirut. The way the Beirutis (and today many people in countries undergoing political upheaval) responded to the coercion of terror and

47. Said, *op. cit.*, p362.

48. *Ibid.*, p361.

49. Denitch, *op cit.*, p160.

50. *Ibid.*, p197.

ethnic cleansing, was to withdraw to the household and sustain themselves through remittances - sending members out into the international labour market. This was an acknowledgment that their world was not amenable to democratic politics but only to the individualisation of one's fate. It is family rather than community that becomes the most versatile linkage in globalisation, offering the possibility of geographical relocation through personalised worlds of reciprocities.

But where does sovereignty lie in such a world? The decentering of global hegemony has led to the decline of state sovereignty but also the proliferation of international organisations to monitor and regulate states experiencing upheaval. It is evident however that these bodies are not capable of reconstituting political and social order of nation-states or substituting supranational institutions of regulation and protection. Instead they seek to contain the impact of civil wars geographically - limiting the flow of refugees, keeping people in place by creating safe havens or providing food aid.

Contemporary civil wars must be understood as the product of fragmentation brought about by changse in the global system. They are extensions of processes of social differentiation and the re-emergence of social reciprocity as the basis for social reproduction and survival as the market fails as a mechanism of social transformation. In particular they are most apparent in the cities where the strategies of urban subsistence and the fragmentation of identities has proceeded with the informalisation of the economy.

The politics of identity and 'ethnic cleansing' are the product of the subordination of the self to the group as the basis of social redemption. Violence brands itself on these cleavages and naturalises them, coercing people into thinking of themselves only as members of a community outside of which there is no protection. Urban warfare reinforces this logic through the fragmentation of the battle according to the urban topography and the advantage of the defenders. The city becomes constructed around siege communities.

The discourse on death in civil wars is that of martyrdom locating the meaning of individual lives in sacrifice for the group. Yet perhaps not everyone is totally persuaded by this. In Beirut defence and death were always first expressed in terms of 'home', the protection of private worlds and women. One's community was the shell of security and bondage.

The Place of Africa in Discourses about the Postcolonial, the Global and the Modern.[1]

Albert Paolini

The human tragedy in Rwanda has once again focused attention on Africa. Yet, like Somalia and Ethiopia before it, such attention has been spasmodic, cursory, and marked by a significant degree of incomprehensibility. Although events in Rwanda have less to do with tribal factors than is commonly assumed, it has been tempting to frame the genocide there as something specific to the 'dark continent': primordial, savage, unfathomable. Africa returns to the spotlight for one of its fleeting, unsettling moments. The stage is quintessentially African; the roles familiar, albeit shocking to the voyeuristic Western audience. However, our knowledge and expectations of African behaviour and identity mask a deep-seated level of cultural misunderstanding. There are long silences concerning what occurs on the African continent between the seemingly random outbursts of violence. This is particularly true of the global media network. The human globe may indeed be shrinking, and the experience of hybridity and ambivalence may capture something common to us all in the late modern age. But within this family of human experience, Africa, like the aberrant relative, remains on the far side of Western comprehension.

What is surprising is that there is little new in this approach to Africa. In *Culture and Imperialism*, Edward Said makes passing reference to an 'Africanist discourse' or 'Africanism', which he describes as a systematic language for dealing with and studying Africa, in the West. This discourse is seen as part of a larger formation of orientalist-type European attitudes and practices toward the continent, involving conceptions such as primativism, tribalism, vitalism, originality and various other exercises in essentialism. Said views this discourse at work in the fiction of Conrad and Dinesen, as well as in the anthropology of Leo Frobenius and Placide Tempels to name but a few. What concerns Said, characteristically, is the continuing practice of normalising, enframing and containing the Third World within a Eurocentric discourse which serves Western hegemony.[2]

To what extent is academia complicit in the continued misunderstanding and enframing of Africa? Is there a refashioned 'Africanism' in the later part of the twentieth century which is equally distorting in its normalising of the African Other? Taking as my focus two recent academic discourses - postcolonialism and globalisation - I would like to argue, provocatively in the case of the former, that an alternate 'Africanism' marks these

1. 'Africa' and the 'Third World' are employed as shorthand for the multitude of cultures and identities under these rubrics. The 'Africa' invoked in this discussion refers particularly to sub-Saharan Africa (excluding South Africa). Similarly, 'postcolonialism' and 'globalisation' are not uniform discourses and encompass different perspectives. However, because they coalesce around certain core assumptions and address a common subject matter, it is possible to speak of them in the singular, if only, once again, as a convenient shorthand.

2. Edward Said, *Culture and Imperialism*, Alfred A. Knopf, New York, 1993, p193.

contemporary discourses. However, unlike the incarnation that Said refers to in which Africa is directly confronted and made sense of in its own, albeit skewed terms, the use and place of Africa in these discourses is decidedly different. Here the specificities of Africa are systematically ignored; it is marginalised by its incorporation into broader insights and theories which are casually, at times arrogantly, carried over into Africa. In fact these are not 'Africanist' discourses at all, although ironically certain key assumptions are made on Africa's behalf. One is consciously Third Worldist, the other Globalist. In the former Africa tends to become part of an amorphous Third World; in the latter, it is lost in certain globalising processes of modernity. Africa figures in both by default. More importantly in terms of this analysis, vital questions of agency and ambivalence are inadequately treated in both. Put simply, such questions are hardly addressed in globalisation, except perhaps in Marxist accounts which attempt to inscribe the materiality of global processes. These critiques, however, display other problems which will be explored later. In postcolonialism, the situation is more complex although no less problematic. The focus on resistance tends to underplay or obscure the capacity for action and change *already taking place* in Africa. Moreover, the postmodern approach to questions of subjectivity which underpins much of postcolonialism, works to narrow a space for agency. A prominent theme in postcolonialism is the focus on the ambivalence of colonialism or colonisers as a process and discourse rather than the ambivalence of the so-called 'subaltern' towards modernity and the West generally.

Postcolonialism and globalisation have dominated literary/cultural studies and sociology respectively, with both making important inroads into the study of politics. As academic discourses they have profound implications for an understanding of culture and identity in the Third World. The former, born out of literary and cultural criticism and infused with French social theory, posits notions of difference and resistance in relations between the West and the Third World, albeit within a framework of intensified hybridity. Gradually the focus on outright resistance has been overtaken by a general acceptance of Derridean ambiguity and contingency. In some respects this has led to certain tensions in the articulation of a postcolonial stance or condition. Notwithstanding its heterogeneity and shifts in emphasis, it can be viewed as a celebration of the particular and the marginal which envisages peoples of the Third World carving out independent identities in a de-Europeanized and hybrid space of recovery and autonomy. Globalisation discourses assume an increasing homogenisation about the world in which Third World cultures lose their specificity and become absorbed in a global (that is, Western) culture. Thus we have quite distinct characterisations about the place of the non-Western world which revolve around the axes of difference and same, heterogeneity and homogeneity. However, I would argue that both these perspectives are flawed with respect to their theoretical assumptions and their treatment, or indeed non-treatment, of particular identities and cultures such as those in Africa.

THE DIASPORA TAKES A POSTCOLONIAL TURN

Postcolonialism has ridden the crest of an academic wave which has established the issues of identity and culture as central in the humanities and social sciences. It has done this, moreover, from the particular stance of giving Third World peoples a voice in Western academe. The focus has been to deconstruct the Eurocentrism of scholarship, as well as attempting to bring the subaltern centre-stage in contemporary analyses of the Third World. Although the discourse has shifted ground and indeed makes a virtue out of its open-endness, it is characterised by an oppositional stance and, at times, a binary frame of reference in its mapping of identity in, through and beyond the colonial encounter. Indeed, the prefix 'post' indicates that issues at the heart of this encounter - relations of domination and resistance, self and other - are seen to persist beyond colonialism, in a strict historical sense, to embody contemporary relations between the West and the Third World. The need to comprehend and reinterpret the colonial experience is integral to an analysis of Third World identity today. Thus the importance of the 'empire writing back', a paraphrase from the title of an early postcolonial collection of essays.[3] This follows the consciously postmodern hue of the discourse: time and space are problematised; past and present blend into one another. Indeed, the prominence of poststructural and postmodern perspectives, particularly evident in the writings of Gayatri Spivak and Homi Bhabha (with their antecedents in Derrida and Lacan) have resulted in an increasingly representational understanding of postcoloniality. Despite the complexity of the discourse, the dual agenda set out by Stephen Slemon can still be viewed as capturing the core of the postcolonial discourse: 'to continue the resistance to (neo)colonialism through a deconstructive reading of its rhetoric and to achieve and reinscribe those postcolonial traditions...as principles of cultural identity and survival.'[4]

These twin concerns have carried the discourse beyond the boundaries of a literary focus to embody more universal concerns about cultural relations emanating from postcoloniality. Tied to this has been the greater prominence given to the postcolonial intellectual. In fact, what is immediately distinctive and potentially problematic about the academic personnel of this discourse is that they mostly form part of a Western diaspora which seeks to speak for the Third World from the crucible of the Western university: Gayatri Spivak, Edward Said, Homi Bhabha, Kwame Anthony Appiah, Arjun Appadurai, Aijaz Ahmad. While Appadurai may have captured a significant feature of the later modern world with his assessment that 'diaspora is the order of things and settled ways of life are increasingly hard to find', he may actually be guilty of reading the general pattern via the particularity of his own position. Indeed he unwittingly captures the underlying problem here with his reflection: 'As I oscillate between the detachment of a postcolonial, diasporic, academic identity (taking advantage of the mood of exile and

3. See Bill Ashcroft, Gareth Griffiths and Helen Tiffen (eds), *The Empire Writes Back. Theory and Practice in Post-Colonial Literatures*, Routledge, New York and London, 1989.

4. Stephen Slemon, 'Modernism's Last Post' *Ariel*, Vol 20, No 4, 1989, p3.

5. Arjun Appadurai, 'Patriotism and Its Futures' *Public Culture*, Vol 5, No 3, 1993, p424.

6. Doreen Massey, 'A Place Called Home?' *New Formations*, Vol 17 (Summer 1992), pp9-11.

7. This is the argument of Ella Shohat in 'Notes on the "Post-Colonial"', *Social Text*, 31/32, 1992, pp101-106.

8. Aijaz Ahmad, 'Disciplinary English: Theory, Third Worldism and Literary Study in India', *Occasional Papers on Indian History and Society*, Nehru Memorial Library and Museum, Delhi, 1991.

the space of displacement) and the ugly realities of being racialised, minoritised, and tribalised in everyday encounters, theory encounters practice.'[5] The 'ugly realities' may be real enough, but to what extent does postcolonial theory meet practice on the basis of the migrant intellectual experience? Appadurai is closer to the mark with his comment that the postcolonial academic takes advantage of the mood and identity of exile in the West. This mood gives postcolonial perspectives a certain currency within Western academe which they do not necessarily have in African universities where exile and diaspora may not be the order of the day, at least not in terms understood by postcolonial critics in the West. Doreen Massey, in a critique of both postcolonial and globalisation discourses, notes how often the characteristic concern with 'place', 'home' and 'identity', and the concomitant feelings of displacement and dislocation evident in writers such as Appadurai 'comes from those who have left'. She prompts us to ask who exactly feels the identity concerns of postcolonial theory and whether or not such concerns are a 'predominantly white/first-world take on things?'[6]

Such questions are especially pertinent as regards the position of Africa. Generally speaking, postcolonialism has little currency in African intellectual circles; it is largely visible in Anglo-American and Indian cultural studies. Indeed, it can be argued that it is peculiar to India for a range of historical and theoretical reasons.[7] The irony here is that the elevation of India in postcolonialism mirrors its exalted status in the imperial experience, suggesting that the consciously anti-imperial postcolonial has unconsciously taken on board the hierarchy explicit in British imperialism. One is reminded of Aijaz Ahmad's remark that in light of the postcolonial ascendancy, the East has become an industry again.[8] Yet to what extent is Africa part of this Western diasporic celebration of Third World identity and culture? The fascination in the West with postcolonialism is certainly not replicated in Africa, excepting only Nigeria (and especially Ibadan) and South Africa, which in some respects is a world apart. Insofar as the discourse is known in Black Africa it is generally dismissed as having little relevance to the problems of Africa. However much postcolonialism may ostensibly be about Africa, it neither springs from nor evokes much interest there. Even in South Africa, there is a strong sense that much of postcolonial theory, underpinned as it is by European social and literary theory, struggles to connect in any meaningful way with the specificities of Africa. One of the core themes of an MA programme in postcolonial literature in the department of English at the University of Natal is the lack of dialogue between Europe and Africa as regards literary theory. The appropriateness of themes emerging from a European grounding but mostly absent from Africa is seen as a key problem for the study of African literature within a postcolonial framework.

A broader problem is the generalisation inherent in both postcolonial and global approaches. In postcolonialism, the need to resist continued Western domination and the related process of identity construction tend towards the creation of binary categories and, at times, journeys into 'otherness' and universality in order to establish, ironically, the particularity of cultures. While this has certain strategic advantages, such universalisms are problematic when certain claims are made about the Third World or postcoloniality simultaneously with their so conspicuously lacking an African dimension. The initial starting point of much postcolonial writing may need to be reconsidered here. The globalising gesture implicit in postcolonialism is all too prevalent across the discourse, even in writers such as Bhabha who attempt to build plurality into their account. In the endeavour to construct a category of analysis that has both a political and theoretical application which can be utilised against a unitary and all powerful villain (be it Orientalism, imperialism, Eurocentrism, or Westernisation), too often the multiplicities of location and temporality are downplayed. Thus the postcolonial collection *The Empire Writes Back* argues for the commonality of imperial rule (ranging from Ireland and Australia to Africa and the Caribbean) and thus the possibility of characterising an inclusive postcolonial experience. The metatheorising evident in this test is guilty of the very sin it ostensibly sets out to redress - universalism in textual analysis and narrative closure. The same charge is levelled in Arun Mukherjee's critique of this and other postcolonial analyses which he views as essentialising an homogenising Third World texts and thus excluding some important insights such as ambivalence.[9] Ahmad's earlier critique of Fredric Jameson's universal claims on behalf of Third World literature is likewise concerned to highlight the diversity of perspectives rather than a bogus commonality.[10] Ania Loomba is uncomfortable with a similar tendency in the work of Bhabha where there is a sliding from the particular to the general, a too easy shift from the semiotic to the social: 'The hybridity of enunciation spills over into becoming the definitive characteristic of all colonial authority, everywhere, at any time.'[11] In setting up a postcolonial condition, such approaches inevitably compress the Third World into a single dimension. As Annie Coombes observes in her analysis of contemporary curating practices, merely celebrating difference and cultural diversity without taking into account actual differences and the specificity of experience 'can ultimately produce a homogenising and levelling effect'.[12] Such levelling is all the more disconcerting when it makes assumptions about whole continents which may not be valid. An academic discourse with universal pretensions about the Third World needs to be grounded in the local and the everyday if it is not to go the way of previous discourses such as dependency theory. Just as Western anthropology has been criticised as lacking a proper dialogue with the ostensible object of its enquiry (that is, native peoples), so postcolonialism can be criticised as having a non-reciprocal relationship with a significant slice of its stated constituency (that is, Africa).

GLOBALISING THE WORLD

Problems of universalising and levelling are endemic to globalisation discourses. The very nature of the subject matter tends inevitably to a

9. Arun Mukherjee, 'The Exclusions of Postcolonial Theory and Mulk Raj Anand's *Untouchable*: A Case Study', *Ariel*, Vol 22, No 3, July 1991, pp27-48.

10. Aijaz Ahmad, 'Jameson's Rhetoric of Otherness and the "National Allegory"', *Social Text*, 17, Fall 1987, pp65-88.

11. Ania Loomba, 'Overworlding the "Third World"' *The Oxford Literary Review*, 13, 1991, p173.

12. Annie Coombes, 'Inventing the "Postcolonial". Hybridity and Constituency in Contemporary Curating"', *New Formations*, 18 (Winter 1992), p42.

globilising gesture. This becomes intensified due to the point of origin of such theorising; unlike postcolonialism which embodies a conscious Third World stance, no matter how problematic, writing about globalisation has been mostly and unashamedly from a First World, Western perspective. With its origins in sociology, the focus on globalisation as the basis for understanding modernity in the late twentieth century is mirrored in world-system theory and more recently, international relations. The uniting thread is the attempt to make sense of the new and profound institutional and social transformations which are occurring in the world at large: new communication and information technologies; universal consumerism; the massive movements of peoples under states; the growth of new social movements based around human rights and economy and increased moves towards global governance. Because of these transformations, it is increasingly felt that the world is shrinking, values are becoming more global, culture more integrated, national boundaries less significant.

Although the focus on a so-called global condition or circumstance is relatively recent, there seems to be broad agreement across disciplines that it is the defining feature of late capitalist society. Pioneered in the writings of sociologists such as Roland Robertson and given theoretical substance in the work of Immanuel Wallerstein and other world-system theorists, the emphasis on globality, global culture and globalisation processes now seems unavoidable in much academic writing - albeit of late there has emerged disagreement about the nature and scope of this global condition, particularly in materialist critiques by Arif Dirlik, Jean Chesneaux, Aijaz Ahmad and Colin Leys, which seek to highlight the North-South dimension of globalisation. According to Anthony King, the term 'global' has assumed a new urgency. King, whose world-economy focus on modern cities and the impact of imperialism and colonisation has incorporated a more cross-cultural and less Western-centric perspective than many other global writers, nevertheless sees the world, particularly in its built environment, as encompassing 'one large, interdependent city', organised through a single, interacting urban system that is the product of a global system of production and international division of labour.[13] Echoing Robertson's famous remark about the world being a 'single place', King points to a greatly increased sense of globalisation in the 1980s. From a similar disciplinary standpoint, Frank Lechner argues that sociology is undergoing a profound change in response to an emergent global order so much so that 'new core problems spring from a basic awareness among contemporary sociologists that we are now living in a truly global society, in a world-system'.[14] Although Lechner hastens to add that this global culture is abstract and open, his insistence on a global focus is mirrored throughout the collection of essays entitled *Global Culture, Nationalism, globalization and modernity*, which were originally contained in a special issue of the journal *Theory, Culture and Society*. The editor of both the collection and the journal, Mike Featherstone, while pointing to the

13. See Anthony D. King, *Global Cities. Post-Imperialism and the Internationalization of London*, Routledge, London and New York, 1990, p4; and *Urbanism, Colonialism, and the World-Economy. Cultural and Spatial Foundations of the World Urban System*, Routledge, London and New York, 1990, pp2,100.

14. Frank J. Lechner, 'Cultural Aspects of the Modern World-System', in William H. Swatos, Jr., ed, *Religious Politics in Global and Comparative Perspective*, Greenwood Press, Westport, Connecticut, 1989, p11.

diversity and variety of discourses under the global banner, nevertheless views the globalisation process as an extension of global cultural interrelatedness leading to a 'global ecumene'.[15]

The writer most associated with this globalisation perspective and indeed the one that has gone perhaps the furthest in globalising gestures, Roland Robertson, argues that the higher degree of 'global density' over the last twenty years means that there is now no denying his earlier observation of the world as a single place. With references to various phases of globalisation, and the possibility of constructing a typology of the contemporary global condition, Robertson not only sees globality as virtually an unavoidable pattern of contemporary life, but calls for a focus on 'explicitly globe-oriented ideologies, doctrines and other bodies of knowledge' that espouse as a central aspect of their message 'a concern with the patterning of the entire world.' The shift in academe toward globality receives its least problematic treatment here. While cognisant of the limitations of world-system theory, Robertson views Wallerstein as having accomplished something of significance in pointing to the world as a systemic and hence singular entity. Such thinking has facilitated a global overview, which, in Robertson's estimation, will likely frame the character of social theory, doctrine, ideology, and culture in decades to come.[16]

Outside this sociological circle, much the same pattern of thinking is evident, albeit at times directed to different conclusions. Fredric Jameson's account of the postmodern age refers to the 'new global space' in which 'we can achieve no distance from it' and resistance is disarmed and absorbed.[17] Indeed Robertson claims that Jameson attunes much of his current work to Wallerstein's world-system ideas. In a critical international relations piece, Stephen Rosow finds common meanings and a 'common reference world' within a global political space marked by fragmentation and diversity. While this commonality is based on a narrow Western modernity, the process of globalisation nevertheless is one that incorporates into it identities outside the boundaries of the world system.[18] In postcolonial vein, Appadurai, who has previously cautioned against conflating globalisation, which he views as true enough, with homogenisation, writes of a 'global force' which is 'forever slipping in and through the cracks between states and borders'. In a more recent article, he goes further along the global spectrum with his notion of an emergent 'postnational' world. While providing some qualifications to his argument, Appadurai states that we are in 'the process of moving to a global order in which the nation-state has become obsolete and other formations for allegiance and identity have taken its place'. Even the USA, that bastion of patriotism and national allegiance, is 'awash with global diasporas' and its increasingly the exemplification of the postnational world.[19] Massey's critique develops a similar thesis, although it is equipped with caveats of certain counter-tendencies and the dangers of universalising. Thus while there is no single condition of postmodernity or globality, there has occurred:

15. Mike Featherstone, 'Global Culture: An Introduction' in Featherstone (ed), *Global Culture. Nationalism, globalization and modernity*, Sage Publications, London, Newbury Park, New Delhi, 1990, p6.

16. See Roland Robertson, 'Mapping the Global Condition: Globalisation as the Central Concept' in Featherstone (ed), *op.cit*, pp25, 26; 'Globality, Global Culture, and Images of World Order', in Hans Haferkamp and Neil J. Smelser (eds), *Social Change and Modernity*, University of California Press, Berkeley and Los Angeles, 1992, pp402-409.

17. Fredric Jameson, *Postmodernism, or, The Cultural Logic of Late Capitalism*, Verso, London and New York, 1991, p49.

18. Stephen J. Rosow, 'The Forms of Internationalization: Representation of Western Culture on a Global Scale' *Alternatives*, Vol 15, No 3, Summer 1990, pp288-294.

19. Arjun Appadurai, 'Disjuncture and Difference in the Global Cultural Economy' in Featherstone (ed), *op.cit*, pp307, 366; and 'Patriotism and its Futures', *op. cit*, pp421, 422, 424.

a truly major re-shaping of the spatial organisation of social relations at every level, from local to global. Each geographical 'place' in the world is being realigned in relation to the new global realities, their roles within the wider whole are being re-assigned, their boundaries dissolve as they are increasingly crossed by everything from investment flows, to cultural influences, to satellite TV networks.[20]

20. Massey, *op.cit*, p6.

The postcolonial world, no less than the so-called postnational world of the West, is caught up in this globalised space, no matter how incoherent or contradictory it may appear.

The widespread conviction that we live in an age of globalisation prompts the critical question: is it possible to over-globalise a world situation in which global processes are obviously of increased and perhaps increasing significance? It would seem that the attempt to arrive at a holistic understanding of contemporary transformations is too often overdone. To be fair, certain qualifications are advanced in order to mitigate such a tendency. Appadurai reminds us that globalisation is constituted around disjuncture as much as homogenisation and conjuncture of culture and ideology. Global forces are inherently unstable. Featherstone emphasises diversity and plurality in his account. Global cultures are to be understood in a plural sense; there is little prospect of a unified global culture. Even Robertson characterises the current phase of globalisation as one of uncertainty, particularly in light of the 'arrival' and 'inclusion' of the Third World.[21] Yet the broad-brush, the sweeping generalisation, the creeping ethnocentrism, the latter no more evident than in Robertson's notion of the 'arrival' of the Third World into the current phase of globalisation, too often mar such writing. Some space is accorded to the particular, yet the move is abstract, the reference non-specific. Featherstone rightly points to the problem of who is defining the global culture, and for what purpose:

21. Robertson, 'Mapping the Global Condition', *op.cit*, p27.

> We are slowly becoming aware that the West is both a particular in itself and also constitutes the universal point of reference in relation to which others recognize themselves as particularities.[22]

22. Featherstone, *op.cit*, p12.

Unfortunately the universal point of reference subsumes the particular. Featherstone admits as such in positing the other as particular only in relation to the universal West. The specific point of reference, the West, becomes universalised. This has led critics such as Massey and Stuart Hall to note how 'un-global' is the perspective from which the nature of the impact of the current phase of globalisation has been analysed.[23] How globalisation is played out on the ground in a specific locale, be it Lagos, Dar-es-Salaam, or the myriad of villages in sub-Saharan Africa, is left out of account, despite the implicit assumption in most analyses that the impact is profound and pervasive.

Ulf Hannerz has highlighted this significant oversight in a series of critiques of globalisation in which he foregrounds the local. He argues that

23. Massey, *op.cit*, p10, and Stuart Hall 'The Local and the Global: Globalization and Ethnicity', in Anthony D. King, ed, *Culture, Globalization and the World-System: Contemporary Conditions for the Representation of Identity*, MacMillan, London, 1991, pp24-25.

one difficulty in assessing the influence and effect of global cultural flows in trying to understand the sense that people in a given place make of these flows. Assumptions are often made without evidence. 'The meaning of the transnational cultural flow is thus in the eye of the beholder; what he [sic] sees we generally know little about.' The consequences of these processes also need to be understood as they unfold over time. Elsewhere he posits the same problem in broader terms: 'There is surprisingly little of a postcolonial ethnography of how Third World people see themselves and their society, its past, present and future, and its place in the world; a cultural analysis of their fantasies and of what they know for a fact.'[24] A global analysis, without a specific and nuanced sense of time and place, tends to merely replicate the Western experience.

More recent materialist critiques compensate in part for this exclusion of the Third World. Such writing is propelled by a more traditional concern to expose the inequality and injustice of the contemporary North-South relationship. The emphasis, not surprisingly, is on the material basis of this relationship and the economic structure of globalisation which underpins it. In this reading, globalisation is accepted as the basis of late modernity and Western hegemony is seen to drive global processes. However, the Third World is not left out of the account. Rather, the marginal and peripheral position of the Third World is directly confronted and held up as indicating the myth of globalisation's universal reach. The critique here is not of globalisation per se, which is accepted as a real phenomenon of the late twentieth century, but its failure to properly address the exploited position of the Third World. Thus, Ahmad, in regarding the Third World in general, and Colin Leys, in focusing on Africa specifically, both attempt to temper the celebratory, triumphal tone of global capitalism. Ahmad argues that globalisation leads not to homogenisation between the First and Third Worlds, but to increased differentiation between the haves and have nots in the global system with the gaps likely to increase as globalisation intensifies.[25] Similarly, Leys' summary of the 'African collapse' paints a bleak portrait of economic weakness and exploitation with the logic of global capitalism merely reinforcing Africa's decline.[26] Jean Chesneaux's critique of global modernity reinforces this reading. Despite the 'decentered' character of the global system, globalisation becomes the 'new master' of the Third World and the West continues to call the tune. While both the West and the Third World are part of the same global system, the Third World is only entitled to a 'cast-off development' and a 'counter-modernity'. Chesneaux admits the precise demarcation between the First and Third Worlds is increasingly complex. However 'what separates the West and the Third World - the two terms are still useful - is perhaps the 'modernity differential' which brings them both into the globalisation circuits but in opposite directions, to the advantage of one and the detriment of the other.'[27] This critical approach to the homogenising tendency of globalisation would appear a vast improvement on the 'Eurocentrism' of many globalisation discourses.

24. Ulf Hannerz, 'Notes on the Global Ecumene', *Public Culture*, 1(2), Spring 1989, p72 and 'The World in Creolisation', *Africa*, 57(4), 1987, p547.

25. Aijaz Ahmad, *In Theory, Classes, Nations, Literature*, Verso, London and New York, 1992.

26. Colin Leys, 'Confronting the African Tragedy', *New Left Review*, 204, March/April 1994, pp33-47.

27. Jean Chesneaux, *Brave Modern World. The Prospect for Survival*, Thames and Hudson, London, 1992.

However, the very pessimism of the analysis not only raises important implications for agency, it ironically undercuts whatever space subjects in the Third World may currently have in mediating and, sometimes, mitigating the combined effects of modernity and globalisation.

LOCATING AFRICA

Africa is often accorded the sign of the exception in academic analysis. It is accorded this status not because there is some overwhelming recognition of its uniqueness as with Japan. Indeed, as I have suggested, it tends to be ignored or incorporated or both. There is a refusal to make sense of it on its own terms. It becomes the sign of the exception precisely because it operates as the repository of certain repressions and projections. The inability of certain Western discourses to accord Africa an autonomous space can be viewed as a process of othering, at least in the Foucauldian sense of repression and normalising. This is particularly evident in globalisation scenarios. However, what is fascinating is that this tendency is not exclusively Western. If one thinks back to the oppositional position of a Frantz Fanon, which has had a profound influence on much postcolonial thinking (particularly on Said and Bhabha), the attempts at carving out an essentialist African identity mask a similar process of repression. While the aim is to hold out a distinct African voice, the polarisation involved in this construction obscures more than it reveals. The curious effect is that such representations of the African self lack much resonance in the face of contemporary pressures and influences on identity. A similar criticism can be levelled at more recent postcolonial representations of the Third World.

I have already noted that Africa is mostly marginalised in postcolonialism, with the significant exception of African writers such as Achille Mbembe and Appiah. As regards the Third World in general, despite rhetoric to the contrary, a lingering sense of otherness comes into play. The Third World is neither repressed, or incorporated here, but becomes what Homi Bhabha (borrowing de Certeau) has referred to in a different context as a 'non-place' in the discourse of modernity. It is not merely 'terra nulla', but a 'time-lag' in the understanding of modernity, 'a lag which all histories must encounter in order to make a beginning'.[28] In this respect, the wish is not to ostensibly deny its place in the modern, but to inscribe its otherness and emphasise its difference. The Third World is seen to exist on the outside of globalisation/modernity as an other which forces the global and the modern to encounter themselves and interrogate and interrupt their assumptions about the non-European world. The desire behind such a reading, also evident in Jameson and Ashis Nandy for example, and indeed prevalent across postcolonialism, is actually to empower the Third World and cast it as a subversive place of resistance to Western hegemony. Nandy, for instance, has argued that the Third World has become the Other of the West and that this otherness opens up, theoretically at least, many possibilities, one of

28. Homi Bhabha, '"Race", Time and the Revision of Modernity', *The Oxford Literary Review*, 13, 1991, p205.

which is that the Third World 'holds in trust the rejected selves of the First and Second Worlds'.[29] Both Bhabha and Nandy, in attempting to confront the Third World directly as part of their taking Western discourses to task, present us with the flipside of the predominant tendency evident in globalisation (that is, incorporation). Yet this flipside is no less problematic; by placing the Third World outside modernity as if it were in some mystical or discursive state of 'non-modernity', they are effectively denying not only its engagement with the modern, but setting up an untenable binarism which effectively marginalises the Third World. The danger here is that the Third World merely becomes a narrative or representational technique of deconstruction, which systematically ignores the key issue of how the many cultures of the Third World already navigate the processes of the global and the modern. As Sara Suleri has noted in a similar context, it becomes part of the 'othering machine'. It is one thing for the marginalisation of the Third World to serve as a discomfort to Western discourses such as globalisation; it is quite another for this so called 'non-place' to imply an existence outside the influence of modernity. Within this context, Africa suffers a double bind. As part of the Third World, it falls within Bhabha's 'non-place' of modernity. Owing to such a postcolonial representation, it is also a non-place in the literal sense that Africa figures peripherally in postcolonialism. As a non-place in the 'non-place' of modernity, it is difficult to locate contemporary Africa in its everyday engagement with modernity.

Between various postcolonial attempts to redress the contemporary effects of imperialism and modernity, which while not all Fanonian's share at least an implied commitment to resisting the West and speaking the language of difference, and considering Western accounts of increasing globalisation, we are left with a dichotomous closure. It is at this juncture that Africa operates not only as the sign of exception but as a place of contestation, a site in between the universalising and exclusionary tendencies of the respective discourses. It is precisely because Africa has been 'overworlded', either postcolonially or globally, that it is able to expose the limitations of much contemporary thinking; it occupies a disjunctive space from which we are able to view the blindspots and indiscriminate presumptions of the academic discourses under review. Nowhere is our vantage point more revealing than through the question of modernity.

MODERNITY

Postcolonial and globalisation discourses are fundamentally commentaries on the modern experience, albeit from opposite poles. Although their starting points may differ, they are both concerned to explore some of the dilemmas and manifestations of modernity: the universal as against the particular; the navigation of individual subjectivity in a world of collective organisation; the shifting sands of identity and culture in the (post)modern age. In globalisation discourses, the global is revealed as the latest stage in

29. See Santiago Colas, 'The "Third World" in Jameson's *Postmodernism, or the Cultural Logic of Later Capitalism,*' *Social Text*, 31/32, 1992, pp258-270. Ashis Nandy, 'Shamans, Savages and the Wilderness: On the Audibility of Dissent and the Future of Civilizations' *Alternatives*, XIV, 1989, p273-276.

the evolution of modernity. Whether it is characterised by a postmodern unease or deconstructive urge to render visible its contradictions, or a more modernist celebration of its possibilities for human governance, the global, to paraphrase Jameson, is the cultural logic of late modernity. On the other hand, postcolonialism can be read as a Third Worldist discourse about modernity critically received. The postcolonial is revealed as the meeting ground of the modern and the traditional; a site of contestation where the two faces of modernity, imperialism and Westernisation, underpin the case for cultural resistance and give voice to the marginal and the dispossessed. As postcolonialism draws heavily on European social theory, in particular postmodernism, an intensified note of negativity has been inherited. Throughout, postcolonialism has been mostly sceptical about, and oppositional towards, modernity. While both discourses are propelled by an engagement with the modern, the question of modernity presents them with obvious pitfalls when it comes to a consideration of Africa. Both display critical blindspots in the way they read, or more accurately, misread how modernity is played out in Africa, and indeed in the Third World generally, particularly when it comes to a consideration of ambivalence and agency.

The postcolonial emphasis on difference (particularly in the African context) and the globalisation assumption of a shrinking world tend to act as binary opposites when in fact the position of modernity is a more ambivalent and complex one. At a general level, notions of resistance and de-Europeanising identity are undermined in the face of the consumption of modernity in the Third World and the inescapable effects of certain globalising processes. Yet these global effects are by no means straightforward. Jonathan Friedman maps out certain local strategies of appropriation as part of 'being in the world'. Modernity is consumed via a process of appropriation. This consumption is viewed as a cultural strategy of self-definition and identity which works as a negotiation between selfhood and the array of possibilities offered by globalisation. In Zaire and the Congo for example, the designation 'Les Sapeurs' has been applied to the outwardly Westernised, predominantly BaKongo, whose preference for French designer clothes and other foreign goods is not merely an imitation of Western taste, but a visible badge of identity and cultural strategy which taps into traditional beliefs regarding appearance and social rank ('You are what you wear'). Clothes are seen as a source of external well-being and life-force; a sign of power. Thus, according to Friedman, there is an appropriation of modernity 'by means of a set of transformed traditional practices' so that the 'Congolese consume modernity to strengthen themselves'. Interestingly, Friedman goes on to describe other strategies for mediating modernity among the Ainu people of Japan and native Hawaiians, suggesting that modernity is played out in a space where cultural specificity, historical circumstances and global position are crucial differentiating factors. There is no single response to modernity.[30]

In this reading, modernity and globalisation are not simply one-way processes, for their various effects are indigenised and creolised. Assumptions

30. Jonathon Friedman, 'Being in the World: Globalization and Localization' in Featherstone (ed), *op.cit*, pp312, 314-315, 323. See also Abdul Maliqalim Simone and David Hecht, 'Masking Magic: Ambiguity in Contemporary African Political and Cultural Practices', *Third Text*, 23, Summer 1993, pp111-112 for the same case study.

of sameness are as precarious and problematic as those of difference. Recent theoretical material on the emergence of a 'Global Culture' both overestimates the homogenisation of world cultures and underplays the increasing diversity of cultural identity in the Third World. Similarly, it often downplays the more ambiguous processes of indigenisation and appropriation, suggesting that the postcolonial subject carves out a meaningful space between the axes of modernity and tradition. Ulf Hannerz's idea about the relationship between modernity and tradition as a two way process rather than a binary opposition is instructive in this respect. The interplay between imported and indigenous cultures is part of an 'intercontinental traffic in meaning' where there is much overlap and cross-cutting. In Hannerz's example of Nigeria, in its popular culture and music in particular, 'an international flow of culture has continuously entered into varying combinations and syntheses with local culture.' Due to the two-way traffic in travel and migration, major Western cities such as London and Paris become part of this creolised world: 'Along the entire creolising spectrum, from First World metropolis to Third World village, through education and popular culture, by way of missionaries, consultants, critical intellectuals and small-town story-tellers, a conversation between cultures goes on.' As Hannerz is at pains to emphasise, this conversation is just that, a dialogue which does not simply signify the impoverishment of local culture. In fact, modernity 'may give people access to technology and symbolic resources for dealing with their own ideas, managing their own culture, in new ways.'[31] In this respect, modernity can be interpreted as potentially empowering for Third World peoples and cultures, an admission that both postcolonialism and materialist critiques of globalisation are loath to make.

31. Hannerz, 'The World in Creolization', *op.cit*, pp547, 555.

From a postcolonial angle, any project of resistance is thus necessarily ambivalent, identity is hybrid, and notions of an authentic self impossibly romantic. Many writers of the postcolonial discourse at times fall into the trap of romanticising the pre-modern and essentialising the self in opposition to the West, focusing too narrowly on rejection. Ashis Nandy, himself veering towards essentialisms regarding the Third World, nevertheless cautions against rejection. He argues that total rejection of the West is impossible as it is akin to denying an integral part of the self. The reception of modernity embodies a love-hate, identification-counter-identification element which is integral to a postcolonial 'strategy of survival'.[32] Nandy writes of India in this particular case; yet his point is relevant to the African context and indeed is evident in Friedman's Congolese example. In this context, an emphasis on difference cannot adequately encapsulate the essentially creolised space of modernity. Outside specific postcolonial debates, African writing on the question of philosophy has mirrored the work of Friedman and Hannerz on the interplay of the modern and the traditional and recognised the powerful dynamics of ambivalence and creolisation in the making of African identities. Both Paulin Hountondji and V Y Mudimbe acknowledge the essential constructedness of African philosophy and

32. Ashis Nandy, *The Intimate Enemy, Loss and Recovery of Self under Colonialism*, Oxford University Press, Delhi, 1983, p107.

identity. They reject notions of a fixed tradition from which a set of beliefs direct contemporary identity. In this context, the traditional and the modern are not dichotomies. Modernity is certainly taken on board but in a close interaction with tradition which is seen as always in the making and constantly re-invented. To the extent that these perspectives can be regarded as part of the broader family of postcolonialism, they are a significant exception to the argument advanced in this paper.[33]

Even when we look to the emphasis on ambivalence and hybridity in the postcolonial discourse, it can be argued that for all the poststructural technique and postmodern sensibility of this writing, the emphasis on resistance and opposition casts a long shadow over key writers in the discourse, such as Bhabha. Said is another case in point, although he is less sanguine about postmodernism. Bhabha is certainly a complex case, but we only need to look closely at his work on mimicry to realise that beneath the Lacanian discarding of a more traditional sense of subjectivity, Bhabha is keen to write his narrative of the colonial discourse as one of resistance and the undermining of colonial authority. Indeed, he views mimicry, which he sets up as the basis of colonial control and disciplinary power, as a 'menace' to colonial power precisely because of the constant reminder implicit in the resemblance and imitation that takes place on behalf of the colonised that colonial authority can only be internalised as *almost the same, but not quite* (Bhabha's emphasis) so that cultural and racial differences cannot be erased and indeed continue to seep through the cracks of colonial domination.[34] Significantly, the ambivalence that Bhabha points to in this regard concerns the colonial discourse itself and by extension, the colonisers. The colonised themselves barely figure as subjects. A similar desire to disrupt authority and domination is evident in the postmodern terrain of Achille Mbembe where the very ambivalence of the power relations in the African 'postcolony' works to undermine and hence resist those ostensibly in control.[35] As in Bhabha, ambivalence is invested in a structure beyond the reach of postcolonial subjects. Thus, the postmodern character of postcolonialism does not cast aside a commitment to resistance; in fact, it attempts to reinscribe it, often uncomfortably, within a poststructural dynamic which ironically undercuts the ability of subaltern subjects to affect the circumstances of their daily lives. This will be developed in the next section.

In attempting to locate Africa within the question of modernity, we therefore need to critically address three key issues: how homogenised is the modern in the spread of certain globalising forces?; how disruptive is the postcolonial to the articulation of modernity?; and what space, if any, is accorded agency and ambivalence in both global and postcolonial discourses? The second question springs from Said's critique of anthropology in which he writes of the revisionist postcolonial effort to reclaim traditions, histories and cultures from imperialism as part of a continuing challenge to the metropole in which the West is forced to take the Other seriously as a 'disruptive articulation'.[36] To what extent has the subaltern, the Other, the

33. See V Y Mudimbe, *The Invention of Africa, Gnosis, Philosophy, and the Order of Knowledge*, Indiana University Press, Bloomington and Indianapolis, 1988; and Paulin Hountondji, *African Philosophy, Myth and Reality*, Hutchinson University Library for Africa, London, 1983 (first published in French, 1976).

34. See Homi Bhabha, *The Location of Culture*, Routledge, London and New York, 1994, chapters 3 & 4.

35. Achille Mbembe, 'The Banality of Power and the Aesthetics of Vulgarity in the Postcolony', *Public Culture*, 4(2), Spring 1992, pp1-30.

36. Edward Said, 'Representing the Colonised: Anthropology's Interlocutors', *Critical Inquiry*, 15, Winter 1990, pp219, 223.

different, achieved this *rupture* in modernity? The Eurocentric formulation of this question aside (that is, the concern is with the effect *on the West* and not the effect of modernity on the postcolonial agent), the consciously oppositional premise evokes a binarism that may not hold in the African context. These issues can best be explored in relation to two significant blindspots in the discourses at hand: the role of ambivalence and agency in African responses to modernity.

REPRESSING AMBIVALENCE AND AGENCY IN POSTCOLONIAL AFRICA

Fredric Jameson, in *The Political Unconscious*, views all narrative as possessing a 'political unconscious', rich with political and social signification, which various textual strategies work to ideologically keep hidden. He writes of the absences and omissions in narrative as 'repressions' and 'strategies of containment' which find their most powerful expression in 'master narratives' and totalising texts.[37] Similar strategies are visible in postcolonialism and globalisation, although they form a different function than in Jameson's Marxist interpretation. The repression is more acute in globalisation discourses due to their point of origin and indeed very subject matter. Although less pronounced in postcolonialism, there has nevertheless been a surprising reluctance to engage specifically with the particularities of the African experience. This can be partly explained by the prominence of India, and the nature of the diaspora which has been instrumental in writing postcolonialism. It also emanates from certain theoretical assumptions that guide thinking on postcoloniality, as evidenced in Bhabha's account of modernity. While postcolonialism is more in tune with Third World sensibilities, it still lacks a specifically *African* dimension. At the literary level, an indication of this is the lack of interest which postcolonialism has shown in indigenous forms such as oral literature, which constitutes a central plank of African literature.

In coalescing around the binarisms of difference and resistance on one hand, and sameness and integration on the other, postcolonialism and globalisation, with the exception of a few key writers such as Friedman and Hannerz, significantly underplay the expression of ambivalence in African responses to modernity. Even where postcolonial writers such as Spivak, Nandy and Bhabha emphasise the theme of ambivalence as central to the colonial encounter, they do so without reference to the African continent, or with reference to the colonisers rather than the colonised. Beyond the colonial encounter, Spivak and Bhabha in particular, tend to avoid discussion of contemporary dynamics and ideas about Third World futures. Said, whose *Culture and Imperialism* touches on Africa and certainly makes claims on its behalf, tends to oscillate between his emphasis on hybridity, and informing ideas about resistance and the recovery of culture. He rightly sees modernity as a major concern in much of the non-Western world precisely because it is

37. Fredric Jameson, *The Political Unconscious, Narrative as a Socially Symbolic Act*, Methuen, London, 1981, pp34, 53-54. Ironically, as previously noted by Ahmad, these repressions are all too apparent in Jameson's attempt elsewhere to construct a universal typology of Third World fiction. See 'Third World Literature in the Era of Multinational Capitalism', *Social Text*, 15, Fall 1986, pp65-88.

far from exhausted and is still a major challenge to cultures dominated by tradition. Yet while hybridity is the new order of things, and presumably informs postcolonial responses to modernity, resistance and opposition persist, so much so that

> The post-imperial writers of the Third World therefore hear their past within them - as scars of humiliating wounds, as instigation for different practices, as potentially revised visions of the past tending toward a postcolonial future, as urgently reinterpretable and redeployable experiences, in which the formerly silent native speaks and acts on territory reclaimed as part of a general movement of resistance, from the colonist.[38]

In this respect, I would argue that there is a tension in Said between the impulse to resistance and an acceptance of ambivalence.

Specifically African studies, most prominently Abdul JanMohamed's analysis of the politics of literature in colonial and postcolonial Africa, highlight resistance and opposition as characteristic of the African response. This would seem to reflect the prominence of the African realist literary canon which has given the spotlight to novelists such as Ngugi Wa Thiong'o, Sembene Ousmane, Ayi Kewi Armah and Alex La Guma, who have tended to reflect, in varying degrees, the Manichean aesthetic which JanMohamed has ascribed to the African colonial and hence literary experience.[39] Critics such as the Ngerian Chinweizu and even some recent comments by Wole Soyinka in his clash with Ali Mazrui would tend to reinforce this oppositional, essentialist reading of African identity.[40]

The Fanonian characterisation of African colonialism as Manichean in organisation and ideology has served an important redemptive role. Yet it has also tended to imprison contemporary approaches within a binary model. Thus JanMohamed invests colonial Africa with a negativity and simplistic antagonism which locks postcolonial responses into a rejectionist mode. The Manichean allegory of colonialism spills over into African texts and gives them a 'fundamental structural uniformity' of opposition between black and white, self and other, subject and object. This has a 'powerful limiting effect' on African literature. JanMohamed makes a token gesture towards the ambivalence of the African native but labels this a colonial contradiction. Similarly, where he admits hybridity between colonial and African cultures, they become merely 'confused hybrids'.[41] This interpretation has profound implications for African agency. At this point it will suffice to make clear the repression of ambivalence, a repression which becomes all the more problematic in light of JanMohamed's bracketing of all African literature into the same Manichean straitjacket.

The postmodern approach to questions of agency and subjectivity within postcoloniality presents a different set of difficulties for an understanding of Africa's place in the postcolonial, modern and global. This is the case, for instance, with Bhabha's account of mimicry and resistance in the colonial

38. Said, *Culture and Imperialism, op.cit,* p212, 329.

39. Abdul R. JanMohamed *Manichean Aesthetics. The Politics of Literature in Colonial Africa,* The University of Massachusetts Press, Amherst, 1983.

40. See Ali Mazrui 'Wole Soyinka as a Television Critic: A Parable of Deception', *Transition,* 54, 1991, pp165-177 and the reply by Wole Soyinka 'Triple Tropes of Trickery' in the same volume, pp178-183.

41. Jan Mohamed *op.cit,* pp4, 9, 263.

encounter and Mbembe's more specific analysis of the African 'postcolony'. Bhabha's Derridean and Lacanian fusion serves to circumscribe the scope for subaltern subjectivity and action. The colonised are necessary only to reflect back to the colonised that they are 'almost the same, but not quite'. This serves to unsettle and subvert colonial authority. Yet the subaltern role is in the Lacanian mirror: they are eternally misrecognised and indeed, unrecognisable. The dynamics of self-identity for the 'native' seem to pale in light of the broader and more significant drama of the colonisers gazing into a troublesome self-image. The process is mostly subjectless and the resistance described strangely 'other-than-subjectivity'. Mimicry resides in the symbolic order of language. The capacity for reflexivity and action unravels somewhat in the play of Lacanian mirrors.[42] Similarly, in Mbembe's journey through the 'chaotic postcolony' of African society (his specific example concerns Cameroon), authority (the 'commandement') is undermined through its very vulgarity and excess. Yet the Foucauldian framework of power and Bakhtin's notion of the 'carnivalesque' serve to condition the approach to the nature of subaltern resistance. The ability of the postcolonial subject to undercut the state's power is appropriately decentred. Resistance is mostly unintentional or 'nonsubjective' in Foucault's terms. Indeed, the subaltern holds a mirror to authority that reflects the debasement of power, 'often unwittingly'. Simulcra frames Mbembe's account of the fracturing of subjectivity under conditions of 'zombification' for both the dominant and the subordinate.[43] In both writers there is a restricted, almost inert and uninvolved quality to the subject's ability to manoeuvre within broader processes of power and hegemony. In both instances the terms of domination are set from above despite the ineffectiveness of this domination and the postmodern desire to decentre the analysis of power. In Bhabha, colonial authority promotes a self-defeating mimicry. In Mbembe, the 'commandement' feeds the fetishization for its vulgar and debased power among the masses. The subject is merely swept up in the ambivalence of (post)colonial discourse; a bit player that responds, rather passively, to the dynamics of mimicry and vulgarity. The impression we are left with is of puppets playing out prearranged roles.

Within the literary province, the exceptions to the types of representation set out above are significant, and considerably undercut the lingering Manichean framework and postmodern problematics of postcolonialism, as well as the repression of ambivalence and agency in globalisation. The turn to fiction enables us to take up Hannerz's challenge and explore the politics of the local and the everyday. Arun Mukherjee's criticism of postcolonial criticism as excluding a significant slice of Indian fiction is mirrored in the African situation if we briefly consider two African novels by Kojo Laing and Dambudzo Marechera. Here the writers allow a greater scope for critical self-reflexivity on the part of postcolonial subjects towards modernity and a more pronounced sense of ambivalence, as well as grounding analysis in the everyday, local level of African particularities.

42. See Bhabha, *op.cit.*

43. Mbembe, *op.cit,* p12.

44. B.Kojo Laing
Search Sweet Country,
Faber and Faber,
Boston and London,
1986, p35.

Laing's *Search Sweet Country* is a vibrant celebration of contemporary Ghana in which the author explores the interplay between the modern and the traditional and never comes down on the side of either one or the other.[44] Indeed, the two are juxtaposed not as binary opposites, but as contemporaneous ingredients of modern African identity. Accra is constantly in motion; its inhabitants living within a hybrid space in which they constantly navigate the exigencies of modernity with reference to the past and the possibilities of the present and future. Kofi Loww, a university drop-out in search of himself, interacts with a whole range of characters who are similarly in pursuit of meaning, ranging from the eccentric Beni Baidoo who wants to return to the village by setting up his own one, and Professor Sackey, a disaffected academic who continually reflects on the dilemmas and ambiguities of modern living. Kofi, propelled by self-doubt, feels only the absence of:

> one thing or one thought as opposed to the other; of one way of life as opposed to an other way; of the collision of decisions and attitudes, one of which would not vanish but would move into a different relationship, a different collision....He wondered whether a quiet persistence to find what he could do with old and new was a sin or a taboo. He ate shitoh, kenkey and doubt: but what was old, what was new, afterall?...The world was open, no matter how many cultures you shut in, including your own. (p36)

For Laing, the quest to find what could be done with both the old and the new, modernity and tradition, is clearly no taboo. Kojo Okay Pol, spying on Professor Sackey for the politician Dr Boadi, reflects that 'Sometimes, caught between the jet and the village, he whistled; he insisted that culture was just what you did, so he was free to do anything' (p49). Professor Sackey, who has no time for either the 'great traditionalists' or the 'modern carpenters of the head', at one point tells his friend Allotey in frustration that you either embrace the modern and become fragmented or remain whole and die, to which Allotey replies 'its a choice I don't accept. There must be a middle way somewhere...no matter who or what is inhabiting me, I want to find this balance!' (pp77, 101). Ezruah, Kofi's father, echoes these sentiments when he claims that some traditional taboos must remain, but then we must continue to modernise: 'look at an old man like me talking about something like modernising. But there's been so much change already in my life that I want more and more! Change everything except the roots that do the changing! And in change we must look both backward and forward...' (p230). Here Laing suggests that the capacity for change is inherent in African society. Sackey warns against the move towards cultural authenticity: be careful about originality, since you may be going against your culture!', and later adds that 'Our soil can grow completely new things here too' (pp288, 290). Laing presages not only the African capacity for innovation and adaptation, but the process of indigenising the modern. The novel ends with the reflection that Accra had a yet unfinished 'sunsum' or soul (p300), which serves to reinforce the consciously open and syncretic tone of Laing's narrative.

Marechera's *The Black Insider* presents a gloomier, more fractured portrait of identity in contemporary Africa.[45] In a text rich with competing and at times conflicting significations, Marechera lays bare, in autobiographical mode, the tensions and insecurities of being an educated, Westernised black moving between Harare and London. The tone is pessimistic and angry, the observations self-deprecating. Marechera writes against 'thinking in straight lines' and emphasises the complexity of being (pp37, 46). Culture, tradition, history, civilisation become 'endoparasites of our mind'. Identity is thus a parasitic process: 'There is a definite degree of tolerance established between host and parasite; each becomes adapted to the other. It is not to the advantage of a parasite to cause serious harm to its host, as thus it is likely to suffer itself' (p33). It is not clear in this equation which is the host or the parasite, the West or non-Western culture. In fact, the statement is deliberately ambiguous; identity is, in Hannerz's formulation, a two way traffic in meaning. Marechera's most bitter broadsides are directed against what he terms the artificial self-image of Africa, particularly that encouraged by the first generation of novelists concerned to recover an authentic identity and resist the West. In the 'real Africa of give and take', one character tells the narrator 'Can't you see, you can't reject everything and everybody?' (pp74-75). Marechera laments that a 'new kind of fascism based on the traditional African image has arisen'. Yet, 'it turned out that the African image which we ourselves were constructing in our novels and poems was as limited and as false as in the white novelists' and poets' descriptions (pp80, 82). Exile and the diasporic experience are doubly complicit in this artificial self-image. Not only do the Africans in London become 'phoney', but according to Marechera, participate in a collective self-delusion, no more apparent than at the Africa Centre in London where there exists 'A test-tube Africa in a brave new world of Bob Marley anguish, Motown soul, reggae disco cool, and the added incentive of reconceiving oneself in a friendly womb' (pp62, 66). In a short story entitled 'The Sound of Snapping Wires', Marechera, again autobiographically, writes of a black writer writing self-conscious 'ethnic' poetry and employing 'the nuances of revolt and black pride': 'When he pared this down to the base of his own personal experience, the anaemic imagery of self-analysis soon revolted him' (p123). Marechera's confronting, self-confessional writing boldly underlines the ambivalence of postcolonial identity, and more controversially, lampoons the artificial authenticity and resistance of the exiled African. *The Black Insider* ends on a typically ambiguous note: the narrator reflects on the modern day, Westernised Africa and comments that 'the whole *looked* like some astounding impossibility' (my emphasis), suggesting that this 'astounding impossibility' could in fact be real (pp108-109).

In the narrative world of Laing and Marechera, the postcolonial does

45. Dambudzo Marechera *The Black Insider*, Boobab Books, Harare and Lawrence and Wishart, London 1990, pp37, 46.

not so much act as rupture or counter to modernity, but a complex site wherein the possibilities generated within the hybrid space between the modern and the traditional are many and by no means oppositional. While Marechera's vision is certainly not as hopeful as Laing's, both see the consumption of modernity in Africa as indigenised and inherently ambivalent for Africans. There is little sense of Africa constituting a 'non-place' in the discourse of modernity: it squarely confronts and interacts with the modern and the global.

In this respect their texts can be read against the assumption in globalisation discourses about a more homogenised reception to modernity in the postcolonial world. Robertson's notion that within a global culture 'all extant societies adopt an orientation to, if not necessarily an acceptance of, the idea of modernisation', seems to denote a one way process that implies Third World submission.[46] But as Appiah reminds us in his partly autobiographical *In My Father's House*, both African and Western cultures 'are all already contaminated by each other' so that the question of what it is to be modern becomes one that Africans and Westerners need to ask *together*.[47] Any notion of an emergent global culture needs to take on board this shared question, as it does the continuing relevance of the diverse traditions in Africa, and what Soyinka and anthropologists such as Robin Horton see as the 'accommodative' nature of many African belief systems such as the Yoruba, which are not only able to devise explanations for new elements, but have a capacity to rework, borrow and integrate foreign ideas. What looks from the outside as Western cultural domination, be it in the form of Christianity or urbanism, on closer inspection reveals a distinctly African negotiation of modernity. As was evident in the example of 'Sape' culture in Zaire wherein Western materialism is liberally borrowed and refashioned to produce quite distinct indigenised meanings which signify neither rejection or absorption, so too the pattern of Christianity in Africa has displayed what Simone and Hecht have called an 'incessant doubleness'. Its spread has been real enough, but it has been met with neither total embrace or outright rejection. Christian churches themselves have recognised the need to 'Africanise' theology and practice, and the passage of African Christianity has been by no means either straightforward or one-way. Thus in the Catholic Church a significant amount of thinking has gone into making the church truly 'African'. The spread of Christianity may indeed form a key part of the globalising processes which have undoubtedly transformed African society, yet its effects have been particularised to the African experience, and the process has involved a significant degree of accommodation and ambivalence on both sides. As Simone and Hecht conclude: 'Christianity in Africa is stronger than ever before, yet its manifestation doesn't necessarily diminish people's awareness of it as an incursion. It is precisely this incessant doubleness, this willingness to live through seeming inabilities and shake the ambiguity of reference and influence which makes contemporary African societies distinctly African.'[48]

46. Robertson, 'Globality, Global Culture and Images of World Order', *op.cit*, p398.

47. Kwame Anthony Appiah, *In My Father's House, Africa in the Philosophy of Culture*, Methuen, London, 1992, pp172,251.

48. Simone and Hecht, *op.cit*, p113.

Mudimbe echoes this argument in his view of the indigenisation of the Christian Church in Africa which he sees as promoting a new discourse based on 'cross-cultural breeding'.[49]

49. Mudimbe, *op.cit*, pp63-64.

The idea of ambivalence in relation to the space of modernity in Africa allows us to read critically discourses about the postcolonial and the global. Global and postcolonial discourses, particularly the former, are complicit in the continued misunderstanding of Africa to the extent that they fail to accord a distinctive, autonomous space for African particularities in their respective representations of the Third World. The most obvious strategy of containment concerns the conspicuous silence regarding what occurs on the ground in the various local settings of the African continent. So far it has been the work of critical anthropologists and some notable exceptions within global and postcolonial circles such as Hannerz, Friedman, Mudimbe and Appiah who have attempted to fill this gap. Fictional works by Laing and Marechera are also effective in portraying everyday situations in which Africans mediate the contours of modernity. Secondly, focusing on the ambivalent nature of modernity's passage into Africa (and indeed into other parts of the Third World) allows us to overcome the hitherto constricting emphasis on Western domination and a Manichean logic. Ironically, postcolonial and global discourses share some common ground here: the postcolonial in its tendency to highlight relations of domination and resistance which works to deny a space in-between; and the global in its often cavalier assumption that the West carries all before it. Thirdly, the ambivalence at the heart of Africa's relationship to modernity, an ambivalence which has as many implications for the West as it does for so-called marginalised cultures, not only brings into focus the irresolution, uncertainty and flux of the postcolonial experience, but draws attention to the processes of creolisation and indigenisation which play key roles in mediating modernity. While writers such as Bhabha and Mbembe effectively evoke the irresolution of postcoloniality, they tend to gloss over what Friedman terms the 'consumption of modernity'. The effects of modernity cut both ways, a feature that postcolonialism and globalisation tend to underplay.

The tendency to misread the ambivalent nature of the modern in Africa has serious implications for an understanding of agency and subjectivity. The capacity for individual and collective action and empowerment, particularly in marginalised cultures, has received little serious attention in Western scholarship. Traditional understandings of power relations have mitigated against attributing an autonomous space for subaltern agents. This is certainly the case with materialist critiques of globalisation. Part of the difficulty lies in the structuralist emphasis of the critique; there is a 'logic' to the system which tends to dictate a subordinate function to the Third World. The Marxist influence is obvious here and while it certainly drives an oppositional sensibility which is directed to resisting global capitalism, it tends by the rationale of its own argument to constrict the space for individual and collective action. This is evident in the very characterisation of globalisation in such analyses, which portray the reach of global forces in such a comprehensive and destructive manner that it is difficult to envisage a way out. The effects of globalisation on the Third World are represented so pessimistically that, despite the calls for resistance, it is almost impossible to imagine what space could exist for any effective counter-offensive. Chesneaux is a good illustration in this respect. His account of the 'whirlwind of modernity' notes certain 'pockets of resistance' worldwide, and he writes of people's choices and the capacity for effective agency in confronting the 'unreason' of modernity. However, his journey through the wreckage of modernity in the Third World and on the environment in general, does not, frankly, fill one with much hope for the way ahead. The apocalyptic vision of 'deculturation' and loss of identity in the face of global forces is bleak. The rather vague and utopian conclusion merely reinforces this. While it is difficult to disagree with the general principles he outlines, the tentative mapping of future pathways pales in comparison with the energy and conviction that goes into convincing us that globalisation is ubiquitous, hegemonic and inert.[50] Much the same is evident in Dirlik and Leys.[51]

The continuing hold of stereotypes regarding African passivity, and one-dimensional images of doom and disaster, nowhere more evident that in coverage of Somalia and Rwanda, merely reinforce these traditional readings of power. Globalisation discourses, particularly those resistant to postmodern reworkings of power, have tended to reflect this traditional demarcation between the powerful and powerless. With the onset of a 'global culture', presumably the options at the disposal of Third World peoples are diminishing. The work of critical anthropologists such as James Scott has sought to challenge such traditional readings: the 'weak' are seen to have their own 'weapons' and resources with which to counter the power of more dominant groups.[52] Certainly one of the major contributions of postcolonialism has been to redirect attention to resistance, and hence the field of possibilities for marginalised groups in the colonial and postcolonial context. In this respect it has attempted to be an empowering discourse for the Third World. However, aside from the obvious problem of a lack of sustained African focus, the postcolonial emphasis on the need for resistance has ironically tended to underestimate agency, or alternately, to render it meaningless under a postmodern reading. The oppositional stance, the insistence on relations of domination, the elevation of marginality, the focus on being dispossessed, the emphasis on the mimicry of power, all work to underplay the autonomy and agency *already in place*. It is precisely because this agency takes place within an ambiguous space and often through an ambivalent guise, on the part of *both* the powerful and the marginalised, that postcolonialism has difficulty reading it. We certainly need to proceed beyond JanMohamed's argument of the colonial subject having a 'limited choice' of either 'petrification' (that is, remaining pure within a static traditionalism) or 'catalepsy' (assimilating yet losing a distinct identity) under

50. Chesneaux, *op.cit.* pp174-182.

51. See Dirlik and Leys, *op.cit*; Dirlik's Marxist reading leads him to conclude that postcolonialism, as an exemplification of a culturalist approach, has 'rendered into problems of subjectivity and epistemology concrete and material problems of the everyday world.' (p356) This line of argument not only reveals a crude and reductionist understanding of the interconnections between the material and the subjective, but a desire to reinscribe the material at the expense of the cultural.

52. See James Scott *Weapons of the Weak. Everyday Forms of Resistance*, Yale University Press, New Haven and London, 1985, and *Domination and the Arts of Resistance, Hidden Transcripts*, Yale University Press, New Haven and London, 1990.

conditions of domination.[58] As for the more postmodern resistance outlined by Bhabha and Mbembe, the poststructural reading of subjectivity which underpins their analyses has serious implications for the capacity of the African postcolonial agent to navigate a way forward out of the enclosure set by a Lacanian hall of mirrors.

53. JanMohamed, *op.cit*, p5.

The problem may be, as Simone and Hecht argue, a peculiar Western inability to see beyond what is visible and certain stereotypes regarding African behaviour. The failure to accord African responses an element of calculation or strategic manoeuvring leads to a one-dimensional understanding. In their examination of the role of ambiguity in African civil society, Simone and Hecht trace certain cultural and political practices in contemporary Africa which highlight the intricate balancing act involved in individual and collective mediation of the state, modernity and tradition. Actors within African societies attempt to manipulate what is visibly political, and what is not, in the process retaining some control over their self-definition and autonomy. Certain masks are utilised, be they ethnic or religious, as survival tactics in a terrain in which both local regimes and global processes compete for ascendancy. Thus agents within civil society practise 'cultural invention' and negotiate meanings, often for the benefit of the outside. The example of modern African cities is emblematic of the inherent ambiguity which Simone and Hecht describe:

> Rapidly decaying infrastructures coupled with ever expanding squalid shanty towns give most cities a sense of impending chaos. Yet the cities are full of hustle and bustle, traffic jams, music blaring, people selling everything they can get their hands on; on the whole a rampant liveliness. The image certainly exceeds that of a people languishing in sterile impoverishment. While the awful conditions under which most urban Africans live are highly visible, not so visible are the means through which people survive.[54]

54. Simone and Hecht, *op.cit*, pp108-109.

Given that many of the cultural and political practices enacted by the postcolonial subject are ambivalent, a recourse to a domination-resistance dichotomy or a focus exclusively on the centre of power, will inevitably ignore this dimension. This is not to deny asymmetrical relations of power or exaggerate the autonomy of the postcolonial subject. One is reminded of Kojo Okay Pol in *Search Sweet Country*, whose feeling that he was free to do anything is tempered by his awareness of factors and situations beyond his immediate control. Agency may be real, but like Kojo Okay Pol, subjects may stumble through it. The complexity of postcolonial Africa provides a fluid context in which individual and collective agency is played out against various constraining elements. Within the 'chaotic plurality' of Africa's postcolony, the important factor to highlight is the capacity for African improvisation and innovation. In this respect Mbembe is insightful, albeit his analysis tends to undercut his inscription of agency: the postcolonial

55. Mbembe, *op.cit*, p2.

subject mobilises several identities 'which must constantly be revised in order to achieve maximum instrumentality and efficacy'.[55] Even if this capacity for action and self-definition is not always effective, at the very least we need to accord some space for critical self-reflexivity.

The fact that both ambivalence and agency are misread in postcolonial and globalisation accounts reinforces the necessity of focusing on particular, specific contexts in any analysis of contemporary identity. What is valid for one culture or society may not carry over into another, even where there are superficial commonalities. The universalising and totalising tendencies of the two discourses under review lead both to paper over significant deviations from their set text. Even when this is done by default, as in the context of Africa, the net effect is a levelling of the diverse and multiple identities that exist under the rubric of the Third World. No doubt modernity is a significant process in the lives of many Africans. But equally, its effects are unseen, evolving, ambivalent. The postcolonial, the global and the modern are all vital clues to the unfolding of African identities. This is all the more so precisely because, as Chinua Achebe has remarked, 'It is, of course, true that the African identity is still in the making. There isn't a final identity that is African. But, at the same time, there is an identity coming into existence.'[56] While I would favour a more plural formulation than Achebe's, his notion of an identity in the making with no finalised form is a salient reminder to discourses that have tended towards a nearer, somewhat static picture of Africa living within the confines of the modern and the traditional.

56. Cited in Appiah, *op.cit*, p113.

The inclination to misread the particularities of Africa, a feature of both postcolonialism and globalisation, has the effect of not only blurring boundaries, but denying an autonomous space for African subjectivity. However, there, readings may be a blessing in disguise. It may be as Simone and Hecht argue, 'that the very limitations inherent in reading African societies provides them a functional space of relative autonomy. Faulty conceptions in the "surveillance of the desperate" might be a resource to the very people observed and analysed'.[57] We are left with the idea that despite the incorporations and silences of Western discourses, African cultures and peoples move ahead making and remaking themselves in a world that has shrunk in magnitude but within which identities are constantly shifting and ambiguous.

57. Simone and Hecht, *op.cit*, p109.

THE CULTURAL POLITICS OF POSTCOLONIALISM

Daniel Goodman

In *Culture and Imperialism*, Edward Said looks to extirpate the still-virulent survivals of imperialism, a project that requires a broadly encompassing historical framework based on a global (not totalising) conception of imperialism.[1] Only such a framework will sustain declarations like the following:

> All the energies poured into critical theory, into novel and demystifying critical praxes like the new historicism and deconstruction and Marxism have avoided the major, I would say the determining political horizon of Western culture, namely imperialism.[2]

Said's further object is to recuperate the works of Western authors, the better to liberate their energies from the oppressing cultural matrix that produced them.[3] He enjoins us to raid the archives of metropolitan culture, refitting canonical works for postcolonial ends - a method he demonstrates in readings of Dickens, Austen, Thackery, Kipling, Yeats, and Conrad.

One can well appreciate that Said, pitting himself against entrenched prejudices and operating on the tricky border between globalised and totalised conceptions, risks lapsing into totalisation, as when he says, 'The great imperial experience has implicated every corner of the globe'.[4] Too often, these lapses prevent him from fully inhabiting his chosen authors, leaving only skeletal versions available for recuperation. Too often, he finds only what his preconceptions dictate, and his critical elaborations are thereby impoverished. Still, it would be exceedingly short-sighted not to ask what causes a critic with such acumen thus to lapse. The short answer is that few critics are engaged simultaneously on so many critical fronts, including a defence of postcolonial studies and a running critique of western Marxism. I am particularly interested in the latter. For while it is true that Said is not sufficiently materialist in his method, he rightly takes western Marxism to task for being a doubtful ally in postcolonial struggles - a clash of antithetical critical practices to which I will return in closing.

One finds the problem writ large in Said's treatment of Joseph Conrad, who figures prominently in *Culture and Imperialism* as a paradigmatic Westerner who, for all his incisive criticism, could see only a world totally dominated by the West.[5] Though Conrad conducted a vigorous critique of imperialism, he harbored residual imperialist propensities, writing as one 'whose Western view of the non-western world was so ingrained it blinded him to other histories, other cultures, other aspirations'.[6] Said sees Conrad's powerfully uneven works as prime terrain for post-colonial writers who

1. Edward Said, *Culture and Imperialism*, New York, Knopf, 1993, p194.

2. *ibid.*, p60.

3. *ibid.*, p269.

4. *ibid.*, p259.

5. *ibid.*, p30.

6. *ibid.*, p24.

address the metropolis using the techniques, the very weapons of scholarship once reserved exclusively for the West. He thus reads *Nostromo* as exemplifying both the reach and limits of Conrad's vision. The novel's core insight is that the newly liberated republic of Sulaco is only a smaller, more intolerant version of the dictatorship from which it sprang. The tyranny of autocracy is succeeded by the tyranny of modern material interests. But because Conrad could see no alternative to this cruel tautology, he perpetuated an imperialist world-view in which every opposition only confirms the West's wicked power.

One can well agree with Said's strategy for recuperating Western authors, while criticising his historical method, particularly the tendency to situate authors within an 'untranscendable horizon of imperialism'.[7] Said is right that Conrad was obtuse about third world realities, but because he seals Conrad within that horizon, he nowhere considers that *Nostromo* embodies an alternative conception of imperialism as capitalist (or neo-) colonialism. Conrad's grasp of neo-colonialism is evident in his depiction of Sulaco's transformation from a Latin American province to a nominally independent capitalist enclave, in a work whose formal mastery underscores capitalism's confident control of the forces of production.

The blueprint for colonisation is laid down in the opening chapters then skilfully woven into the narrative fabric. The opening words, 'In the time of Spanish rule', mark Costaguana's history as beginning with the Spanish, whose brutal regime decimated the indigenous peoples. Periodic allusions to the Spanish reinforce the idea that it was they who savaged the country and pacified the populace. By thus scapegoating the Spanish, Conrad deflects criticism from the Anglo-Americans, who come upon a beleaguered country caught in ruinous civil war, a country whose turmoil is a mandate for Western intervention. Said sees Sulaco as a banana republic; rather, it is a to-be-colonised - a set-piece in Conrad's ironic depiction of maximally efficient colonisation.

The Anglo-Americans are cast in a favorable light because the San Tome silver can only be recovered using advanced (read 'Western') methods. Centuries of brutal inefficiency have rendered the mine inoperable: 'It was no longer an abandoned mine; it was a wild, inaccessible, and rocky gorge of the Sierra'.[8] The mine is ruined by the Spanish, by a succession of corrupt governments and peasants revolts, and finally by Nature itself: "The very road had vanished under a flood of tropical vegetation as effectually as if swallowed by the sea'.[9] Nature further abets the Anglo-Americans by warding off competitors:

Sulaco had found an inviolable sanctuary from the temptations of a trading world in the solemn hush of the deep Golfo Placido as if within an enormous semi-circular and unroofed temple.[10]

The implacable calm of the Golfo Placido bars competitors until modern

7. *ibid.*, p30.

8. Joseph Conrad, *Nostromo*, New York, Holt and Reinhart, 1966, p45.

9. *ibid.*, p45.

10. *ibid.*, p5.

steamships can penetrate the Gulf, thus sparing the Anglo-Americans any inter-colonial competition. When Sulaco secedes from Costaguana, the mountains act like perforations in a cardboard cut-out, separating Sulaco from the host country and making it an enclave accessible only to the West. The groundwork has been laid: a labor force lies ready, the silver requires liberation, and the beleaguered country calls for modernisation. The Anglo-Americans need only quietly back the 'independence' movement then consolidate their gains by creating an infrastructure that facilitates the extraction of silver, thence to be shipped north and converted into the capital that further accelerates the extraction of natural resources in a self-augmenting cycle.

Stated thus baldly, the ploy seems obvious, but Conrad, replicating the cunning of neo-colonialism, weaves these conditions into the narrative fabric so that readers come away satisfied that colonialism has withstood the test of history. For all the semblance of history in the making in this roiling novel, colonisation is a foregone conclusion and is thus normalised in the reader's experience. Conrad works this sleight of hand by forging a narrative style that maintains the maximum complexity compatible with a unified point of view. The novel's many strands are 'subsumed in the study, concretely rendered of the play of moral and metaphysical forces, politics and personal motives, in the founding of the Occidental Republic'.[11] Conrad pushes digression to the limit then catches up the loose ends with bursts of sure-handed exposition that affirm the novel's unity. Just as Sulaco cedes control to the Anglo-Americans, so the reader cedes control as apparent disorder is disciplined progressively into the fulfillment of prophecy.[12]

Observe how Conrad deceives readers into thinking they have seen the worst of mine labour:

> The miners mingled together with a confusion of naked limbs, of shouldered picks, swinging lamps, in a great shuffle of sandalled feet on the open plateau before the entrance of the main tunnel. It was a time of pause...the screeners and ore-breakers squatted on their heels smoking long cigars; the great wooden shoots slanting over the edge of the tunnel plateau were silent; and only the ceaseless, violent rush of water in the open flumes could be heard, murmuring fiercely, with the splash and rumble of the turbine wheels, and the thudding march of the stamps pounding to powder the treasure rock on the plateau below. The heads of gangs, distinguished by brass medals hanging on their bare breasts, marshalled their squads, and at last the mountain would swallow one-half of the silent crowd, while the other half would move off in long files down the zig-zag paths leading to the bottom of the gorge.[13]

I quote at length (this is less than half the passage) in order to convey the structure of this compendious paragraph, with workers broken down according to shift, function, and rank (as signified by brass medals), thus

11. F.R. Leavis, *The Great Tradition*, New York, New York UP, 1969, p186.

12. Eloise Knapp Hay, *The Political Novels of Joseph Conrad*, Chicago: University of Chicago Press, 1963, p37.

13. Conrad, *op. cit.*, p83-4.

foregrounding the integration of men and machinery. Screeners and ore-breakers (these are categories of workers but could also be machines) are fused with shoots, flumes, and turbine-wheels to form an ore-extracting apparatus. The energy coursing through the passage echoes the deeper violence done to the men and distracts us from the crucial sleight of hand when the narrator mentions in passing that the mountain would 'swallow up' half the crowd. The montage effect gives the impression of full disclosure, but we never enter the mine, never witness the crushing reality of subterranean labour.

One would think such an elision would be obvious, but the tell-tale phrase is embedded in a paragraph that makes considerable demands on our attention as we move from disorder (the mingling confusion of limbs) to the unified man-machine and from dispersal to the coordinated change of shift. Caught up in shifting perspectives and variable intensities, we rely on the narrator's command of the scene, our attention deflected from the crucial phrase. The thicket of symbolism surrounding 'the mountain would swallow' further distracts us from the crucial phrase. Numerous digressions weave a complex pattern around the mine and introduce, together with their life histories, Don Pepe, Father Corbellan, Hernandez, and Guzman Bento, whose brutal dictatorship dwarfs the hardships of mine labour. Conrad is a master at concealing what he appears to be disclosing in this novel whose amplitude and sweep induce readers to relax their vigilance, thus replicating the cunning of neo-colonialism.

Nothing better attests to Conrad's design than his use of an omniscient narrator who ranges freely over time, space and other minds. The narrator can adopt a loftily distant viewpoint, as when he surveys Sulaco's timeless landscape, or delve immediately into scenes of the most intimately private kind. The narrator governs unobtrusively, allowing the secondary (or proxy) narrators to lend their voices, but only on condition that they not overstep their bounds. The result is a bonus of readerly pleasure, combining the richness of a multivocal work with the range and mobility of an omniscient narrator who takes on the colouration of individual sensibilities as needed.

This division of narrative labour helps to explain the novel's most brutal scene: the spiritual annihilation in the Golfo Placido of Charles Decoud, the most audacious of the proxy narrators. Decoud, his wit sharp and his jibes well-aimed, is an ironist for whom the revolution is but a badly played farce. But Decoud, who prides himself on being immune to illusions, is brutally stripped of all illusions: 'Both his intelligence and his passion were swallowed up easily in this great unbroken solitude of waiting without faith'.[14] The narrator adds:

14. Conrad, *op. cit.*, p412

It was generally believed that the young apostle of separation had died striving for his idea by an ever lamented accident. But the truth was he died from solitude...The brilliant Costaguanero of the boulevards had died from want of faith in himself and others. The brilliant 'Son Decoud' was unfit to grapple with himself single-handed.[15]

15. Conrad, *op. cit.*, p413

Decoud succumbs to the 'disillusioned weariness which is the retribution meted out to intellectual audacity'[16] - the retribution reserved for those who overstep their bounds. The narrator governs his fictive domain with the same quiet authority with which neo-colonialism governs the nominally independent Sulaco. True, the new regime has its critics, but they are so co-opted and confused that the regime could not ask for a more accommodating 'opposition'. Just as the Golfo Placido swallows Decoud, so the opposition are folded back into the unified narrative. *Nostromo* is not, as Said contends, a failed critique; it is an object-lesson in containing critique. My further point is that because *Nostromo* demonstrates a more thorough-going grasp of imperialism than Said allows, we require a more nuanced historical analysis than he provides.

16. *ibid.*, p413

The force of Conrad's breakthrough is underscored by the marked contrast between *Nostromo*, which grasps history whole, and the preceding *Lord Jim*, which is so awash in its own content and so saturated with the colonial presence in the eastern Pacific that one is hard-pressed to tell whether it critiques colonialism or is simply mired in it. Although *Lord Jim* is replete with instances of the colonialist economy, it is never clear whether we are catching intermittent glimpses of an economic system in this novel that is so full of digressions and perspectival shifts that the reader labours simply to maintain continuity. There are persistent hints of a system at work - including references to the shipping industry, international and inter-regional trade, labor recruitment, the communications and finance networks, legal and regulatory agencies, etc - yet the novel remains maddeningly equivocal, handing us the requisite pieces with the instructions, some assembly required. These two novels, one equivocal the other adamantly unified, give the measure of Conrad's quantum leap in historical understanding - a leap that calls for an inquiry into the conditions of possibility (the space) that enabled Conrad to break with the dominant ideology.

If personal and authorial exigencies are prerequisite for achieving such a break, Conrad was overly endowed. During this crucial stage in his career (1897-1902), this self-described 'homo duplex' who suffered 'from a sense of unreality, from intellectual doubt of the ground on which I stood', sought to center himself in the firm of William Blackwood and Sons.[17] He looked to the firm as his mainstay: a hedge against market pressures and a privileged space wherein to compose himself. Blackwoods seemed the best of both worlds: a traditional firm with a long-standing reputation for publishing Literature, yet a firm that commanded the capital with which to maintain a competitive advantage - modern publishing with a human face. Conrad, mesmerised by the system, was ripe for a falling out. Blackwoods was one of the Seven Leviathans who spearheaded the transformation of the British publishing industry into an integrated system (the Net Book Regime) centering on the Net Book Agreement.[18] This system was the model of

17. Joseph Conrad, 'Letter to Cunninghame Graham', 14 March 1900, in *Joseph Conrad's letters to R. B. Cunninghame Grahame*, C.T. Watts (ed), Cambridge, CUP, 1969, p173.

18. John Sutherland, 'The Institution of the British Book Trade', *The Development of the English Book Trade*, Robin Meyers (ed), Oxford, Oxford Polytechnic Press, 1981, p75.

19. Colin Sumner, *Reading Ideology*, London, Academic Press, 1979, p271-2.

monopoly capitalism: the carefully coordinated production of a multi-form commodity by a few hierarchically structured firms with extensive control over the production and dissemination of their product. At a stroke, the Net Book Regime established economic orderliness, took booksellers out of the competition, and placated authors with guaranteed royalties and a firm copyright.[19] The genius of the system lay in its ability to accommodate each party's interests without calling undue attention to the concentration of power in the hands of a cartel with unprecedented industry control. Conrad was an astute observer: those self-augmenting cycles whereby the Anglo-Americans secured their hold on Sulaco mirrored the cycles (the seamless integration) of the Net Book Regime.

One can well imagine how the system beckoned to Conrad; however, the industry had spawned a whole new apparatus through which authors were incorporated. A writer working for a major firm was like a hand-loom weaver working in a factory, a space wherein the publisher could incorporate an author's output into the larger tapestry. Authors might 'own' their literary property, but publishers had near total control of the printing, formatting, disseminating, and marketing of the texts.[20] Now more than ever, the industry could produce that Literariness Conrad coveted, but only at the cost of being absorbed into this capital-driven system.

20. John A. Bull, *The Framework of Fiction*, Clifton, Barnes, 1988, p155.

Conrad, looking to centre himself in Blackwoods, found himself buffeted by the conflicting demands of the system while rankling under its constraints. He launched into his career just as the publishing industry was consolidating into a confident structure of capitalist control and colonialism was maturing into a global economy. Conrad was well positioned to see that, just as the author's nominal ownership of his literary property masked his alienation from the means of production, so a country's nominal independence masked its lack of control over the chain of production extending from the colonialist core to the periphery. Conrad's hard-won insight - that both systems favour capitalist control over outright coercion - propelled him into the writing of *Nostromo*, whose pact with the reader (relinquish control and be amply rewarded) mirrored the pact between coloniser and colonised and between authors and the publishing industry.

The point is not to make Conrad into a hero of anti-imperialism but to outline the conditions of possibility that enabled an author rightly situated to grasp the correlation between literary production on the home front and neo-colonialism abroad. A further condition is that there be sufficient antagonism within the world system to expose its fault lines. As was certainly then the case: the world had reached a juncture where, because the surge of colonisation had nearly exhausted the globe, competing powers could no longer defuse tensions simply by apportioning themselves unclaimed territory - a limit-condition that exacerbated tensions and necessitated new modes of domination. Further, although the British empire was now considerably overextended, England was driven to expand as a hedge against aggressive international competition. To this we can add England's complicity in Leopold's rape of the Congo and the cruel futility of the Boer War. Whether England was seen as approaching the apex of empire or beginning its decline, it was clearly pressing at a limit. This historical juncture, together with a raft of personal and authorial exigencies, paved the way for Conrad's quantum leap. It is this mode of materialist analysis that Said's totalising conception of imperialism precludes.

Yet Said rightly pegs Conrad's blindness to other histories, other cultures, other aspirations. Indeed, one is struck by the anomaly of an author who could grasp far-reaching structural symmetries but could not shake that 'paternalistic arrogance of imperialism' whereby 'the outlying regions of the country have no independence or integrity worth representing without the West'.[21] The play of blindness (to imperialism's negation of the Other) and insight (into the cunning of neo-colonialism) is the expression of an author caught in precipitous shifts between incommensurable horizons - which is to say that this anomaly in 'Conrad' reprises the competing interpretive frames of Marxism and postcolonialism. Which returns us to the distinction between globalised and totalised conceptions of imperialism. For I take it that Said means by the former that it can (indeed must) be ranged against alternative conceptions (including capitalism as world system) in a reciprocal dynamic that provides a check on both frameworks. Said certainly requires such a check, as when he claims, 'Modern imperialism was so global and all-encompassing that virtually nothing escaped it',[22] and:

> The culmination of this process is imperialism, which dominates, classifies, and universally commodifies all space under the aegis of the metropolitan center.[23]

Just as Said pegs an essential lack in Conrad but seals him in an untranscendable horizon, so he gives a searching critique of contemporary critical theory - but from a totalising standpoint that precludes reciprocal engagement. Said claims as a principle advantage of his method that it recuperates Western critical theory, refitting it for the work of postcolonialism. Surely a crucial test for any such operation is that the target theory retain sufficient integrity to sustain a critique of one's own standpoint. To be sure, Said rightly criticises Western Marxism as a doubtful ally in postcolonial struggles and as being implicated in the same invidious universalism that connected culture with imperialism for centuries. Western Marxism, with its metropolitan underpinnings, has consistently scanted imperialism as inessential to an understanding of capitalist expansion and 'has routinely bypassed the confluences between its own findings and the liberationist energies released by resistance cultures in the Third World'.[24] Said faults Marxism for the alternatives it has foreclosed. Still, he does not test his own standpoint against a mature conception of Marxism. Benita Parry observes:

21. Said, *op. cit.*, XIX

22. Said, *op. cit.*, p68.

23. Said, *op. cit.*, p225.

24. Said, *op. cit.*, p304.

The very range of a perspective that presumes to transcend the restrictions of eurocentric interpretations, loses sight of the changing modes of western capitalist penetration into other worlds.[25]

25. Benita Parry, 'Resistance theory/ theorizing resistance', *Colonial discourse/postcolonial theory*, Francis Barker (ed), Manchester, Manchester University Press, 1994, p24.

Because he greatly underestimates the reach of transnational capital and the mounting disparity between the telematically advanced and telematically disadvantaged powers, Said greatly underestimates the structural forces arrayed against postcolonialism, leading him to make pronouncements like the following:

> First of all, there's a sense of the fragility of the culture industry or the dominating apparatus. After all, just as it was put there, it can also be There's nothing inevitable or even necessary about it; it's there, it can be taken apart.[26]

26. Said, *op. cit.*, p240.

Such prescriptions are tantamount to sending sword-bearing troops against a mechanised army. They result from a bad circularity: because Said lapses into a totalising conception of imperialism, he does not appropriate crucial elements of 'Western' theory, including a critical theory of capitalism. Said offers a compelling historical vision wherein the progressive forces released by the surge of decolonisation transform first world critical practice, but he is surprisingly unconcerned about the prospect that what he champions as postcolonialism has been radically recontained by neo-colonialism - not the abolition but the reconfiguration of earlier forms of domination.

In order to understand why Said tilts towards totalisation, one must see that he is fighting on at least two fronts: one explicit, the other implicit and therefore not well understood. On the explicit front, Said, convinced that a broad-based postcolonial movement is underway, adamantly opposes **any** critical practices which impede that movement, including those stemming from Nietzsche, Freud, and Marx. In order to locate such theories as being of the West and liberate their energies from the cultural matrix that produced them, Said requires the leverage of imperialism conceived as world-system:

> The constitution of the European self, by defining and encoding its colonies as Other, is privileged over Europe's diverse modes of self-presentation that were reassembled in the triumphalist culture of imperialism, and in permuted form has persisted in a cultural hegemony where Western norms and values are equated with Universal forms of thought.[27]

27. Said, *op. cit.*, p34.

28. Gyan Prakash, 'Writing Post-Orientalist Histories of the Third World', *Comparative Studies in Society and History*, 3, 1990, p403.

How else can one counter the universalising pretensions of contemporary critical theory? How else crack the casing that seals such theory against the postcolonial revolution that is 'penetrating the inner sanctum of the first world in the process of being "third-worlded" - arousing, inciting, and affiliating with the subordinated others in the first world?'[28] Precisely because

Said is bent on recuperating Western critical theory, even with all its entrenched prejudices, he must push his counter-history to the limit.

Said is well aware that, in challenging the very constitution of history from the standpoint of a border intellectual overseeing the metropolis, he risks lapsing into totalisation. He is aware, yet something pulls him out of orbit. Clearly, he is subject to other vectors stemming from other battles, including the defence of postcolonial studies, a discipline now entering into a difficult maturity. Significantly, Said, who 'stands at the headwaters of colonial discourse theory', seldom refers to the discipline per se, which can only be construed as a strategy of implicit address - of surmounting the increasingly fractious disputes while providing a platform from which to mediate them.[29]

Critics see postcolonial studies as having grown inflated (taking all oppositional practices as its purview) while growing attenuated from political struggles 'on the ground'. These twin trends raise serious questions, not least of which is why postcolonial studies is not more critical of its institutional underpinnings. This is not to say that the discipline has become a decompression chamber for radical critical practice, but neither has it shown an aptitude for rigorous self-critique. This indifference as to the terms of its ascendancy feeds the perception of a bad circularity where postcolonialism has suppressed the necessity of even considering its complicity by repudiating a foundational role in history to any system of domination other than imperialism.[30] This insularity is intensified by a strong poststructuralist drift:

> Since postcolonial criticism has focused on the postcolonial subject to the exclusion of an account of the world outside the subject, the global condition implied by postcoloniality appears as at best a projection onto the world of post-colonial epistemology - a discursive constitution of the world.[31]

Now, if Said is attempting to speak to the problem of a discipline supposedly grown attenuated from politics, he must also speak to a discipline riven with dissension. The debate (if that is the word) between Homi Bhabha and Aijaz Ahmad gives some measure of this polarisation.

Homi Bhabha's poststructuralist postcolonialism, already well established in the field, has been cemented with *The Location of Culture*. And clearly, a critic who takes his stand on the 'shifting margins of cultural displacement' and takes 'the cultural and historical hybridity of the postcolonial world as the paradigmatic place of departure',[32] is far more concerned to advocate a politics of contingency than to guard against the threat posed by any (putative) systems of domination. One could say that Bhabha is optimistic about the potential of a politics that harnesses 'the forms of cultural identity and political solidarity that emerge from the disjunctive temporalities of culture'.[33] The forward thrust of his politics is to make felt the sudden shock of the successive, nonsynchronous time of

29. Stephen Slemon, 'The Scramble for Post-colonialism', *De-scribing Empire*, Chris Tiflin and Alan Lawson (eds), London, Routledge, 1994, 120.

30. Arif Dirlik, 'The Postcolonial Aura: Third World Criticism in the Age of Global Capitalism', *Critical Inquiry*, 20, Winter, 1994, p331.

31. Dirlik, *ibid.*, 336

37. Ahmad, *ibid.*, p1

32. Homi Bhabha, *The Location of Culture*, London, Routledge, 1994, p21.

33. Bhabha, *ibid.*, p151

signification. Still, one waits for the other shoe to drop. Are history and system really so unbearably light? Is it discourse all the way down? Is Bhabha so certain that 'all cultural statements and systems are constructed in the contradictory and ambivalent space of enunciation' that he states, without qualification, that his object in specifying the enunciative present is to 'provide a process by which objectified others may be turned into subjects of their history and experience?'[34]

34. Bhabha, *ibid.*, p178.

The answer is evident not only in pronouncements like those above but in Bhabha's deconstruction of Fredric Jameson, the designated Marxist. He rightly pegs conflicting strains in Jameson but ignores the strategic commitments that drive him to conjoin radically divergent critical methods. Bhabha observes that, although Jameson looks to open Marxism to structures of ambivalence, he cannot, finally, abide a politics of contingency. Jameson has one foot on the pedal and one on the brake. But when Bhabha ascribes these contradictions to Jameson's 'anxiety of enjoining the global and the local', and describes him as 'a kind of Marlow in search of the aura of Mandel';[35] when Jameson's 'primal fantasy of late capitalism' is said to trigger a 'retreat into the teleological spaces of global capital',[36] Bhabha is projecting a shadow Jameson wholly severed from his political moorings. Thus, where Bhabha speaks of Jameson's dogmatic adherence to class as a foundational category, Jameson's point is that, as a practical matter, political alliances structured around class are more durable than those structured otherwise. Similarly, when Jameson speaks of the 'unimaginable decentering of global capital', he is not invoking some Conradian phantasm but arguing that, with socialism now routed and capitalism hegemonic, we lack the very means (material, cultural, conceptual) to comprehend capitalism. Bhabha nowhere considers that the proper antidote to Jameson's (admitted) totalising bent is not deconstruction but constant exposure to the exigencies of political struggle.

35. Bhabha, *ibid.*, p216

36. Aijaz Ahmad, 'The Politics of Literary Postcoloniality', *Race and Class*, 3, 1995, p220.

Bhabha's deft deconstructions, together with the forward thrust of his politics, speak to certain segments in postcolonial studies. Yet one can also see how he exasperates those with even modest materialist commitments. Aijaz Ahmad, who himself criticises Jameson for his homogenising notion of 'third world' literature and politics, is appalled at Bhabha's glibness in first depoliticizing Jameson then claiming him as a postcolonial critic.[37] Ahmad sees Bhabha as emblematic of postcolonialism's attenuation, the discipline having become 'postmodernism's wedge to colonise literatures outside Europe and its North American offshoots'.[38] He traces the discipline's decline from its origins in focused debates about the post-colonial nation-state to its present vacuity. This latest variant of poststructuralism only gestures parasitically towards an oppositional politics that is everywhere and nowhere. Postcolonial critics deny the structural endurance of history, and 'speaking with virtual mindless pleasure of transnational cultural hybridity, and of the politics of contingency, effectively endorse the cultural claims of transnational capital itself'.[39]

38. Ahmad, *ibid.*, p12

39. Slemon, *op. cit.*, p29.

Not surprisingly, Ahmad's aspersions and intransigent stance towards the discipline have drawn considerable censure; however, the discipline's drift does warrant criticism, nor can an activist/critic of Ahmad's standing be dismissed out of hand. Indeed, one is struck as much by the tenor of the dispute (including the exasperation vented on Ahmad) as by the issues themselves. Such rifts feed the perception of a deadlocked discipline where the other is always neo-colonialist:

> At heart, what seems to structure these oppositions is a pattern in which proponents of post-colonial archeological work are trained to criticise anti-colonialist counter-discourse theory for a residual neo-colonialism, and in return find themselves criticised by anti-humanist post-colonialists who have trained themselves to link that form of research to a neo-colonialist function through an allegorization of methodology.[40]

40. Bruce Robbins, 'Comparative Cosmopolitanism', *Social Text*, 31/32, 1992, p30.

Against such perceptions, *Culture and Imperialism* stands as a summa cementing a broad historical perspective wherein post-colonial studies cannot be dismissed as an academic enclave riven by turf wars. The strategy of implicit address (of keeping above the fray) allows Said to stand as a semi-autonomous point of reference who cannot be pegged as an insider because he holds the discipline accountable to an overarching historical perspective.

Said also provides a platform that mediates the Ahmad-Bhabha dispute. He can match Bhabha's forward thrust but without depending on poststructuralist premises. He seeks to maximise openings for a politics of contingency but insists that these openings stem from a broad-based historical movement. He shares Bhabha's conviction that culture is the crucial terrain of contestation, but on historical grounds. That is, because culture has long been the privileged instrument of imperialism (conditioning even our most mundane experiences), and because it retains much of its force and remains largely normalised, postcolonial critics must work to crack that aura of normalcy. Conversely, while Said shares Ahmad's concern about the discipline's drift, he denies that it has grown attenuated. On the contrary, precisely because the postcolonial movement is an on-going, uneven historical process, postcolonial studies, the intellectual arm of that movement, is necessarily an uneven and expansive field. Ahmad, who wants his politics too punctual and his theoretical commitments sealed in advance, refuses the transformative potential of this historical movement.

Said's stance allows him to check polarisation within the discipline, counter the perception of deadlock, and contest those critical practices that impede the postcolonial movement. All of which helps to explain, but does nothing to correct, those lapses into totalising conceptions of imperialism. Nor does it answer the criticism that post-colonial studies has sealed itself off from rigorous critique. Now, at this point, I can offer no solutions except to reiterate that Said's own objectives are best served when he ranges his own conceptions against competing ones. For example, he is rightly credited with putting his status (his capital) in service of the discipline:

> The concept of cultural capital makes a valuable stab at translating an otherwise vague 'guardianship of the archives' into a dynamic economy of cultural resources. And this import-export model brings out some distinctive features of the authorizing story of the intellectual that Said calls "the voyage in": the movement of Third World writers, intellectuals, and texts into the metropolis and their successful integration there.[41]

41. Said, *op. cit.*, p259.

Said is uniquely qualified to author this narrative, but it is one that depends crucially on the further premise that postcolonial intellectuals 'represent an extension into the metropolis of large-scale mass movements'.[42] But do they represent such an extension? And if so, by what networks of agency are they so linked? Here Said's own account of cultural transmission (of 'movements and migrations') proves inadequate, resting on geo-demographics (the sheer mass of people crossing borders) and on an underdeveloped conception of culture as an aquifer through which influences flow. What is (crucially) lacking is any account of the contravening impact of the media-finance network and its impending enclosure of national and public space. One can well grant the broad force of Said's critique, while regretting that he greatly weakens his own case by ignoring such powerful intervening factors. Here, at this crucial juncture in a narrative meant to underpin the postcolonial movement, Said proves damnably complacent about capitalism's counter-offensive: the forging of a global telecommunications network that so outstrips the regulatory capacity of nation-states that we struggle even to take its measure. Said's narrative would gain credibility were he to acknowledge that this counter-offensive threatens to vitiate many postcolonial advances.

Here Marxism could prove a strategic ally, but neither can postcolonialism simply borrow as needed from Marxism in order to bolster its own historiography. The figure of Conrad, caught in precipitous shifts between incommensurable world-views, reminds us of that. For his part, Said might well respond that correcting any alleged blindspot is far less important than the imperative to oppose all impediments to the still-nascent postcolonial movement - including the impediment of a First World Marxism that projects a greatly exaggerated global capitalism. And here I step aside from the fray.

Facializing the Nation: The Digger's Face, 1918-1945 and 1995

Fiona Nicoll

The period between 1919 and 1945 saw the face of the World War One (WW1)'digger'(a popular and generic term for the Australian soldier which encompasses all ranks) arrive upon the scene of Australian cultural representation. The digger's face functioned as a site over which contesting views of nationalist subjectivity were articulated. This article takes the emergence of the digger's face in interwar nationalist discourse as a point from which to formulate some broader connections between nationalist subjectivity and the face. Interwar debates over the morphology of the digger's face alert us to a deeper tendency within Australian nationalist discourse to render a nationalist subject that is inextricable from a specific embodiment. This tendency cannot simply be dismissed as 'historical'; it continues to echo through contemporary nationalist discourse, as can be judged from events surrounding the celebration of Anzac Day in 1995. Anzac Day is an Australian public holiday which commemorates Australia's entrance upon the historical stage of WWI at Gallipoli.[1] The occasion of the fiftieth anniversary of the end of World War Two (WWII) 1995 was a year marked by various attempts on the part of the state to reinvigorate a fading 'Anzac' myth for incorporation within a contemporary, 'proto-republican' version of nationalist subjectivity.

1. Benedict Anderson, *Imagined Communities: Reflections on the Origins and Spread of nationalism*, Verso, London, 1983.

THE DIGGER'S FACE DEBATE

'...the most handsome men the world had ever seen' - Sir Thomas Legge.
'...mostly a sweet faced, round faced mamma's boy' - Sir John Monash.
'...I believe the digger was gaunt. I believe he was haggard' Will Dyson (Fig. 1).
'It is the face of a man of action but not of ideas' - Norman Lindsay.

Newspapers are a significant cultural site from which the modern nation daily (re)produces an 'imagined community'. They continually reinscribe 'the nation' by addressing particular issues to a reader presumed to be a national subject. In 1929 the face of the WWI digger emerged as an object of debate in the national press. The question over which the following debate raged was: what did the digger's face *look* like?

The ostensible 'cause' of the digger's face debate

Fig.1 Will Dyson, 'Digger', Adelaide Register

was Sir John Monash's unexpected response to the comments of Sir Thomas Legge in his 1929 address to the London Society of Arts concerning the impressive physical appearance of the first Australian Imperial Forces (AIF). According to Legge the first batch of diggers to arrive in London were:

> The most handsome men the world had seen. They had narrow faces, straight foreheads and noses, high cheekbones, short upper lips, strong chins, thick hair and magnificent figures.[2]

2. *Register*, Adelaide, 26 February 1929.

Sir John Monash, Commander-in-Chief of the AIF in France, took public issue with Legge's characterisation, claiming that rather than being 'handsome' ... 'In the matter of looks, the Digger is mostly a sweet-faced, round-faced Mamma's boy.' He went on to criticise the artistic representations of the digger which were currently in circulation,

> I think artists like Will Dyson, Norman Lindsay and others have failed to reproduce the typical 'Digger' face. They make him a gaunt, haggard man with harshness written on every facial line. They're wrong.[3]

3. *Telegraph*, Sydney, 21 February 1929.

Sir John Longstaff, official war artist, then entered the fray affirming Legge's

original characterisation, denying (with Monash) that the digger was 'gaunt and haggard' but claiming (against Monash) that it was the *Americans*, not the Australians, who had the round faces.[4]

4. *Sun*, Melbourne, 22 February 1929.

5. *Register*, Adelaide, 23 February 1929.

Fig.2.
Photograph from the Angus Weekend Magazine, *Melbourne*

Official war artist Will Dyson then wrote in defence of his depiction of the 'gaunt and haggard' digger, accusing Monash and his fellow generals of expecting '... their men to behave like lions and look like lambs ...'[5] Norman Lindsay entered the debate, submitting a drawing of the digger's face with a statement concerning the 'racial type' and 'characteristics' which could be read off the digger's visage. Lindsay compared the digger with the 'legionary of Caesar's time' but concluded somewhat bitchily that 'It is the face of a man of actions but not of ideas...The Australian has a fine head for action. When he allies ideas to action this will be a fine country to live in'.[6]

6. *The Sunday Sun*, (no date provided).

'Rip', a traveling British cricket caricaturist ventured the opinion of an 'outsider' accompanied by his own drawing of the 'digger type',

> ...if I may intrude, I would like to say that in my opinion neither of them [Monash and Dyson] is quite right ... Clean-cut, keen-eyed, tight lipped lads they were, with little of the 'mammy's boy' about them and less of the soulful youth portrayed by Will Dyson, as far as I could discover.[7]

7. *Herald*, Melbourne, 25 February 1929.

There are, to begin with, two obvious points which emerge from a consideration of the above debate. The first is that the 'digger's face' issue was in 1929 obviously able to sell papers. A glance at the headlines of the various national newspapers illustrates this.

'Diggers Like "Mammas' Boys," Says Monash; But in Fight!'[8]
'Digger's Face Discussed: Sir J. Monash Says It Is "Sweet"'[9]
The Real Digger Was Not Cherubic: Sir John Monash Answered'[10]
'Were Lean and Handsome: Diggers Stood Out For Looks Artist Says'[11]
'Real Digger Not Cherubic: Famous War Artist Says He Was Haggard'[12]
'What Is Australia's National Face?'[13]
'Diggers as Beauties'[14]
'The Digger Face: Sir John Monash Stands To His Guns'[15]
' "Mild": Diggers' Faces: Monash Sums Up'[16]

8. *Sun*, Sydney, 1 March 1929.

9. *Sun*, Melbourne, 21 February 1929.

10. *Herald*, Melbourne, 21 February 1929.

11. *Sun*, Melbourne, 22 February 1929.

12. *Adelaide Register*, 23 February 1929.

13. *Sunday Sun*, Melbourne.

14. *Sun*, Melbourne, 22 February 1929.

15. *Herald*, Melbourne, 28 February 1929.

16. *Sun*, Sydney, 1 March 1929.

That the digger's face was able to function as a 'hook' for selling papers is also apparent in the way that the issue was harnessed to news items which were only tenuously connected to it. For example, a 'sporting' story about a shooting competition at Williamstown in Melbourne bore the headline: 'DIGGER FACES AT WILLIAMSTOWN. Thrills on the Ranges. RIFLEMAN AT 87 GETS BULLSEYES.' (*Herald*, Melbourne, March 6, 1929). And, as late as 1934, the Melbourne *Sun* was using the digger's face to add interest to a 'medical' story. 'The Digger Face. Need of Vitamin D Says Doctor.' The fact that only the first sentence of the article was connected to the digger didn't prevent the *Sun* from providing a photograph of a serviceman's head simply captioned, 'The Digger'.

The other point to note in the digger's face debate is the degree of public participation it was able to mobilise. In the course of the debate Monash presented a photograph from the AWM's official collection to substantiate his vision of the 'smiling, mild, gentle and round featured digger'[17] (Fig 3). In an attempt to further fan the fires of controversy, the press reproduced alternative photographs of diggers encouraging readers to draw their own conclusions. The Melbourne *Sun* for example presented a photo of weary

17. *Herald*, Melbourne, 1 March 1929.

Fig. 3. Photograph reproduced for the debate in the Herald, *Melbourne, March 1929.*

Fig.4. 'Weary
Diggers',
photograph
reproduced in the
Sun, *Melbourne,*
22.2.29.

18. *Sun*, Melbourne,
22 February 1929.

19. Kapferer, Bruce,
Legends of People:
Myths of State,
Smithsonian
Institution Press,
Washington, 1988,
p195.

Fig.5. *Sketch*
submitted to
Western Mail's
competition,
18.8.32.

looking veterans, rhetorically asking its readers, 'Are these diggers sweet-faced, round-faced Mumma's boys?...What do you think?'[18] (fig. 4) That the digger's face issue drew active participation from the reading public is demonstrated in the overwhelming response to the *Western Mail's* 1932 readers' competition inviting sketches of the digger's face to determine which was 'the most popular type'.(fig. 5) The three most popular sketches were subsequently reproduced in the paper.

EMBODYING NATIONALIST SUBJECTIVITY

In his reading of the rituals surrounding the celebration of Anzac Day, Bruce Kapferer registers a sense of the strong connection which Australian nationalism establishes between identity and a specific body:

> There is a tension toward *the substantialization*
> *of identity in egalitarianism, identity becoming*
> *integral to being, part of one's very substance* ...
> Australian nationalism carries the powerful
> ... notion that the ideals of a perfect society
> are already *embodied* within the individual,
> the Australian, male individual...[19]

This is an important point: the years following the federation of Australia saw the formulation of a range of policies specifically aimed at the national *body*. For example, the 1901 White Australia policy, the Aboriginal Protection and later Assimilation policies were designed to stem and/or regulate the movements of 'black', 'brown' and 'yellow' bodies, whilst the 1903 Report into the White Birth Rate was concerned with encouraging recalcitrant Australian women to make their bodies available for the reproduction of large quantities of little (white) Australians. Such national policy objectives could hardly be furthered at the level of cultural representation if the national spirit was unfettered from a specific embodiment.

Emannuel Levinas' 1934 attempt to theorise the particular type of nationalist subject produced by National Socialism bears relevance to the Australian material I will be examining here. Levinas argued that National Socialism could be understood as a particularly tragic means of resolving the long-standing Western philosophical split between 'body' and 'spirit', in favour of the former. 'This possibility is inscribed within the ontology of a being concerned with being'. Such a being would reject the concept of a *disembodied* national spirit in favour of positing a '...spirit ... that is chained to the body'. Levinas goes on to argue, 'A society based on consanguinity immediately ensues from this concretization of the spirit. And then, if race does not exist, one has to invent it!'[20]

20. Emmanuel Levinas, , '1933-1934: Thoughts of National Socialism: Reflections on the Philosophy of Hitlerism', reprinted in *Critical Inquiry*, Autumn, 1990, pp63, 69.

Levinas' formulation is useful insofar as he suggests that National Socialism is characterised by the dominance of a peculiar type of *signifying regime*. What distinguishes the National Socialist regime of signs is its *site* of inscription. Whereas a signifying regime that is racially 'unmarked' inscribes identity upon the *spirit*, in National Socialism identity is carved directly into the *body*. And, because these signifying regimes articulate meaning and value in different, often mutually contradictory ways, the strategies intended to resist or subvert their efficacy will necessarily differ.

FACING THE NATIONALIST SUBJECT

It is not the individuality of the face that counts but the efficacy of the ciphering it makes possible...Certain assemblages of power (pouvoir) require the production of a face, others do not.[21]

21. Deleuze, Giles, and Guattari, Felix, *A Thousand Platteaus: Capitalism and Schizophrenia*, Vol2 2., University of Minnesota Press, Minneapolis, 1987, p175.

It is necessary to situate the above debate in relation to the cultural context of 'digger-nationalism' in which the digger's face was initially formulated. The locus for the production of digger-nationalist iconography between the wars was the as-yet-unbuilt Australian War Memorial. The most significant exponent of interwar digger-nationalism, and the driving force behind the establishment of a National War Memorial, was official WWI historian and war correspondent CEW Bean. In anticipation of a National War Memorial, Bean instigated an official war art commissioning scheme and supervised the collection of war 'relics', soldiers' diaries and other 'records' during the war. After the war he strenuously lobbied the federal government to help fund and provide a site for the Australian War Memorial in Canberra. For Bean it was of crucial importance that the Memorial should occupy a privileged position among the monuments of the national capital. The architectural prominence of the war memorial would reflect the view of digger-nationalists that the battlefields of Turkey and France were the birthplace of a nationalist subject. As Bean put it in the introduction of his second volume of the official history of WWI: 'In no unreal sense it was on the 25th of April, 1915, [when the first AIF. landed on Gallipoli] that the consciousness of Australian nationhood was born'.

The Australian War Memorial was to *embody* this nationalist subject in paintings, sculptures and dioramas and to *enshrine* it by encasing these representations, along with the 'relics' of war, in a quasi-sacred architectural space. As a source of representations of the digger, the WWI war art scheme played an important role in the digger's promotion to the status of an exemplary nationalist subject. The scheme commenced in 1917 when war cartoonist Will Dyson was commissioned to cover the activities of the diggers in France. By the end of the war 17 artists had received commissions. As the scheme was able to recruit many of the leading figures in the local art world, such as Arthur Streeton and George Lambert, it received widespread public attention. And in WWII the aesthetically conservative scheme was at the centre of considerable controversy as the 'modernist' Contemporary Art Society attempted to gain commissions for its members. Considering the scale and profile of the scheme, together with the aesthetic homogeneity of its output, it is reasonable to claim that the object of the scheme was to produce the digger as a *hegemonic* nationalist subject.

In utilising the products of the official war art scheme, Bean was concerned with maintaining a clear distinction between the 'portrait' and the 'digger's face'. The most obvious distinction between these categories lies in the *composite* character of the 'digger's face', in contrast with the *individual* emphasis of the 'portrait'. Bean ensured that the symbolic organisation of the Australian War Memorial was emphatically structured around the figure of the average 'digger'. A corollary of this, at the level of representation, was the relative marginalisation of those figures who occupied the upper echelons within the military hierarchy, on one hand, and the particular, 'heroic', individuals who emerged in the course of the war (such as Victoria Cross winners) on the other.

> Bean insisted that the Memorial would resist the 'cult of the individual' ...[and imposed] strict limits on the number of named individuals to be hung in its galleries.[22]

22. McKeran, Michael, *Here Is Their Spirit: A History of the Australian War Memorial*, 1917-1990, UQP. with AWM., 1991, p254 *ibid*.

Similarly Bean 'strenuously opposed' a 1948 proposal to establish a portrait gallery of VC winners within the Memorial.

Bean wanted to dedicate a gallery to Will Dyson's representations of the 'average' digger. Plans submitted for the memorial's architectural competition had to include 'A minimum of 650 running feet of wall space required for the pictures, *of which 200 were to be allocated to Dyson's drawings*'. Bean's preference for Dyson's composite diggers over military portraits can be easily related to certain characteristics of the 'Anzac myth' that Bean was so instrumental in formulating. The Anzac myth is structured upon an opposition between an egalitarian community of 'diggers', on one hand, and the 'Tommy', on the other, who is represented as victim of an entrenched and deeply hierarchical British military system that is as inefficient as it is inhumane. But Bean's desire to limit the display of portraits also needs to be understood in relation to the *actual* volume of portraits produced by the official artists. A huge stream of portraits, well in excess of the exhibition space allocated to them, flowed into the Memorial. Many war artists, rather than capturing the qualities of the average digger, found themselves commissioned to paint portraits in the field. And as these commissions were usually issued by their superior officers, the artists were unable to refuse them. The irony of this situation *vis a vis* the egalitarian Anzac myth is obvious and neatly demonstrates that despite Bean's disavowal of 'the cult of the individual' in the symbolic (and, arguably, utopian) space of the memorial galleries, even in the *Australian* military some diggers were more important than others.

If Bean's preference for the generalised, 'representative' digger's face over the individual 'portrait' was not a straightforward reflection of the 'innate' egalitarian tendencies of the Australian military, what was at stake in his preference for the former? It is not simply a matter of Bean's personal prejudices here; to what pre-existing nationalist logic must Bean have had recourse to mobilise the necessary support for this particular preference? I will argue that Bean's valorisation of the digger's face is symptomatic of a particular moment in Australian nationalist discourse in which the official portrait's project of putting 'faces' to the 'names' of a national 'history' was less pressing than that of fitting the nation with a definitive 'face'. Bean's fervent opposition to the tradition of military portraiture and the celebration of war heroes is a powerful assertion of 'difference' from a British cultural tradition. This assertion of 'difference' is at once a basic precondition for and an inevitable consequence of 'facializing' the nation.

Now *if* the official war art scheme, and, in particular, the works of Will Dyson, are seen as important elements of the digger-nationalist project of fashioning a nationalist subject from the experience of the Great War, the stakes in the digger's face debate become clearer. At issue in Dyson's virulent defence of his work against Monash's criticism is the *authority* of the official art work. The terms in which Dyson defended his 'gaunt and haggard' digger make it clear that, in the artist's view, his work transcended the sphere of mere representation. Thus, rather than defending his *representation* of the digger, Dyson interprets Monash's criticism as a criticism of the *digger*, writing, 'Some bitter things have been said about the digger but so far nothing so bitter as John Monash's statement that ... the digger is "mostly a sweet faced, round-faced mamma's boy"'.[23] To criticise the digger's face posited by Dyson, is to criticise the nationalist subject *immanent* in the artistic representation. Dyson here is removing the official representation from the domain of the arbitrary signifier by which mere 'representation' (and its critique) is circumscribed. This move is necessary to guarantee that Dyson's

23. *Observer*, Adelaide, 2 March 1929.

face can effectively function as the *authoritative* vehicle of nationalist subjectivity. That is to say, the digger's face must be shown to be *necessarily* rather than *contingently* 'gaunt and haggard'. The digger's face simply *could not be* that of a 'round-faced, sweet-faced mamma's boy'.

FACES AND RACES

> The face is not a universal. It is not even that of the white man: it is White Man himself...At every moment, the machine rejects faces that do not conform or seem suspicious...the first divergent types are racial: yellow man, black man, men in the second or third category.[24]

24. Deleuze and Guattari, *op. cit.* p176.

> In his closing address at the Hyde Park Anzac War Memorial, Mr Priest struck out at the 'politically correct' idea of multiculturalism: 'A diverse cross-section of the Australian community chose for a variety of reasons to leave their shores to defend this country and its way of life. They all had one common bond - they were Australian and they loved their country, they had no need of politically or socially correct words such as multiculturalism'.[25]

25. *The Age*, 26 April 1995.

'Melbourne's Annual Day of Tribute and Play' - these *The Age* headlines convey a sense of the ecstatic possibilities available for nationalist identification on 25 April.[26] The nationalist-identified subject can attend the Anzac Day ceremonies, go to the footy at the MCG and watch Collingwood and Essendon play or - better still - both.

26. *The Age*, 25 April 1995.

The football field has become an increasingly important site from which indigenous Australians' demand for recognition and respect is articulated, with Aboriginal players insisting that racial vilification laws be enforced on-field. In the course of a tense match, Collingwood's Damien Monkhorst called Essendon's Michael Long a 'black bastard'. In a 'mediation session' organised by the Australian Football League, rather than apologising, Monkhorst told Long 'You took it the wrong way mate'.[27] According to Bill Gammage, a prominent Anzac historian, when the Australians arrived on Gallipoli they,

27. *The Age*, 26-30 April c. 1995.

> ...showed their foes little mercy ... They shot every Turk on sight, firing on enemy burial parties ...[and]...striking down men attempting to cross the line in surrender, and exclaiming after a successful shot, *'Take that you black bastards.*[28]

28. Bill Gammage, *The Broken Years: Australian Soldiers in the Great War*, Penguin, 1974 p91.

One of the several elements in Monash's description of the digger's face most consistently opposed was 'roundness'. Why were nearly all of the other participants in the digger's face debate concerned with replacing Monash's 'round-faced' digger with a 'gaunt', 'narrow-nosed', 'hard-angled' or 'aquiline' version? The digger's face debate emerged at a moment in Australian nationalist discourse in which the 'difference' of the 'Australian type' from its British, prototypical counterpart was frequently expressed through the language of 'race'. In September 1939, just weeks after the outbreak of WWII, the *Argus Weekend Magazine* provided the following caption to a full-page illustration of a 'hard-featured' digger's face,

> The digger of the Great War was the incarnation of Australia's nationhood, and this striking study of an IF Light Horse man shows the characteristics of the *Australian race* of which strength and independence predominate. In the article below, however the question is asked whether, as well as being a nation, we are *a separate people*.

The 'face' and the 'head' were sites upon which 'difference' was seen to be most densely inscribed in popular theories of racial types circulating from the mid-nineteenth century to the early twentieth century. Important markers of racial difference included hair-type, head size, facial-bone structure, facial hair and nose-shape. The 'Caucasian' type was described in a *fin de siecle* Victorian state school geography textbook as,

> The Caucasian race is distinguished by the following attributes: an *oval head, oval face, regular features,* arched forehead, cheek bones not too prominent, mouth small, skin generally of a light colour...*The facial angle is greater in this race than in any other*, and the brain is usually heavier and of a greater size, hence the superiority which this race has always maintained over the others.[29]

29. Reproduced in D. M. Gibb, *The Making of White Australia*, Victorian Historical Association, Melbourne, 1975, p14.

The drawings, photographs and written descriptions which were submitted in the course of the digger's face debate, reflect consensus on the point that the digger's face was 'long', 'hard' and 'narrow-nosed'. In this context, the outrage sparked by Monash's 'round-faced' digger can be understood in the following terms: the digger was being posited as the exemplary instance of the Australian race and, since the face was a privileged signifier of racial distinction, it was crucial to get it right.

For early twentieth century nationalist artists and writers, the 'Australian race', constituted a reinvigorated, *improved* version of a British prototype. As David Walker puts it,

> The Australian mission was to restore exhausted English bodies in the great sanitorium of the south, providing a thorough overhaul of blood, lungs, bone and muscle. In the process, Australian bodies were drawn back to the earth and were depicted as the products of a new soil and a new climate.[30]

30. David Walker, 'Modern Nerves, Nervous Moderns: Notes on Male Neurasthenia', *Australian Cultural History*, No. 6, ANU, 1987, p50.

Following this nationalist logic, it is not surprising that the digger's face should be presented as a new, 'improved', 'hyper-Caucasian' type.

The racially overcoded form of the digger's face suggests the function it was made to perform in early twentieth century nationalist discourse. The digger's face debate entered nationalist discourse at a moment when the question of identity was being posed in relation to a recently constituted *federal* sphere. Symbolising a united patriotic endeavour, capable of transcending interstate rivalries, the digger's face is, above all, a federal face. Federation was the occasion of a systematic reorientation of white Australia's attitudes towards those who had been constituted as its racial 'others'. It is significant that the first session of the national parliament was spent formulating legislation to ensure the 'purity' of a white Australian race. As the member for Darling Downs put it:

> ...the question of a white Australia [is] really a vital one, and I can say emphatically that I believe [it] has given an impetus to our national life ... it is no mere sentimental question; it is a question striking deeply into the principles of this new Commonwealth ... We are just at the eve of our national life, and it behoves us at the very beginning to decide who are going to be the citizens of the Commonwealth ... I believe that we want the whole of Australia for the white races ... and we should stop the flow of coloured races to this land at the very beginning and ... we should do it decisively and firmly.[31]

31. D. M. Gibb, *op cit*.

The emergence of the 'digger' in nationalist discourse between the wars enabled the policies concerned with racial purity inaugurated with federation to be facialized. The digger's face is a Janus-face. On one side the 'hard' and 'narrow' features look out to sea like a coast-guard prepared to repudiate the arrival of 'Asian' faces and races. The other side of the digger's face is turned censoriously inwards, given the task of preventing an 'Aboriginal' face from coming into view and making its claims upon the nation.

At the very moment the digger's face was coming into the national view, 'protection' policies were being implemented to 'contain' Aborigines in missions and reserves located beyond the horizon of white Australia's gaze. The claim that white Australians were evolving as a distinct 'race' of people went hand in hand with the assertion that the Aborigines were 'dying out'. The digger could only be posited as the unique product of Australian soil insofar as more substantive Aboriginal claims to that soil were marginalised. School children were taught from 1911 that,

> The story of our winning of Australia is a peaceful one. It is a story of fine colonization. *In this case there were no powerful tribes of natives to oppose our settling in the land*; the original inhabitants were few in number, and of a very low order of civilization. *Their occupation of the country was of such a sort as to strike no roots in the soil*[32].

32. John Finnemore, *Black's Literary Reader*, Adam and Charles Black, London, 1911, p33.

In this account, Aborigines fail to attain the status of 'indigenous' peoples with 'roots in the soil'; their occupation is presented as merely ephemeral. Characterisations such as this conveniently cleared the way for subsequent representations of white Australians as the continent's true 'indigenous' inhabitants.

NO 'MAMMA'S BOY'

'Moral' Perversions: The experience of the AIF in these very important matters was slight, so far at least as records reveal. There is no evidence pointing to any significant homosexuality in the force. The records of the AIF therefore provide no contribution to the place of the homosexual in a total war effort.[33]

On 29 March, Anzac Day officially became the 'national day of commemoration' of those who served and those who died for Australia in wars and other conflicts ... Such official status has the effect of representing military combat as the pre-eminent form of national service, and thereby privileges a pursuit from which women have been deliberately and formally excluded. The decision has the effect of confirming women's status as second-class citizens.[34]

I have shown that the digger's face was articulated in relation to a wider imperialist discourse of 'race'. Within this discourse 'difference' was held to be inscribed upon the body, and the face was a site upon which its signs were to be found in particular abundance. The hegemony of a nationalism which was articulated through a language of race enabled the digger's face to simultaneously embody a national territory and constitute a domain of 'others' both within and outside of its borders. Similarly the hyper-masculinity of the digger's face could be held up as a kind of phallic talisman in digger-nationalism's negotiation of the fraught relationship between nationalist subjectivity and the feminine.

The resistance to Monash's description of the digger's face as that of a 'mamma's boy' would seem to reflect a desire on the part of digger-nationalists to distance the digger from a 'feminine' sphere. As several writers have pointed out, the 'vitality' of the nationalist body was eulogized in relation to an existing discourse of 'masculinity'.[35] In this context the special attributes of the digger's face, such as 'hardness' and 'length'(!), could be made to signify a 'hyper-masculinity'. And in a more psychoanalytic register, 'mamma's boy', in connoting a specifically *feminine* identification, might be seen as a threat to the dominant construction of the digger's sexuality as hyper-masculine - and, by extension - hyper-heterosexual.

Secondly, Monash's use of the term 'mamma's boy', enabled the question of the proper owner of the digger to be posed. The language of proprietorship implicit in 'mamma's boy' opens up a discursive space in which 'the digger's mother' emerges as a figure with a claim on the digger. This raises the nationalist spectre of a state of affairs in which the claims of the 'digger's mother' come into conflict with those of 'the nation'. This

33. Grahame Butler, *Official History of the AIF Medical Services, 1914-1918*, AWM, 1943 p137.

34. Marilyn Lake, *Age*, 24 April.

35. See David Walker, David, *op. cit.* and Caroline Jordon, 'Designing Women: Modernism in Art and Australia and The Home', *Art in Australia*, 1994.

spectre is banished by positing a 'hyper-masculine' digger, impervious to any claims that might issue from a devalued maternal sphere.

Finally, the suggestion of youth attached to the 'mamma's boy', works against the nationalist project of using the digger to assert a sense of national maturity in the decades following Federation. Connoting a certain naiveté and inexperience, the 'mamma's boy' is rejected in favour of a national face upon which the struggle to attain the valourised qualities of independence and decisiveness is clearly registered.

MONASH: A 'SWEET-FACED, ROUND-FACED MAMMA'S BOY'?

A striking feature of the digger's face debate is that the qualities attributed to the digger and, by extension, the nation which he is called to embody, are *never* called into question. At no point does Monash suggest that the digger *is* a sweet-faced, round-faced mamma's boy:

> Their faces were round and smooth and innocent-looking - I said innocent-looking - and for all the world they appealed to me as mother's boys. But see them operate with bayonet upon a thirteen-stone Turk and hurl him over the shoulder and then you get another impression of the digger...that sweet, round face of his tricked more than one unhappy warrior on the other side.[36]

36. *Sydney Telegraph*, 21 February 1929.

What Monash presents is a *paradoxical* digger's face; a face which functions as a deadly mask concealing a fierce, fighting spirit which lies just beneath the surface. The official war artists, according to Monash, have 'failed to reproduce the typical "Digger" face [by making]...him a gaunt haggard man *with harshness written on every facial line*. They're wrong!'[37] By inscribing the 'harsh' qualities which distinguished the digger's performance upon the latter's face, artists, according to Monash, have failed to register the paradoxical point that the digger's *appearance* is at odds with his *essence*. Monash posits the discrepancy between essence and appearance, then, as an additional and important attribute of the digger.

37. *ibid.*

Monash's construction of a digger's face that was totally at odds with the official version had the effect of loosening the mystical bond between signifier and signified which Dyson believed lifted his work out of the realm of mere 'representation'. This raises the question of why Monash, an ardent digger-nationalist himself, would attempt to interrupt the seamless articulation of identity/presence which Dyson had inscribed on the digger's face? This question cannot be easily answered. Monash claimed at the time to be genuinely surprised at the outrage sparked by his 'chance' remarks.[38] In spite of this, however, he continued to staunchly defend 'his' digger's face.

38. *Sydney Sun*, 1 March 1929.

Regardless of his conscious intentions, Monash's introduction of a paradoxical face to the national media constituted a serious challenge to the powerful, and deeply *racist* strain of nationalist discourse that the digger's face was increasingly being made to articulate. As a Jewish Australian, Monash was only too aware of the anti-semitic flavour of wartime and post-WWII Australian nationalist culture. This underlying anti-semitism exploded onto the surface of the local art world a few years after the 'face' debate in Lionel Lindsay's book *Addled Art*. In this text Monash was actually singled out as one of a handful of 'good' Jews. But, significantly, Lindsay's attack on Sigmund Freud as the embodiment of a 'bad' Jew was supported by a reading of the latter's *face*.

> Glance at Freud's face. The look of concentration in the eyes is confounded by a general expression of sulky disquietitude and their sadness tempered by a vague hostility. It is the face of a man soured and ill at ease with himself or the world.[39]

39. Cited in Bernard Smith, *The Critic as Advocate*, OUP, Melbourne 1989, p500.

Similarly, while Monash's indisputable brilliance as a military strategist was acknowledged, Bean's appraisal of the general was, nonetheless, less than enthusiastic. Monash, the official historian implied, was an anomalous digger, characterised by too much intelligence and too little propensity for physical risk taking. As a particularly intrepid war correspondent, Bean had cynically noted that Monash was 'the best leader from whom to seek information before a fight but the worst to go to afterwards'.[40] While it is never actually *said*, the derogatory 'mamma's boy' echoes resoundingly beneath both Bean and Dyson's representations of the general. In view of the anti-semitic and anti-intellectual subtexts through which Monash found himself refracted in interwar nationalist discourse, it was certainly in the interest of the round-faced general to emphasise the deceptiveness of appearances.

40. Cited in Robin Custer, *The Heroic Theme in Australian War Writing*, Melbourne University Press, Melbourne 1987, pp69-70.

REARRANGING THE DIGGER'S FACE

> Finally, the face or body of the despot or god has something like a counterbody: the body of the tortured, or better, of the excluded. There is no question that these two bodies communicate...[41]

41. Deleuze and Guattari, *op. cit.*, p115.

Judith Butler accounts for the constitution of subjects in discourse in the following terms:

> [The] exclusionary matrix by which subjects are formed ... requires the simultaneous production of a domain of abject beings, those who are not yet 'subjects' but who form the constitutive outside to the domain of the subject. The abject designates here precisely those 'unliveable' and 'uninhabitable' zones of social life which are nevertheless densely populated by those who do not enjoy the status of the subject. This zone of unlivability will constitute that site of dreaded identification against which - and by virtue of which - the domain of the subject will circumscribe its own claim to autonomy and to life.[42]

42. Judith Butler, *Bodies That Matter; On the Discursive Limits of Sex*, Routledge, London and New York 1993, p3.

As a significant locus of the production of subjectivity in Australian inter war nationalist discourse, the digger's face represents an exemplary case in point. The debate about the appropriate form of the digger's face reveals the particular desires and anxieties attending a nationalist subject-in-construction. The material I have presented indicates that Monash's 'sweet-faced, round-faced mamma's boy' threatened his opponents with the very dissolution of the nationalist subject. The collection of traits attributed to the digger's face point directly to the latter's 'constitutive outside'. In this context, even the 'chance' or accidental attribution to the face of traits associated with the domain of abject beings by which it is circumscribed is able to derail the articulations of the digger-nationalist signifying regime.

An examination of the official digger's face in conjunction with some of its contemporary 'abject' alternatives further demonstrates this. In the remainder of this article I will look at the ways in which two war artists, one official and the other unofficial, rearranged the features of the digger's face.

THE DIGGER'S FRACTURED FACE

43. Deleuze and Guattari, *op. cit.* p115.

The one who is tortured is fundamentally one who loses his or her face...[43]

MacLure was a brilliant and original surgeon with amazing technical skill. To watch him make an incision was to realise that here was a man who knew exactly what he was going to do and why...There was no indecision - a knife directed by a mind that was clear and full of confidence - and so it went on through all the stages of an operation.[44]

44. Daryl Lindsay, *The Leafy Tree*, F.W. Cheshire, Melbourne 1965, pp116-7.

Daryl Lindsay enlisted in the AIF in 1915, serving in France as a driver until 1917 when he was transferred to divisional headquarters to work as a batman for his brother-in-law, Will Dyson. In 1918, Lindsay was also given a commission and sent as a 'medical artist' to Queen Mary Hospital at Sidcup in Kent. Queen Mary Hospital was opened in 1916 and it was here that the Empire's facial injuries were sent to be treated by means of a new treatment - 'plastic surgery'. In a series of over 100 watercolour 'portraits', Lindsay documented the 'success' of the new surgical techniques (Fig 6).

As instances of official war art, Daryl Lindsay's watercolours are ambivalent objects - part-medical record, part-official portrait and part-digger's face. Recalling Dyson's 'digger' in technique, Lindsay's watercolours can be read as skilfully executed, 'academic' portraits. But they differ from the work of other official artists in that they don't depict individual 'high ranking' or 'heroic' diggers. Nor do they present a 'composite' digger. Rather the subjects of Lindsay's portraits are those individual diggers who happened to 'get it' in the face. Lindsay's watercolours can be viewed as a site upon which the respective meta-narratives of 'nationalism' and 'medicine' converge. This meta-discursive convergence potentially threatened the

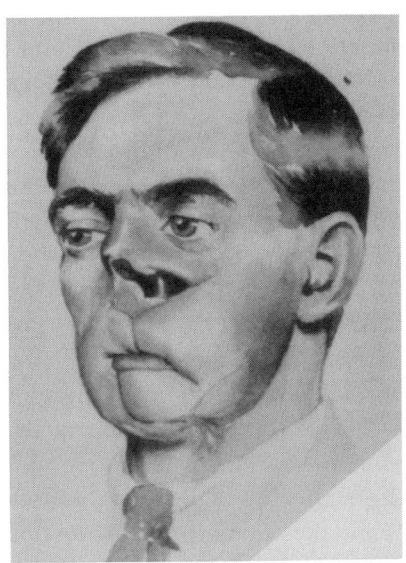

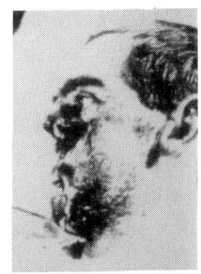

Fig. 6 (left). Watercolour, Daryl Lindsay 1918, Royal Australasian College of Surgeons, Melbourne.

Fig. 7. Photographs, 1918 (anonymous), Royal Australasian College of Surgeons, Melbourne.

official digger's face produced by a nationalist signifying regime.

The medical team at Queen Mary Hospital were pioneers in the field of maxillofacial surgery. Trench warfare produced a continuous stream of fractured faces upon which the new techniques of sterilisation and skin grafting could be tested and refined. The volume and variety of cases, combined with the experimental nature of their treatment, necessitated a rigourous regime of recording. Lindsay was involved in various stages of the overall recording process. In addition to executing the watercolors, he took photographs of staff, patients, buildings and grounds at the hospital and produced immaculate diagramatic illustrations of the new surgical procedures.

In most of Lindsay's watercolours the face is depicted following the successful intervention of the plastic surgeon. In doing this, Lindsay focuses upon the triumphant point 'after' the surgeon has completed his work within an implicit temporality of 'before' and 'after' which structures a wider medical meta-narrative. The task of picturing the face 'before' is largely left to the photograph which records various stages in a *continuous* process. And because most of the patients were subjected to a series of operations before the facial reconstruction was deemed 'complete', the photographic record captures the painful and arduous nature of this lengthy process (fig 7). A similar sense of the sitter's trauma can be found in the written records. For example,

Private X, Age: 19, Service: 11 months
Patient seems somewhat confused mentally and still in a highly nervous state. There is a *large ragged dirty wound* at left corner of the mouth opening up the cheek and both lips are swollen and slightly wounded ... Owing to nervous condition of patient no minute examination of lower jaw has been made...[45]

45. Patient record, Royal Australasian College of Surgeons, Melbourne.

The few watercolours Lindsay executed depicting the face 'before' surgery are worth examining as they shed some light on the function of the 'after' portraits. In his construction of the pre-operative face Lindsay removes the traces of chaos and horror which are evident in the early sequences of the photographic record. In this sense, in translation from photograph to watercolour, the face is figured less as the site of a chaotic *wound* and more as a surface which is marked by a *hole* (Fig 8). By substituting the ragged-edged, chaotic, often septic and, above all, *traumatic* 'wound' for a clean, clearly delineated 'hole', Lindsay is able to articulate a triumphant medical meta-narrative-narrative celebrating plastic surgery's pioneers. Put schematically, the surgeon initially transforms the 'wound' into a 'hole' through a process of sterilisation and cutting. The 'hole' is then more or less successfully 'filled' by means of the new technique of skin-grafting.

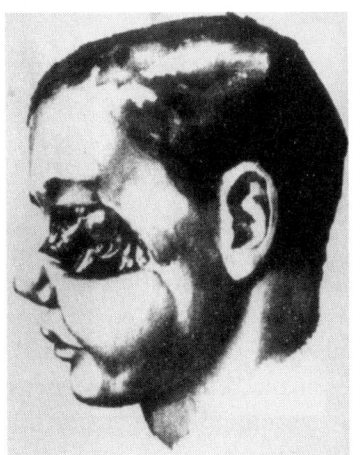

Fig 8. Daryl Lindsay, watercolour, 1918, Royal Australasian College of Surgeons, Melbourne

Although the watercolours, written records and the photographs all function within a medical discourse, it is necessary to establish the different discursive domains within which each are called to signify. The continuous photographic and written records of each 'case' belong to the sphere of medical *practice*. As such, they register significant points in the transition from the 'wound' to its surgical 'erasure'. The watercolour, in contrast, is called to signify within the meta-discursive domain where the representation of surgery itself is at stake. As a *medical* artist then, Lindsay had this in common with Dyson and his other 'official' colleagues: both medical and nationalist meta-narrative-narratives posit a subject predicated on the overcoming of the trauma of war. In this sense, Lindsay's watercolours can be seen to celebrate a subject upon which the triumph of 'nation' and 'medicine' are simultaneously inscribed.

The question raised by Lindsay's work is whether the medical and nationalist meta-narratives which converge upon these artworks are *necessarily* mutually exclusive. From the moment of their execution to the present time of writing, the watercolours have circulated and been exhibited within the strict confines of a medical discourse. In 1919, the watercolours were loaned to the Pathology Department at the University of Melbourne where they remained until 1952, when they were transferred to their present location - the basement of the Royal Australasian College of Surgeons. Having commissioned a medical artist to record the achievements of Australian medical practitioners, the Australian War Memorial demonstrated a surprising lack of interest in the products of this particular commission. In spite of the fact that the memorial actually featured a small 'medical' gallery, Lindsay's digger's faces were never hung in this space of nationalist representation.

It is not as though the reconstructed face was an inherently unsuitable vehicle for the expression of a triumphant nationalist subject. The reconstructed digger's face enjoyed an altogether different status in post-war France. The *mutiles de guerre* were given the honour of leading the victory parade in Paris on 14 July 1919. In this context, the reconstructed face, in addition to celebrating the surgical achievements occasioned by the war, was obviously made to signify a resilient national spirit. And it is interesting to note that in 1927, three years prior to the eruption of the digger's face debate in the Australian press, the French illustrated news magazine *L'Illustration* told the story of a group of more than 5,000 veterans with *severely damaged* faces called the Union Gueules Cassees (Union of Bashed Faces) [which] included photographs and a wrenching description *from a physician* (fig. 9).[46] A comparison with the situation in France would seem to indicate that the low profile of Lindsay's watercolours is connected to the specific requirements of *Australian* nationalism between the wars. In this context, how are we to understand the particular threat that the surgically reconstructed face posed for an interwar nationalist discourse in search of a face?

It is clear that *any* face which didn't embody the digger's essential attributes in a *transparent* manner was a threat to the official digger's face, the paradigmatic form of which was established by Dyson. It was not the 'unattractive' appearance of the reconstructed face which made it so threatening. For the digger's face debate demonstrated that a 'gaunt and haggard' face was infinitely preferable to a 'sweet' and 'round' face. Rather,

46. Cited in Sidra Sich, *Anxious Visions*, Berkeley Art Museum, San Francisco 1990.

Fig. 9. Daryl Lindsay in his studio at Sidcup, C.1918, Royal Australasian College of Surgeons, Melbourne (anonymous).

the problem posed by the reconstructed face was that both the initial 'wound' and the surgeon's intervention rearranged the face in *inconsistent* and *unpredictable* ways. The form of embodiment offered by the reconstructed face, then, was dangerously *arbitrary*. The reconstructed face raised the destabilizing possibility that the war, rather than providing a pretext for the nation's *facialization*, might, from another perspective, be construed as the occasion of its *defacialization* or *refacialization*.

THE DIGGER'S PSYCHO-FACE

Whether the term or the concept 'shell-shock' came first from the medical service or from the soldiers themselves will probably never be known...[but]...the concept of 'shell-shock' was immediately and enthusiastically accepted ... 'Shell-shock' provided for the overwrought soldier a more or less conscious escape from the stigma of the essentially feminine failing 'hysteria' which itself is an unconscious escape into disease from an emotional tension and conflict that has become unbearable. So 'shell-shock' became a respectable way of escape from the conflict between 'fear' and 'duty'. In each case, the motivating impulse, conscious or unconscious is advantage.[47]

We were all treated as weirdoes and not quite right in the head...so there was no way of getting in [to the official war art scheme].[48]

47. Grahame Butler, *op. cit.*, p100.

48. Transcript from author's interview with Albert Tucker, 2 June 1994.

At the outbreak of WWII, Albert Tucker was a founding member of the Contemporary Artists Society. The CAS was a loose coalition of 'modern' artists opposed to the 'academic' artistic establishment from which official war artists were largely recruited. From the perspective of a modern artist such as Tucker, the war, rather than providing the 'testing' conditions which enabled a coherent nationalist subject to emerge, simply produced extreme forms of alienation. Such an attitude was anathema to the Australian War Memorial project where architecture, relics and official texts all converged upon the digger's body which was, in turn, a metonym for the larger unity of the nation. The tendency of 'modern' war art, in this context, was to disembody or dismember the nationalist subject which the Memorial was attempting to secure.

Tucker was conscripted in 1942. Fortunately, due to the intervention of his superior officers, Tucker was never sent to participate in the 'butchery' of the New Guinea campaigns. He was placed, however, in a perfect situation to unofficially record the results of this 'butchery'. The first six months following Tucker's recruitment were spent in camp at Wangaratta where he was given the task of copying photographs and drawings of war injuries onto large sheets of cartridge paper for use in lectures instructing nurses, orderlies and stretcher bearers. After this, Tucker was transferred to Heidelberg repatriation hospital where he executed a series of portraits called *Psychos*. At Heidelberg, Tucker had the opportunity to observe the effects of the war upon a range of diggers, ranging from POWs and plastic surgery cases to the victims of shell-shock. 'I had a full panorama. I was given a peculiar, spectator, tourist experience of the whole thing.'(Fig. 10)[49]

49. *Ibid.*

It is useful to compare Tucker's digger's face with that of Dyson. Dyson was very explicitly concerned with registering the trauma of trench warfare on his 'gaunt and haggard' digger's face. This notwithstanding, his digger's face represents the coherent sense of nationalist subjectivity occasioned by the *overcoming* of this trauma. In contrast, the digger's face delineated by Tucker is that of a nationalist subject *constituted* by trauma. Tucker accounts for his *psychos* as follows:

> ... a series of portraits of what we called then 'bomb happys'. Their nervous systems were shattered. They were a most awful mess. There were 40 of these characters who'd covered the British withdrawal from Greece and they'd been bombed to smithereens...one wonders what their eventual fate was. There they all were twitching and in quite a mess, shaking from head to foot *with no self-control*. They were given insulin injections every morning for a month. [The nurses] tucked bibs around their necks and they'd be dribbling. To see a whole crowd like that, dribbling mouths and snow-white faces, was quite horrendous in itself.

Not only is Tucker's psycho face incapable of embodying a triumphant nationalist subject, it presents us with the spectre of the latter's disintegration.

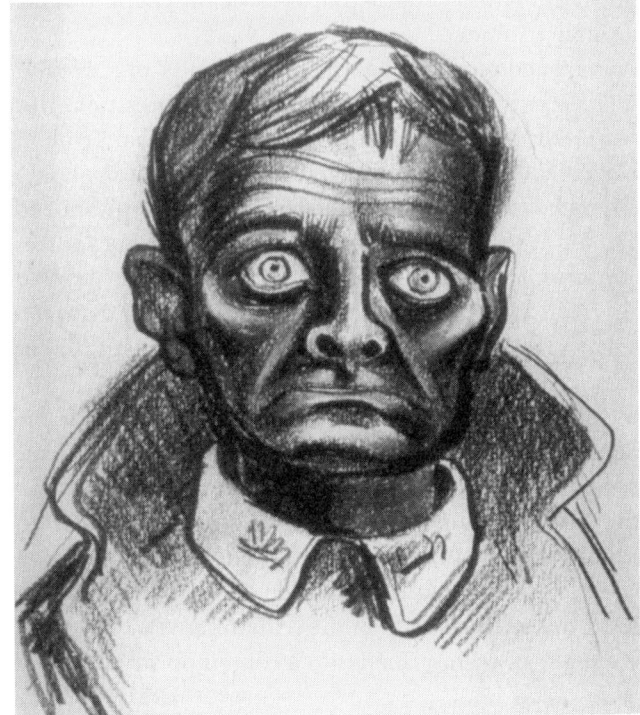

Fig. 10.
Psycho, *Albert Tucker, 1942, drawing, Australian War Memorial, Canberra.*

Tucker's psycho face bears testimony to a double alienation. In addition to representing the loss of *national* identity, this digger represents the loss of identity *per se*. A parody of the nationalist subject, this 'twitching, shaking, dribbling psycho with no self-control', can hardly be seen as a subject at all. The psycho face shows how little remains of the subject after its exposure to the trauma of modern warfare.

Perhaps the most important point to emerge from this examination of the digger's face is the inherently tenuous nature of facialization. It would seem that no 'significant' 'subjectifying' face is produced without eliciting the spectre of an 'asignifying', 'asubjective' counterpart. For the digger had barely been established as a national facialization when he was 'de-faced', initially, and, to some extent, inadvertently, by Monash and Lindsay and later, deliberately, by avant-garde artists such as Albert Tucker.

The faces we have looked at deconstruct the official face in different ways: Dyson's official face has no 'inside'; its facial features directly reflect its essential attributes; Monash's face consists of a series of signifiers which need to be inverted to reveal the digger's character; Lindsay's reconstructed faces suggest that war makes the face into an unprecedentedly malleable surface, open to the various inscriptions of bullets, shells and scalpels. And finally, by bringing the psychic (or interior) disintegration of the digger up onto the surface of the digger's face, Tucker presents an alienated subject that is radically incompatible with a collective nationalist subject.

Michael Taussig has argued recently that the 'monuments' of a 'secular state' issue a powerful invitation to 'defacement'.[50] This peculiar vulnerability to defacement, Taussig suggests, resides in the ambivalent relationship such objects establish in relation to what he calls the 'sacred'. The Australian War Memorial as it was imagined by CEW Bean epitomized a 'sacred site' designed for a 'secular state'. Taussig's formulation captures something of the paradoxical status of the digger within Australian nationalist discourse. That is, whilst the digger is posited as a sacred embodiment of nation, the reason that the 'nation' itself is constituted as sacred remains unclear.

'Defacement' of the digger may take many forms ranging from academic criticism or the laughter of schoolchildren on an excursion to anti-Anzac Day protest marches. Consciousness of this is registered in most Australian war memorials in the form of signs reminding visitors to refrain from smoking, eating, drinking and loud talking. (Fig. 11 and 12) But *what* is in danger of being defaced? It seems that this question arises with particular urgency now, as, with the impending death of the remaining WWI veterans, the digger is being energetically reinscribed into a contemporary vision of nationalist subjectivity.

50. Lecture delivered at University of Melbourne, June 1995.

Figs. 11 & 12. Signs at Anzac Memorial, Sydney. Photographs by Fiona Nicoll, 1994.

1995: 'Australia Remembers'. A series of commemorative visits and speeches as Australian statesmen urge us, and the rest of the world to remember. Television, radio and newspaper advertisements, documentaries and commentary. Events designed to reinforce memory down the generations - the visit to Gallipoli of the descendants of the first 'diggers', press photographs of young boys dressed in AIF uniforms wearing their grandfathers' medals.(fig 13) Record attendances at Anzac Day ceremonies. Vietnam veterans finally destigmatised and taking pride of place in the Anzac Day parades. 'Australia Remembers'; in 1995, the Anzac myth reappears with the force of Adorno's '...provocative lie which does not seek belief but commands silence.'[51]

With the temporary(?) reinstatement of the digger-nationalist signifying regime criticism becomes defacement. To criticise past and present representations of the digger is to speak or to write in bad faith. To criticise the signifier is to criticise, and thereby deface, the digger. The digger is not a 'sign'. To recall Will Dyson's response to Monash's criticism of his *art*: 'Some bitter things have been said about the digger, but none so bitter as..'. The power of the nationalist signifying regime consists in its capacity to transform the

51. Theodore Adorno, 'Cultural Criticism and Society', in Paul Connerton (ed), *Critical Sociology*, Penguin, Harmondsworth 1976, p275.

Fig. 13 Grandsons in Anzac Day Parade

critique of representation into defacement. In this context, the critic becomes s/he who would deface the war dead. It is therefore appropriate to give a digger the last word:

> I was in Vietnam carrying on the proud Anzac tradition that had been forged in blood and suffering through two world wars and Korea. Proving yourself in war was a very personal thing for me as I came from a family with a proud history as citizen soldiers.

> ...I slowly pulled the body over to match one of those faces in the photographs. To my horror, I discovered there was no face. A head, but no face. The face had been sheared off almost surgically by a red-hot piece of shrapnel. It seemed that even death refused to reveal my enemy to me. That experience was the perfect metaphor for Australian involvement in Vietnam. We didn't know our enemy, and *killing the Vietnamese brought us no closer to knowing them.*[52]

52. Terry Burstall, *The Age*, 29 April 1995.

A CINEMATIC LANDSCAPE IN LOS ANGELES:
A GRAVEYARD TOUR OF CINEMATIC SPACE AND SPECTACLE

Vicki Callahan

Many tours of Los Angeles are mapped out according to a 'grid' of the Hollywood landscape. While these excursions may be organised around a formalised studio tour, the ubiquitous 'map to the stars' homes,' or a coach trip through the celebrity haunted city, there is, nonetheless, something quite peculiar about this 'map'. The oddity resides not only in that the location of much of the tour ventures into areas that are external to Hollywood proper, but is also due to a certain ambiguity or indeterminacy of the space examined, or indeed, with the very notion of 'location' in itself. On arrival, it is not always clear to the tourist what there is to see or to do at a given site. Maps to the stars' homes are guides to mansions typically hidden from view or to places long since vacated by the great film stars (due to death, public disfavour or disinterest, and downward mobility) and now occupied by lesser known or non-celebrities.

Studio tours seem to face similar problems of locating a tangible space associated with the Hollywood aura. Warner Brothers' studio - already out of 'place' by their suburban Burbank location - offers a 'personalised' tour of the site. Golf carts whizz you past the corporate offices and production facilities into the world of the backlot, scattered with film and television sets in various stages of mutation. Though the trip does include some time in set and costume design, and even a rehearsal for a low-profile television sitcom is on display, many of the details of production are omitted e.g., on set filming, editing, sound and special effects work. The tour ends at the final archive - the gift shop - to commemorate the visit in a more directly corporate and consumerist manner.

Universal Studios, geographically less disavantaged (as it is, in fact, located in Hollywood), but equally estranged from the material base of film production, offers an alternative tour. In the place of a 'working studio' the visitor is plunged into a multi-dimensional entertainment complex which includes a theme park, movie theatres, and an outdoor mall for shopping and dining. The theme park itself mimics a studio tour (complete with trams and over narration), but is more appropriately seen as a high-tech amusement ride that travels through animated movie 'scenes' (e.g., *Jaws*, *King Kong*) or disasters (the viscerally accurate earthquake ride). However, even here the scenes are not precise re-enactments from films, but represent scenes based on the visitor as a participant in the film.

The city then, I would argue, maps out a topography not unlike the cinema itself. My reference, here, does not refer solely to the thematic level of celebrity fixation and the generalised fictionalised universe that Angelenos are said to inhabit, but also to the formal properties of the cinema. To illustrate my point, I would like to propose another tour of the city, this time of a space less explicitly aligned with the Hollywood machine, but no less representative of the cinematic landscape that defines Los Angeles. My choice of locale is the well-known cemetery, Forest Lawn. While a graveyard might seem an unlikely site to situate a discussion of Hollywood cinema, Forest Lawn offers a unique opportunity to examine some distinctions between the photographic and the cinematic image and, moreover, to highlight the city's understanding of the cinematic landscape as fundamentally based on the classical Hollywood model of cinema.

On one level, Forest Lawn appears to be a space defined by the photographic image. As Christian Metz has noted, photography shares a certain affinity with death:

> Photography is linked with death in many *different* ways. The most immediate and explicit is the social practice of keeping photographs in memory of loved beings who are no longer alive. But there [is] another real death which each of us undergoes every day, as each day we draw nearer our own death. Even when the person photographed is still living, that moment when she or he *was* has forever vanished. Strictly speaking, the person *who has been photographed* - not the total person, who is an effect of time - is dead: 'dead for having been seen'...[1]

1. Christian Metz, 'Photography and Fetish', *October*, Volume 34, 1985.

Thus, both photography and death create a sense of completeness or fixity to the image. Walter Benjamin's comment that a person's 'real life...first assumes transmissible form at the moment of his death' suggests a similar relationship, i.e. the 'form' *becomes* image at the moment of death.[2] The death of a person serves to present us with a temporally bounded entity that can be reconstructed by those who survive. These reconstructions can, of course, vary, but the key point is that the person faced with the process of interpretation and reconstruction assumes a finality to the sequence of events.

2. Walter Benjamin, 'The Storyteller', *Illuminations*, Schocken, New York, 1969, p94.

However, any tour of Los Angeles including one of Forest Lawn usually offers ample evidence of Benjamin's claim that bourgeois society has effectively *erased* the public markers of death.[3] This creates a problem with the finality and clarity of the image suggested by the photographic perspective. Indeed, what Los Angeles offers the observer is the creation of a space, in which the city's own negative image is included; that is to say, a cinematic form of representation. Again, Metz's discussion of the photograph includes the distinction between this particular medium and the cinema:

3. Benjamin, *op. cit.*, pp93-94.

> ...film is less a succession of photographs than, to a large extent, a destruction of the photograph, or more exactly of the photograph's power and action.[4]

4. Metz, *op. cit.*, p85.

Hence, the cinematic space cannot be fixed, cannot be located, cannot be temporally bounded *in itself*; it requires some other mechanism to provide time and logic (i.e. classical narration).

As a *photographic* space, Los Angeles locates and acknowledges time through a strategy of inversion. Here, the city imprints and fixes the image by its ongoing efforts to arrest or reverse the effects of aging. If Los Angeles's particular variant of immortality has not provoked necessarily a sense of eternal youth, it has, at least, presented the option of a 'preserved' life. In 'The Ontology of the Photographic Image,' André Bazin argued that the original impetus behind the plastic arts was a desire to defeat death. Tracing the beginnings of painting and sculpture back to ancient Egyptian culture, he noted that these works served as a type of embalming, or freezing, of the body at a particular moment in time.[5]

5. Andre Bazin, 'The Ontology of the Photographic Image'. *What is Cinema*, trans. Hugh Gray, University of California Press, Berkeley, 1967, p9.

The preservation of life takes on a variety of forms in Los Angeles. In its most pragmatic permutations there are the numerous services designed for physical 'preservation' of individuals. Health clubs, cosmetic surgeons, and hair transplant specialists are ever present establishments - if not in the literal space of our neighbourhoods, then filling the imaginary space of advertising.

More appropriate to our discussion are the numerous places in Hollywood - again, speaking as both a 'real' and an 'imaginary' site - that deal with another sort of 'physical preservation'. In this case, the preservation tends to take the form of some artifact, some tangible entity 'left behind' by an individual. These artifacts, or *traces*, by their very physicality serve to 'freeze' our memory at a particular moment in time. Again, all this would be consistent with the photographic image.

Moreover, the Hollywood 'artifact' typically takes the form of the 'celebrity' photo. Serving as both a type of endorsement and 'historical' souvenir, the celebrity photo is part of the requisite furnishings of a neighbourhood's business. The variety of establishments that feature these photos include portrait studios, restaurants, and even mailbox businesses.

A more interesting variation on this practice includes the celebrity imprint. The most famous practitioner of this is Graumann's Chinese Theatre. Here, the hand- and foot-prints of numerous stars are preserved for us in concrete, accompanied by a signature that 'authenticates' the indentations. This tradition has been copied by Hollywood's newer class of celebrity - the rock star - at a well-known guitar shop on Sunset Boulevard. In each case, the imprint guarantees an artifact of the 'star' at a specific moment in time. Not only does this serve as a type of historical evidence of the 'event' (the star visit), but also the individual is forever preserved for us as they were at that moment. This explains the significance of some sort of dating device at the Graumann theatre - a specific date or a filmic reference - that accompanies the imprint.

At the Graumann theatre another sort of 'mechanical reproduction' demonstrates the drive towards preservation. Surrounded by the hand- and foot-prints of numerous stars is a machine that for a small fee ($1.00) will produce a replica of the theatre in wax 'before your eyes'. The detail in the reproduction is of interest; it features not only the well-known exterior of the movie house, but also a space in the centre of the figure with the site's most distinguishing feature - star imprints, yet another celebrity turn.

Consistent with this photographic base and the desire for preservation is the Forest Lawn memorial park. The cemetery consists of five different sites, making it, in effect, a 'chain' of graveyards. The space has 'inspired' a number of writers, for example Jessica Mitford, Umberto Eco, and Evelyn Waugh, to a range of commentary on the landscape. Generally speaking, most of the writings - despite the cemetery's unabashed commercialism - stop short of outright condemnation (with perhaps the exception of Mitford's *The American Way of Death*).[6] In part, the begrudgingly favourable response can be attributed to the very lushness of the landscape in an otherwise often bleak urban environment. However, the continuing fascination and admiration of the 'memorial park' must also be the product of its recurring invocation of the preservation theme. But it is the very *repetition* and *variation* of the fixed and preserved images that makes this a cinematic, rather than merely a photographic, object. As we move from site to site through the park, we experience a metonymic slippage from one cultural icon to the next - e.g. Jesus, David, Washington, da Vinci - and it is precisely this *movement* that defines this cemetery as a cinematic landscape. A similar process is described by Thierry Kuntzel with regards to the cinema machine: 'The most astonishing characteristic of this apparatus resides in its movement...everything happens as if it were inscribed and erased on the screen without stop...'[7]

The movement is facilitated by several factors: the uniformity of the landscape, the style of transportation through the park (i.e. the automobile), and an ever present and unifying narration (through written text and recorded voice and song). It becomes difficult to remember that Forest Lawn is, in fact, a cemetery. There are the graves, headstones, mausoleums, and acres of green grass that we associate with any such site. Yet, from the initial entry through the 'World's Largest Wrought Iron Gates' (proclaimed by the colorful cemetery brochure/tour map) to the viewing of a 'performance' of the 'Crucifixion' and 'Resurrection', a trip through Forest Lawn underlines the site's uniqueness.

Although Forest Lawn does contain the usual statuary and other 'art' objects that one generally associates with a traditional cemetery, it is the specific technology and ideology behind the production of these works that sets the space apart from others like it. Forest Lawn as a landscape and as a repository for art and 'artifacts' is structured around a narrative, which is itself shaped by the use of 'mechanical reproduction' in a postmodern, consumer society.

The process of mechanical reproduction offers two major advantages over manual procedures: exactness and efficiency. These two features are essential to Forest Lawn's identity and marketing strategies. Once through the gates, the principle of efficiency is immediately apparent. On the right

6. Jessica Mitford, *The American Way of Death*, Simon and Schuster, New York, 1963, p148-160.

7. Thierry Kuntzel, 'A Note Upon the Filmic Apparatus'. *Quarterly Review of Film Studies*, Vol. 1.3, 1976, p266-271 (this quote is p269).

hand side of the road is the flower shop, mortuary, and executive offices of the cemetery. As the brochure/map notes, 'Forest Lawn Mortuaries offer many distinct advantages because *everything is in one place....*' The advertisement points out that this centralisation of facilities is not only more convenient, but also saves time and money. In addition, this arrangement has a certain democratising function in that Forest Lawn, because of its overall efficiency and supposed policy of affordability, is available to 'people in all income brackets'.[8] Forest Lawn is clearly a 'good buy' for consumers regardless of their particular needs of the moment. The cemetery's marketing strategy recalls Guy Debord's description of the commodity:

8. See the Forest Lawn - Hollywood Hills brochure.

> ...concentrated capitalism orients itself towards the sale of 'completely equipped' blocks of time, each one constituting a single unified commodity which integrates a number of diverse commodities. In the expanding economy of 'services' and leisure, this gives rise to the formula of calculated payment in which 'everything's included'...[9]

9.Guy Debord, *Society of Spectacle*, Red and Black, Detroit, 1977, p152.

The ongoing references to the park's efficiency and affordability provide a certain narrative cohesion. As such, several places in the cemetery can be labelled as 'performance sites', or 'exhibits', which incorporate various levels of theatrical or cinematic spectacle. In its simplest form, these sites will include an 'art' work and some sort of narration. For example, our next stop on the tour brings us to 'The Great Mausoleum'. Outside the mausoleum is the statue entitled: 'For such is the Kingdom of Heaven'.

With the push of a discreetly placed button, the spectator can begin a recorded narration that tells us the 'history' of the art object itself, the 'history' of the particular biblical event or passage in question, and finally, a not-so-discreet sales pitch for a final resting place at Forest Lawn. Here the narration around efficiency overlaps with the Tayloresque ideal stated in the brochure and on the park entrance sign - '*One call makes all arrangements*' (see Fig. 1).

Fig. 1

The 'Kingdom of Heaven' statue is interesting not only for this advertising blurb, but also for its introduction of the idea of journey as pilgrimage - which proposes a narrative trajectory in and of itself. The narration for the 'Kingdom of Heaven' notes that the 'founder' of Forest Lawn, Hubert Eaton, searched throughout Europe for a statue of a 'smiling Christ'. Eaton's journey takes him from one studio to another until finally he finds '...not my smiling Christ, but a kind Christ'. The benevolent Christ is surrounded by numerous contented and happy children.

The possibility of 'happy children' in the context of a graveyard setting was an important one for Eaton. 'The Builder's Creed', an engraving opposite the 'Kingdom of Heaven' on the other side of the entrance to 'The Great Mausoleum', suggests that the notion of an upbeat cemetery was also crucial to Eaton's 'vision' for Forest Lawn. Setting itself apart from other cemeteries that are '...full of inartistic symbols and depressing customs', 'The Builder's Creed' promises a 'different' environment. According to the Creed, Forest Lawn will be a place:

> ...devoid of misshapen monuments and other customary signs of earthly death, but filled with towering trees, sweeping lawns, splashing fountains, singing birds, beautiful statuary, cheerful flowers, noble memorial architecture with interiors full of light and color, and redolent of the world's best history and romances....where lovers new and old shall love to stroll and watch the sunset's glow, planning for the future or reminiscing of the past; a place where artists study and sketch; where school teachers bring happy children to see the things they read of in books...

This 'vision' of Forest Lawn is underscored by a statue in front of the engraving that depicts two children and their puppy looking up to the 'creed' (see Figure 2).

Fig. 2

In a rather bizarre inversion of Bazin's principle of preservation, a sales brochure features a photograph that *replicates* the statue through the placement of two 'real' children next to the work. The children are, of course, not an *exact* copy of the statue in that they are missing their pet. However, this absence is easily explained by the park's numerous restrictive 'guidelines' within this 'place for the living', a policy that includes a ban on pets.

As we leave 'The Builder's Creed' and enter the 'Great Mausoleum', a clearer sense of the Forest Lawn

Fig. 3

narrative emerges. Inside the mausoleum is the family tomb of Hubert Eaton, the 'founder' and 'builder' of Forest Lawn as a memorial park. According to information that accompanies Eaton's tomb, in 1916 Eaton decided to transform the cemetery he was managing into a 'memorial park'. Essentially, his plan was twofold; the replacement of traditional headstones with bronze tablets as grave markers, and, the replacement of the usual graveyard statuary with 'works of art'.

The use of bronze tablets significantly changes the landscape of Forest Lawn. First, not only are the tablets uniform, eliminating the numerous variations in individual headstones (for a look at the area of Forest Lawn that appears to pre-date Eaton's vision see Figure 3), but the bronze markers are the epitome of groundskeeping efficiency. The markers lie horizontal enabling quick and consistent lawn maintenance on a large scale. A quick glance around the grounds sees only immaculately kept, seemingly unending green space (Figures 4 and 5). According to Evelyn Waugh the park was

Fig. 4

Fig. 5

10. Evelyn Waugh,
'Half in Love With
Easeful Death', *The
Essays, Articles and
Reviews of Evelyn
Waugh*, ed. Donat
Gallagher, Little,
Brown and
Company, Boston,
1984, p332.

planted only with evergreens, thereby eliminating the untidiness, of dead foliage.[10]

What is missing from this picture is, of course, recognition of the surrounding gravesites (Figure 6). The elimination of headstones is more than an effort to remove the depressing reminders of death that surround us in a cemetery; they are part of Forest Lawn's essentially classical Hollywood narrative technique. The elision of complex and multiple lines of potentially disruptive narrative action allows for the insertion of a continuous and cheery meta-narrative in their place. Even 'The Builder's Creed' sets up an opposition between dreary death and the 'happy eternal life' (for those 'who believed in Him').

To return to the inside of the 'Great Mausoleum', death is reconfigured in the use and presentation of 'works of art' - an

Fig. 6

important component of Eaton's plan. In part, art at Forest Lawn serves to collapse the distinctions between high and low culture. Within the confines of a space that is, theoretically at least, affordable to all, are to be found the works of the 'great masters'. This said, Forest Lawn does offer a mix of artistic styles, though the High Renaissance period of art dominates the landscape of the park. This period is particularly useful for the Forest Lawn setting since commentators have emphasised both the acts of individual 'genius' and 'creativity' behind these works of art and, furthermore, the 'divine' inspiration that motivated these artists.[11] The artist is, in this instance, a transcendent figure. In some sense, Forest Lawn's use of the 'great' artist can be seen as a replacement for the erasure of the individual; enacted in the landscape.

11. H.W. Janson, *History of Art*, Harry N. Abrams, Inc., New York 1974, p346.

The art object can be seen to fulfil contradictory functions in the context of Forest Lawn. That is, they represent both 'timeless treasures' and artifacts that point to a specific time period - a temporal tension we have already established as embedded within the cinematic apparatus. As in 'The Kingdom of Heaven' each work of art is presented with a 'history', or narrative trajectory, to obfuscate this tension. Inside 'The Great Mausoleum' is featured a variety of works and their history: the reproductions of 'La Pieta', 'Moses', 'Twilight and Dawn', 'Day and Night', 'Madonna of Bruges', and 'Medici Madonna and Child'. Of course, what appears to be the most famous art work in the mausoleum is the stained glass representation of da Vinci's 'The Last Supper'.

Rosa Moretti's stained glass 'Last Supper' stands as another performance site at Forest Lawn. Located in the area designated as the 'Memorial Court of Honor', the stained glass work is stored behind curtains except for selected viewing times throughout the day. Seating is arranged in front of the curtains as in a theatre, with the above mentioned 'masterpieces' surrounding the audience. The viewings, or perhaps more accurately, the screenings, are accompanied by background music, over-narration, and even special effects. All of the performance is automated from the opening of the curtains to the narration and effects. The narration features the only reference to the objects' status as reproductions. The works are never labeled as copies, but rather as 'exact re-creations'. Here the language and ideology of mechanical reproduction is implemented even if the technology does not literally participate in the process of replication.

In the case of 'The Last Supper' the re-creation appears particularly 'authentic' because it is taken from Leonardo's 'original drawings'. In fact, as the narration points out, the stained-glass version of the piece is even *superior* to the original da Vinci painting because the decaying effects of time - the fading and chipping of paint - and other artists' intervention (retouching) have destroyed the work. To quote the brochure, '...at Forest Lawn the painting lives again...' - it is re-born. The language recalls Kuntzel's and Metz's description of the photograph's erasure or 'decay' within the cinematic space, and the notion of rebirth becomes yet another counter-narrative to displace this ongoing loss.

In part, the idea that da Vinci's 'Last Supper' now 'lives again' can be seen as a repetition of the 'eternal life' narrative discussed earlier. More specifically with regard to Christian theology, eternal life is the product of a 'resurrection' - an idea that will be carried to its logical and spectacular conclusion at the last stop on the tour at the 'Hall of The Crucifixion-Resurrection'.

More specifically, mechanical reproduction, whether as ideology or technology, serves to preserve the original art work for its Forest Lawn 'resurrection'. Moreover, the notion of an 'original' work is a very difficult one to maintain in the park. As in the Memorial Court, few works are clearly designated as 'real' or 'reproduction'. Even the accompanying background material frequently alternates between a discussion of the original's and the copy's history. In the darkness of the theatre, before the curtains open we hear of the difficulties Moretti, the artist, had with forming the stained glass figure of Judas. At one point, we are told, Moretti almost abandoned the project because of problems with the figure. Then, as the curtains open to view Moretti's 'Last Supper' we are given a history of da Vinci's difficulties in finishing the project. In fact, once the curtains open there is no longer any mention of the 'original artist' (Moretti), and her name does not appear anywhere on the work (although da Vinci's name and 'Forest Lawn' can be seen in the bottom right hand corner). Here the metonymic slippage outlined earlier functions even at the level of the artist - all aesthetic practice becomes equivalent in this context.

The memorial court itself is the preferred viewing site for the 'Last Supper'. The site's superiority to Milan is due to the opportunity Forest Lawn offers the spectator of a completely controlled environment for the viewing experience. As a consequence, during the course of the 'program' the audience is able to see the work as it appears at various times of the day. A series of shutters have been installed behind the stained-glass that recreates changing light conditions and enables us to view the transformation of the piece. As the day grows dark, supposedly only the Christ figure remains visible. Shortly after this brief description, the shutters perform their magic and the illuminated Christ figure glows from the centre of an otherwise darkened portrait. The entire 'performance' of the 'Last Supper' suggests Baudrillard's discussion of simulation: 'It is no longer a question of imitation, nor of duplication, nor even of parody. It is rather a question of substituting signs of the real for the real itself....'.[12] Here, the manipulation of 'time' through the use of the shutters and the overall 'historical' context now functions to 'authenticate' the simulacrum.

Despite efforts to ensure 'authenticity' through a variety of mechanisms, Forest Lawn, and moreover the technology of reproduction, are plagued by the issue of uniqueness - a problem that, of course, calls to mind Benjamin's discussion of 'aura':

12. Jean Baudrillard, 'Simulacra and Simulations', *Selected Writings*, Ed. Mark Poster, Stanford University Press, Standord 1988, p167.

...that which withers in the age of mechanical reproduction is the aura of a work of art. This is symptomatic of a process whose significance points beyond the realm of art. One might generalise by saying: the technique of reproduction detaches the reproduced object from the domain of tradition. By making many reproductions it substitutes a plurality of copies for a unique existence.[13]

13. Benjamin, *op. cit.*, p221.

Appropriately enough, Forest Lawn attempts to recapture the sense of 'aura' through the introduction of yet another copy. In this case, the reproduction is no more just an object, but rather of a reproduction of an institution - the Westminster Abbey.

As the viewing of the 'Last Supper' ends, a final walk through the room reveals an 'honor court' directly beneath the now covered (the curtains are drawn after performance) stained-glass work. According to the accompanying plaques, the court is the cemetery's version of Westminster Abbey. Like its famous British counterpart, the court contains the remains of renowned, or in Forest Lawn's words 'immortal', persons. In order to qualify for burial inside the court, Forest Lawn's Council of Regents (a vaguely defined entity itself) must pronounce and proclaim the individual as 'immortal'.

The individuals chosen for the court are an odd mixture of professions: a musician, a popular songwriter, a physicist, and a painter (Jan Styka, responsible for the painting 'The Crucifixion' on view at another building). Each person chosen for the court is featured on a plaque that gives a brief description of their work. These personal histories are usually signed by a well-known public figure (eg, Billy Graham, Dwight Eisenhower, Richard Nixon). To ensure our understanding of the uniqueness of each individual, and simultaneously, to erase Forest Lawn's status as yet another commodity, one plaque notes that an immortal's final resting place will be in a crypt which, it claims, 'money cannot buy'.

14. Richard Alleman, *The Movie Lover's Guide to Hollywood*, Harper and Row, New York 1985, p298-300. According to Alleman, the list of stars supposedly buried at Forest Lawn - Glendale is extensive and impressive. Here is a brief list of some of the more noteworthy inhabitants: Humphrey Bogart, Clark Gable, Jean Harlow, Sid Graumann, Carole Lombard, Marie Dressler, and even Walt Disney. As Alleman notes, Walt Disney's place of internment is unclear since, according to modern folklore, Disney has been frozen until an unnamed, but presumably, medically superior point in the future.

Fortunately for the general public (and Forest Lawn), there are still numerous places in the cemetery which money *can* buy. Many areas within the mausoleum - as well as other areas of the cemetery - are demarcated as off-limits except for 'property owners'. These restrictions are enforced by a number of means: locked and roped off areas, security guards, and the use of surveillance cameras - in effect, gated communities for the dead. At the same time, the park makes an effort to describe these controls in a positive light, in one instance by an imbrication of financial wherewithal and fond remembrance - a locked courtyard notes that its entrance 'is restricted to those possessing a golden key of memory, given to each owner at time of purchase'.

The security arrangements return us directly to the cinematic spectacle; that is, Forest Lawn is, in large part, known as the cemetery for celebrities.[14] Celebrities serve an important function in this space in that 'stars' aid in the replacement of the machine age's lost 'aura'. As Benjamin points out in his discussion of cinema, the replacement gives us a new sort of object:

> The film responds to shrivelling of the aura with an artificial build-up of the 'personality' outside the studio. The cult of the movie star, fostered by the money of the film industry, preserves not the unique aura of a person but the 'spell of the personality', the phony sell of the commodity (Benjamin, *op. cit.*, p231).

As a commodity, the celebrity is particularly useful to the Forest Lawn environment because stars relay to the consumer the attributes of both the 'unique' and the 'ordinary'.[15]

15. Pam Cooke, 'Star Signs', *Screen*, Vol 20, No. 3/4, Winter 79/ 80, p83.

The mythology of stars as ordinary people works in conjunction with a number of signs of 'democracy' throughout the park to promote Forest Lawn's ideology that this is truly a cemetery for all. Although the Hollywood Hills Forest Lawn is specifically organised around the theme of American democracy, the Glendale branch of the cemetery also invokes this idea. After leaving 'The Great Mausoleum', a road sign in the shape of a bible (Figure 7) serves to guide us through the narrative and towards our next sites - 'The Court of Freedom' and the 'Freedom Mausoleum'.

Appropriately enough, the 'Freedom Mausoleum' ('dedicated to the spirit of American Liberty') does not have restricted access areas. Segments of the mausoleum are divided into separate rooms and labelled in accordance with the overall theme; for example, 'The Sanctuary of Liberation', 'The Sanctuary of Allegiance', and 'The Columbarium of Patriots'. Outside the mausoleum are statues of George Washington and 'The Republic' while across the way there is a large mosaic representing 'The Declaration of Independence'. In the face of this public demonstration of democracy, it is important to note that at one time the cemetery had a 'white only' policy.[16]

16. Mitford, *op. cit.*, p128 and also Waugh, *op. cit.*, p336.

However, as one walks through the 'Court of Freedom' today, one notes the Asian names on the tombs that border and frame the 'Declaration of

Fig. 7

Independence' mosaic - evidence of the cemetery's efforts to accommodate the demographic shifts in the Los Angeles landscape. History, though, has its limits, and the icons of American democracy are still rather narrowly defined; i.e as European and male.

The next area of the park features more examples of 'works of art'. The 'Court of David' contains a full-size 're-creation' of Michelangelo's 'David'. According to Jessica Mitford, the statue at one time featured a fig leaf in the interests of public decency.[17] However, Forest Lawn appears able to adjust with the times, and the anatomical 'censorship' has since been removed.

Fig. 8

17. Mitford, ibid, p149.

Michelangelo is the artist of choice for the cemetery, with a separate segment of the Forest Lawn 'museum' set aside for a display of his 'work'. The 'Court of David' provides an excellent photo opportunity for the tourist (according to the brochure there are more than one million visitors a year) with the lush greenery surrounding the sculpture and the nearby 'Mystery of Life' garden and sculpture. This 'Mystery of Life' site comes complete with lyrics from a Jeanette MacDonald song on a nearby marble tablet. Absent, of course, is any *direct* reference to the work's cinematic heritage. On the opposite side of the piece a separate text points out that the sculpture was 'carved...expressly for Forest Lawn, because Forest Lawn has solved the "mystery of life".' This same courtyard features a return to the 'happy children' narrative with the sculpture entitled 'Baby's bath' - an examination of the 'mystery' from the other end of the life chain (Figure 8). Waugh notes that the recurrent motif of childhood at Forest Lawn represents a dramatic theological shift:

> We are very far here from the traditional conception of an adult soul naked at the judgment seat and a body turning to corruption...Hell waited for the wicked and a long purgation for all but the saints, but Heaven, if at last attained, was a place of perfect knowledge. In Forest Lawn, as the builder claims, these old values are reversed. The body does not decay: it lives on, more chic in death than ever before, in its indestructible class A steel and concrete shelf; the soul goes straight from the Slumber Room to Paradise, where it enjoys an endless infancy...[18]

18. The "Slumber Room" is the name of the space used to view the deceased. See also Waugh, *op. cit.*, p336-337.

Our arrival at paradise brings us logically, then, to the last stop on our tour - to the backlot of the park: the Forest Lawn Museum and 'Hall of Crucifixion

Fig. 9

and Resurrection'. The 'Hall of Crucifixion' (Figure 9) is unusual in that this enormous building was expressly designed to house *one* painting. The front of the hall looks very much like the facade from a Hollywood outdoor set. Although the body of the building is clearly visible from the front, it appears unrelated to the church-like facade that serves as the entranceway to the hall (Figure 10).

Fig. 10

Next door to the hall is the cemetery's museum. The museum continues the syncretism of the 'real' and the 'simulated' with its presentation of 'authentic' and 'imitation' objects side by side - often without a clear explanation of the origination of a work on display. As you enter the museum, the front room is completely dedicated to the 'work' of Michelangelo. A text accompanying the exhibit announces that Forest Lawn is the optimum site to view Michelangelo's work, since the cemetery is the only place where all of his important works can be seen together.

The museum has 'collected' copies of numerous drawings, fragments from a 'David' reproduction (to enable us to see the detail of the sculpture) and a replica of 'The Sotterraneo' - a room that has been exactly reproduced (through the aid of photography) complete with the wall sketchings that Michelangelo made in the space while in a period of hiding. The pamphlet that accompanies Forest Lawn's version of the room is written by the popular 'historical' novelist, Irving Stone (whose books include a 'biography' of Michelangelo). The emphasis in the brochure is placed on the reproduction's authenticity with the text continually moving back and forth between a discussion of the original site and the replica.

> When you step into that room, as you look at the drawings Michelangelo did with his little carbon sticks on the walls, you are living with Michelango in 1530.

> It's a real miracle. Because you're looking at something absolutely authentic. I know the drawings are authentic, because I've studied Michelango's work all my life. The Italian and the German art critics agree.

> There is no other room like Forest Lawn's Sotterraneo in the world, except the one in Florence....

As always, the Forest Lawn version of the Sotterraneo is the superior one not only because of its placement alongside so many other Michelangelo 'art works', but also due to the unrestricted visitation policy which contrasts to the restricted policy of the Medici chapel's original 'Sotterraneo'.

The rest of the museum is very similar to the Michelango exhibit in that the demarcation of 'original' and 're-created' works is never quite clear. A 'gift shop' that separates the Michelangelo exhibit from the rest of the museum perpetuates this confusion in that they offer, in effect, copies of copied material: for example, 'La Pieta', 'Moses', 'Last Supper' can be found in a variety of formats (slides, paperweights, postcards, 'collector' spoons, and art miniatures). All of the park's 'treasures' are thus available to the visitor as an explicit commodity. The accessibility of essentially all goods is, in some sense, yet another variation of the park's 'efficiency' and 'democracy'.

All of these factors come into play in the last two rooms of the museum. The selection of materials is truly eclectic with no visibly apparent organising principle behind the collection. The range of material includes: an exact reproduction of Ghiberti's 'Paradise Doors', replicas ('made expressly for Forest Lawn') of the British 'Crown Jewels', an ancient coin collection (complete with maps and historical summaries), a piece of 'primitive' art sculpture from Easter Island, and a selection of bronze statuary on the American West (their status as copies or originals is unclear from both the accompanying text and park brochure). Again, the metonymic slippage is clearly at work for the only coherent element behind these diverse materials is the notion of the collection as artifacts *qua* artifacts. Each artifact is equal to any other, thereby allowing for the commodification and accumulation of these 'goods' at random.

Although the signs of the commodity are everywhere, the cemetery also makes an effort to downplay the more explicit examples of cash transactions. The 'Hall of Crucifixion-Resurrection', located next to the museum, is the only 'performance site' in the park with an admission price ($1.00). This admission has been relabelled as a 'donation', yet a ticket booth and controlled access verify that the donation is not voluntary. Perhaps the most peculiar aspect of the admission is that despite the presence of the booth and a ticket agent, no money changes hands. Instead, the audience must drop money into a box before admittance is permitted into the theatre.

The admission's strange mixture of church 'collection box' and cinema 'box office' sets the stage perfectly for the upcoming event. The 'performance' of the 'Crucifixion-Resurrection' contains elements from both an evangelical crusade and a cinematic spectacle. As you enter the theatre, which holds approximately 700 to 800 people (although there were no more than 30 people in the 'audience' during either of my visits), it is difficult to remember that this vast space (and, in fact, the *entire* hall) was built exclusively for a painting - Jan Styka's 'Crucifixion'. The painting is, like the stained glass 'Last Supper', concealed behind a curtain that is only withdrawn during carefully orchestrated and automated 'performances'.

The rest of the room plays off this tension between performance site and religious space. There is a 'quiet room' where less than solemn children may be taken to prevent any disruption of the services. There are also other 'exhibits' within the space itself. A case contains a programme from the 'opening night' of the painting's unveiling at Forest Lawn (March 23, 1951 on 'Good Friday'), some brushes and a palette that belonged to the artist, and Styka's 'original' model for the 'crown of thorns' seen in the painting.

Strangely enough, the artist responsible for the second painting in the 'programme' - 'The Resurrection' is not mentioned - the impression is that the work is an extension of the first painting by Jan Styka. The two works are presented as one coherent unit. As the theatre darkens, the audience is told by automated narration to take a seat in preparation for the performance. While the room is completely dark, the narrator tells us the painting's (Styka's 'Crucifixion') history. The pilgrimage narrative is invoked again; this time as the artist's journey through Jerusalem (following Christ's travels in the city), and the founder's (Eaton) journey to bring the painting to Forest Lawn.

As the curtains open, only parts of the painting are lit in succession: the 'history' of the painting now shifts to a recounting of the crucifixion saga. The performance takes on the characteristics of a multi-projector slide show with the appropriate parts of the painting lit as the story unfolds. In addition, the narration is now complemented with sequences that are 'acted out' or perhaps more accurately dramatically 're-created' on the sound track complete with crowd noise and dialogue from a variety of participants including Roman soldiers and Mary Magdalene. Throughout the entire stay in the theatre there is also background music. However, the music appears to shift from standard 'classical' pieces accompanying the pre-performance time to stock Hollywood film score music during the narrated sequences.

The 'slide show' ends after the figure of Christ is lit in the centre of the work and the whole painting is, then, illuminated. The effect of the complete illumination of the painting is akin to Cinemascope.[19] This is enhanced no doubt by the dimensions of the work - 195 feet long and 45 feet wide - and the accompanying sound track and special effects. Christ is seen standing between two posts used during the crucifixion. As the brochure notes, the painting captures the 'intense emotional moment before Christ was nailed to the cross'. The actual moment of Christ's crucifixion is not seen, in fact, this part of the story is told in complete darkness. As a transition device to the next painting ('The Resurrection'), the audience that is seated in the darkened and cavernous theatre is treated to a variety of effects: simulated lightning, thunder, and even a minor earthquake (a particularly unnerving event for Californian residents).

As the story of the resurrection unfolds, with the second painting now on view, there is one last effect. A bright cross is illuminated behind the work and continues to shine even after the curtains are drawn over the painting. The performance is complete. Automation continues to control the audience by turning on the house lights, flashing 'Goodbye and God Bless You' on the closed curtains, and a fairly rapid dimming of the lights in order to hurry the audience from the room.

With the completion of this grand cinematic spectacle, the tour and the narration of the park has reached a type of closure. It is important to remember that *any* cinematic event cannot in itself effect closure. For to return to Kuntzel's commentary on the cinema:

> The writing disappears at the instant it appears and does not cease vanishing until, at the end of the projection, the screen returns to its initial whiteness. The writing remains elsewhere as permanent traces: it is conserved on the film strip, capable of reappearing when the strip is reinserted in the projector's path.[20]

While the photographic moment in this particular cinematic landscape - and throughout the Los Angeles area - provides a temporary respite from this process in the form of preservation, it can never remain 'still' or complete within this context. Thus the idea of preservation must be situated elsewhere, that is, at the level of narration. However, it is instructive to reiterate what has been preserved in this narrative - an eternal resting place firmly settled within the boundaries of a rather narrowly defined Western discourse - not unlike classical Hollywood narration. This is not to say, that there are not ruptures in this discourse - for surely the almost manic drive to implement this narrative within the park (and one could argue also within the Hollywood cinema) represents some ongoing disturbance of this idealized homogeneity. But such disturbances often will lead us only to another site, another scene, another tour, another 'happy ending'.

I would like to thank Teshome Gabriel, Alison Mckee and the New Formations *readers for their suggestions and comments on earlier drafts of this essay.*

19. I am grateful to Alison McKee for pointing out not only the similarities in the painting's format and presentation to Cinemascope, but also the initial viewing date's (1951) proximity to Hollywood's introduction of the widescreen format.

20. Kuntzel, *op. cit.*, p269.

BEYOND CRISIS, BEYOND NOVELTY: THE TENSIONS OF MODERNITY

John Rundell

1. J-F Lyotard, *The Postmodern Condition*, (trans Geoff Bennington and Brian Massumi Manchester University Press, Manchester 1984; N. Luhmann, *The Differentiation of Society*, chicago University Press, Chicago 1980, and 'The Two Sociologies and The Theory of Society', *Thesis Eleven*, Number 43, 1995, pp28-47.

2. See G. Markus, 'A Society of Culture: The Constitution of Modernity', G. Robinson and J. Rundell (eds), *Rethinking Imagination*, Routledge, London 1994, pp15-29; D. Roberts, 'Beyond Progress: The Museum and Montage', G. Rose, 'Architecture to Philosophy - The Contradictions', in *Theory, Culture and Society*, Vol 5, Number 2-3, June 1988: Ihab Hassan, Indeterminancy and Immanence: Margins of the (Postmodern)Age *Humanities in Society*, Vol. 1, 1978, pp51-85; Richard Kearney, *The Wake of Imagination*, Hutchinson, London 1988.

It is usually assumed that there is a conceptual gulf between the images and notions of modernity and postmodernity which can be summed up, at least in societal terms in a shift in language from that concerning social integration to that of polycentric disaggregation. Both draw on an image of the increasing functional differentiation of society; from this vantage point the main distinction between the modern and the postmodern revolves around a capacity and cultural ethos for integration and co-ordination at both the social and systemic levels, problems of which are couched in terms of dysfunction and crisis (the modern image), or disaggregated, disorganised or *autopoeitic* systems and cultures (the postmodern image) problems of which are viewed in terms of feedback or cybernetic blockages that require novel solutions.[1]

Moreover, both modernity and postmodernity view themselves as cultures of creativity. In this context, the distinction between modernism, rather than modernity, and postmodernism, rather than postmodernity, is more accurately an *aesthetic* distinction that emerge in painting by the 1920s and in architecture by the 1930s as a response to both the nature of cultural production (orthodoxy of style), and the nature of creativity itself. From the vantage point of modernism, the creativity of culture referred to the autonomy, and inner and imaginative origin of the work of art which became the bearer and symbol of high culture, as well as the reference point for the utopic reconciliation of beauty and freedom which had been alienated from one another. From the vantage point of postmodernism, creativity of culture also referred to the autonomy of culture, but without its utopic dimension. Moreover, the modernist emphasis on imagination and creativity *sui generis* is replaced by an emphasis on parody and pastiche, irony and repetition, in which the distinctions and boundaries collapse between the styles and content of high and mass/popular culture.[2]

In addition, the languages of both modern and postmodern social theory are indebted to images of societal totalisation. Both have suggested that, as well as an increasing differentiation or disaggregation there is also an increasing tendency towards a totalisation that results in a social and cultural levelling and reduction of complexity. Horkheimer and Adorno, writing in the 1930s from the vantage point of classical social theory, argued that the outcome of modernity's own logic of capitalist development which was anchored in the production of industrial goods, was a rational mastery of commodity production which extended to all other social relations and dimensions of social reproduction, especially culture.[3] Postmodern social theory of the later part of the twentieth century has argued that the outcome of the postmodern logic of development is polycentred-domains of power organised around the infinite expression, control and consumption of signifying or discursive practices. Lyotard, for example, emphasises a release from totalisation and an emphasise on novelty. Yet, as will be argued below, the postmodern image of polycentrism is still overlaid by totalising motifs that project a *particular* narrative *retrospectively* onto the terrain of modernity as a whole, or *prospectively* onto the postmodern condition, itself.

Nonetheless, the notion of novelty remains within the postmodern discourse, not only as one that refers to the aesthetic condition of postmodernity, but also as one that points to a sometimes concealed, sometimes explicit, argument about democracy, its nature and the practices that constitute it. This aspect will be further explored through a further analysis of Lyotard's work, which also entails that the question of postmodernity's self-understanding of its own *historical* novelty can be raised.

However, neither the images of crisis, totalisation, nor novelty adequately illuminates the variegated landscape of late twentieth century societies, not only of the west, but also in the eastern, northern and southern parts of the globe. The deployment of each image, and the theoretical strategy that stems from it, results in a levelling of the historical, cultural and systemic fields that constitute the modern period from the Renaissance to the present. In this context, the distinctions between modernity/postmodernity and modernism/postmodernism are symptomatic of a wider and deeper set of issues.

The idea of 'tensions of modernity' is an attempt to posit an image of modernity which can be viewed from three different vantage points simultaneously - a shift from virtue to post-virtue cultures, the differentiation of modernity into irreducible fields of activity, and a differentiation of human self-images which a modernity may produce and call its own. In this light, too, the modernity presented here refers the modernity of the western hemisphere, with its own arguments and traditions. Moreover, this modernity stands in tension not only with itself, but also with other societies and civilisations that may create their own modernities and their own tensions.

FROM CRISIS TO THE NOVELTY OF THE PRESENT

Jean François Lyotard's *The Postmodern Condition* marked a turning point. Prior to its publication (in French in 1979 and in English in 1984), there was certainly the perception of a crisis. It has been suggested, though, that serious theoretical reflections of this sense of crisis had not only denied 'the novelty of the present situation', but also relied on classical nineteenth century sociological formulations which viewed society as capitalist and/or industrial. Paradigmatically, these formulations were shared by both

3. See T. Adorno and Mac Horkheimer, *Dialectic of Enlightenment*, (trans John Cumming) Verso, London 1979; J. Connerton (ed), *Critical Sociology*, Penguin, Harmondsworth 1976; A. Arato and Gebhardt (eds), *The Essential Frankfurt School Reader*, Urizen Books, New York, 1978; T. Adorno, *Negative Dialectics*, (trans E.B. Ashton) Routledge, London 1990, Andrew Benjamin, *The Problems of Modernity*. Adorno and Benjamin, Routledge, London 1989.

historical materialism and functionalism. Bauman argues that in denying the novelty of the present situation these works could be seen to be traditional, or classical, in a double sense:

> they deny the existential autonomy of postmodernity as a separate type of society [and] they also deny the need and legitimacy of the search for a *postmodern* sociology ... [For them] the idea of crisis suggests that while society requires certain resources for its unhampered self-reproduction (and for retaining its own identity over time), it is not, for one reason or another, capable of producing such resources, or of producing them in sufficient quantity.[4]

4. Z. Bauman, 'A Sociological Theory of Postmodernity', *Thesis Eleven*, Number 29, 1989, pp39-40; 'Is There a Postmodern Sociology?; *Theory, Culture and Society*, Volume 5, Number 2-3, June 1988.

Bauman argues that this sense of crisis sketched by classical sociology had developed along three paths: the inner contradictions of capitalism, the limits of rationalisation, and the dynamics and historicity of identity formation. Notwithstanding the insights gained from these three paths, their diagnostic language still alluded to images of social health and illness, which, as Habermas had pointed out in *Legitimation Crisis*, was itself, internal to the metaphor of crisis. This internality of the metaphor and the analysis, however, indicated an underlying reliance on a functionalist image of society with its counter-image imbedded in the idea of pathology or dysfunction, through which social conflict was analysed, either normatively, as in the Parsonian tradition, or as a function of an underlying system of production, as in the Marxian one. Moreover, alongside this heightened sense of crisis there was an increased sensibility and visibility of different sites and forms of social conflict that neither involved, addressed nor were conceived in functional terms. Whilst these conflicts were always present, they often went unnoticed from the normative perspective or class constituted discourses. It is suffice again to mention three: the women's movement, the environmental movement, and the conflicts between the juridico-administrative-therapeutic state, its actors and its clients.

Lyotard cannot be accredited with systematically analyzing the complexity of this contemporary situation with its sites and dynamics of social conflict. His aim and argument in *The Postmodern Condition* was different. He gave a name to this new constellation - postmodernity. In so doing he dissolved the language of crisis. For him, postmodernity indicated a fundamental structural and cultural shift; from an integrated social system with a coherence and belief in the veracity of its meta-narratives, to one that was not so much disintegrated, but disaggregated or functionally differentiated, in which multiple (rather than singular) centres of social power become visible. Moreover, an incredulity towards meta-narratives also accompanied this disaggregation - plurality also meant a de-totalisation and de-legitimation of what were seen as modernity's predominant two unifying cultural fictions - science and universalism. Hence, for Lyotard, the emergence of new sites and zones of social conflict and consequently of new social movements, indicates neither societal dysfunction, nor of real or imputed radicalism. Accordingly, we have moved beyond an historical moment, one that belonged quintessentially to the eighteenth and nineteenth centuries, with its own narratives of capitalism, nation-state formation, class conflict, individualism, and have entered a contingent world with other possibilities and perspectives.

The pluralisation of sites of conflict, as well as the formation of new ones, indicates a 'normalisation' of the essentially paralogic or agonistic social relations that inform and constitute each differentiated sphere and its field of knowledge and code of conduct, in its own specific or particular way. Postmodernity, in Lyotard's view, is polymorphous, and heterogenous. It is also polysemic, in that there is a permanency of the conflict of interpretations.[5] In his closing remarks to 'What is Postmodernism' Lyotard gives what he sees as the apt formulation for this new situation: 'let us wage war on totality; let us be witness to the unpresentable; let us actuate the differences and savour honour of the name'.[6] Lyotard's war against totality is, for him, a democratisation by other means. In other words, the politics that emerge from this postmodern condition are those that not only recognise plurality; they are constituted through it. For him, *modern* politics is nostalgically sublime, obsessed with a restless, ceaseless, ultimately terroristic quest for a reconciliation of concept and experience, of rendering the opaque transparent, unable not only to recognise plurality (in other formulations - différance), let alone *live it*.

Postmodern politics, though, lives plurality; it has no pre-established rules, nor a universal addressee to whom, or for whom, it speaks. In Lyotard's terms, it is *pagan*. In an attempt to develop a post-transcendental formulation of pragmatic politics, its pagan ethos is a:

> calculating reason, as a strategy; it is a mode of strategy but one in which the issue is not how to conquer but how to achieve parity between people. This is the difference. In every instance one must evaluate relations: of force, of value, of quantities, and of qualities; but to evaluate them there are no criteria, nothing but opinions'.[7]

This is a 'case by case' approach to questions of political judgment, justice and the competing tastes between competing styles of life.

Lyotard is somewhat different from other postmodern writers because, for him, the collapse of meta-narratives does not mean the existence of a myriad of disembodied opinions and strategies between power saturated players. Rather, these opinions are, themselves, *narratives* or *traditions*. They are the imbedded set of world relations which become the 'pole of reference' for the interlocutor. For Lyotard, the postmodern feature of this formulation of pagan narratives is that they are never static: identity with difference intermingle as the narratives get repeated, and as they do so they are never identical to what came before. In this way, they are stories without a

5. This is also an unacknowledged verification of hermeneutics own insight in its post-transcendental register. For two different accounts of this sensibility see C. Taylor, 'The Hermeneutics of Conflict' in James Tully (ed.), *Meaning and Context: Quentin Skinner and His Critics*, Polity Press, Oxford, 1988, pp218-228; Paul Rabinowm, 'Repersentations are Facts: Modernity and Postmodernity in Anthropology' in James Clifford and George E. Markus (eds), *Writing Culture: The Poetics and Polictics of Ethnography*, University of California Press, California, 1986, pp236-261.

6. Lyotard, 'What is Postmodernism', The Postmodern Condition 1984, *op. cit.*, p82; see also his *Just Gaming* (with Jean Loup Thbaud), (trans Wlad Godzich, University of Minnesota Press, Minneapolis 1985, esp. 'A Politics of Judgement' and 'The Faculty of Political Ideas'.

7. *ibid.*, p27

8. Lyotard, *op. cit.*, pp31-13.

beginning, with no originary point in time, and with no end.[8]

However, notwithstanding postmodern politic's flight from teleology, it is nonetheless not only a politics beyond good and evil, but also beyond pain and pleasure. In Lyotard's construction of a postmodern politics, politics is beyond suffering, beyond crisis. It is the politics of abundance and novelty. Read *positively*, postmodern politics is one of a generation and its sons and daughters who have lived through the horrors of war and deprivation and rebuilt their lives beyond *ressentiment*. Read *negatively*, it is simply the politics of a West that is in danger of a self-centredness, which refuses to see the death and suffering in other parts of the world. Its danger is not necessarily relativism, but *indifference*.

And this is the difficulty of Lyotard's critique of grand narratives — the question concerns their grounding and their meaning. In terms of the latter, Lyotard reads them as only holistic and totalising *uber-Geschichten*, equates them with redemption and totalisation and projects them onto modernity as whole. In terms of the former, he equates them with Kant's transcendental move and thus collapses together transcendental argument with univesality. Before pursuing this strain in Lyotard's thought further, though, we need to look at two other postmodern analyses of the current condition - one stemming from the works of Baudrillard and Eco, and another from the work of Foucault. In each, and beginning from the vantage point of novelty, an image of totalisation is developed which is also projected onto society as a whole. The image of totalisation is thrown into relief more clearly if we begin this part of our discussion, not from the vantage point of systemic disaggregation, but from the specifically *aesthetic* response to the question and crisis of high culture, that is postmodernism.

TOTALISATION

9. F. Feher, 'The Status of Postmodernity' in *The Grandeur and Twilight of Radical Universalism*, Transaction Publishers, New Brunswick 1991, p 541. See also his 'Redemptive and Democratic Paradigms in Politics', *Telos* 63 Spring 1985, pp 147-156 and Joel Whitebook, 'The Politics of Redemption' in the same issue of *Telos*. See also D. Kellner, 'Postmodernism as Social Theory: Some Challenges and Problems', *Theory, Culture and Society*, Vol. 5, Number, 2-3, June 1988, pp241-269.

The term postmodernism, as distinct from postmodernity, initially emerged as a counter-critical discourse concerning the status of art and its relation to life, and especially politics. In its status as a cultural-critical discourse, postmodernism represented the final critique of the marriage of high culture and the redemptive paradigm. This marriage attempted to re-sacralise the *this-worldly* activity of modern art and politics after their internal differentiation, as well as after their initial liberation from Church and Absolutist State. The attempted re-sacralisation of high culture occurred under the category of *Kunst*, which 'denote[d] the rationalistic unification of extremely heterogenous activities as well as their subsumption under a common category'.[9] The catechism of this aesthetic re-sacralisation included placing art beyond or above the realms of all other activities, and, thus, replicated and reproduced the divide between the sacred/sublime and profane. The catechism of *Kunst* also reinforced the cults of the genius and expert, as well as the distinction between them. The redemptive paradigm, for its part, had three characteristics that addressed modernity specifically.

It personalised politics by locating political authority in a personified character (e.g. Napoleon). It wished to reduce the inherent complexity of modernity. In the face of its differentiation, the redeemer, attempts to reconnect and co-ordinate the spheres that had become differentiated. Thus, the redeemer re-orders the crises, lack of order and permanent instability which inevitably emerges from this type of differentiation, and places his hyper-rationality and hyper-authority beyond question. Related to this, the redemptive paradigm homogenised society as a whole. The re-integration, re-ordering of society dismissed and illegalised the 'intrinsic heterogeneity of complex modernity. [Thus, the Redeemer opposed] the particularistic existence of groups and units, individual autonomy and political pluralism'.[10] The state becomes the vehicle for this homogenisation which subjects and subsumes civil society to its prerogative.

10. F. Feher, *op. cit.*, p148.

Postmodernism represented the autonomisation of aesthetics from its long held subordination or subsumption to religion, as well as romanticism's attempt to create a this-worldly sacred moral mission for art and literature. High culture was also released from the Jacobin fusion of art and politics where *together* they were seen as the correct expression of sacralised meaning in the face of generalised commodification. Postmodernism, thus, provided a basis for a critique of the re-sacralisation of art and the redemptive paradigm. Following Feher, this critique resulted in art's 'internal liberation'. This liberation involved a double process: 'the dismantling of canonic expressions [and] the theoretical and practical dismantling of the unified concept of art'.[11] According to Bürger's reconstruction of the historicity of postmodernism in *The Theory of the Avantgarde*, whilst Surrealism and Dada's attempt to subvert the emergent separation of art and life and art and politics failed, it nonetheless created the conditions in which art persisted as an institution, yet without aesthetic norms.[12] Moreover, the collapse of the idea of *Kunst* also entailed that each art form was able to move and develop in its own medium. This resulted in a multiplication of styles, genres and media without the clamour for the need to claim either political legitimacy or authenticity. This has been accompanied by the decline of art works to 'demand' authority, and of the critic to demand respect. Everyone becomes potentially both an interpreter *and* an artist.

11. F. Feher, 'The Pyrrhic Victory of Art in Its War of Liberation: Remarks on the Postmodernist Intermezzo' in A. Milner, P. Thomson and C. Worth (eds) *Postmodern Conditions*, Berg, New York 1990, pp84-85.

However, this thesis of art's internal liberation is overlaid by another one. In a case of historical repetition, the *limits of rationalisation* thesis, which Bauman argued was part and parcel of the language of crisis, is replaced, but played out homologously as a *limits of signification* thesis. The specificity given to the counter-aesthetic forms, and the struggles that resulted in a release from, and dismantling of, the redemptive paradigm, is now minimised. Only the production and consumption of signs, instead of commodities, are read and projected onto the postmodern condition as a whole. Through the deployment of the notions of hyper-reality and the simulacra, Eco and Baudrillard, respectively, emphasise a totalisation of signs that denies a novelty to the current postmodern condition.

12. Peter Berger, Theory of the Avante-Garde, Minneapolis University Press, Minneapolis 1984; Introduction, Postmodern Conditions, *op. cit.*, pp ix-xv. See also Albrecht Wellmer, 'The Dialectic of Modernism and Postmodernism: The Critique of Reason Since Adorno' in *The Persistence of Modernity*, Polity Press, Cambridge 1990; S. Lash, 'Discourse or Figure? Postmodernism as a 'Regime of Signification,' *Theory, Culture and Society*, op. cit. pp312-336.

Eco's notion of hyperreality revolves around the issue of high cultural production and its purported demise. High culture, from this perspective, has simply become a site where it, mass culture, and democratic society, have collapsed together. In his 1975 essay 'Travels in Hyperreality' Eco argues that the distinction between the real and the fake collapses 'in the absolute production of fantasy', and in the collapse people can no longer discriminate; judgment disappears.[13] The art museum becomes the institutional nexus and reference point from which the social world is read and reconstructed. As in Marcuse's work, there is also an underlying Heidergerrianism grounded in the questions of authenticity, historicity and critique of technical and commercial civilisation. As Eco states: 'the frantic desire for the Almost Real arises only as a neurotic reaction to the vacuum of memories; the Absolute Fake is offspring of the unhappy awareness of a present without depth'.[14]

13. Umberto Eco, 'Travels in hyperreality' in *Faith in Fakes*, (trans. William Waver) Secker and Warburg, London 1986, p43.

14. *ibid.*, p 73.

This account is replicated in its entirety in Baudrillard's 1986 *travelogue* through America. Using the desert as a background motif, Baudrillard constructs a play of images located between sterility and fecundity - death and life. The western desert has exceptional qualities, for him, because it combines 'the most ancestral of hieroglyphs, the most vivid light, and the most superficiality'.[15] Each desert image, in its own way, is infused with an artificiality: 'microprocessive and instantaneously obliterated'.[16] The artificial representation of the desert - because, for Baudrillard, there are only representations - is a world of hyperreality - neither dream nor reality. Baudrillard marries the idea of the constant and irredeemable mediation and re-presentation of reality with the idea of the artificiality of contemporary mechanised forms of representation. For him, the pronounced artificiality of these representations results in a 'utopia' of simulations. This utopia of the sign-world has been accomplished, according to Baudrillard, on the one hand, by 'a frantic self-referentiality' in which the mirror phase has given way to the 'video phase' (the object mother has been replaced by the object video).[17] This phase of self-referentiality, accordingly, only heightens the generalised inability of a population to distinguish between phantasy and reality. On the other hand, and in an argument against de Tocqueville and Arendt, Baudrillard argues that American society has achieved its utopia of simulations by cultivating no 'origin or mythical authenticity ... it lives in a perpetual present' of violent artificiality. For Baudrillard,[18]

15. Jean Baudrillard, *America*, (trans.) Chris Turner (Material Word), Verso, London, 1988, p70; see also p99.

16. *ibid.*, p73.

17. *ibid.*, p37.

18. *ibid.*, p76.

the American way of life is spontaneously fictional, since it is a transcending of the imaginary in reality ... All we [Europeans] do is dream and, occasionally, try to act our dreams. America by contrast, draws the logical, pragmatic consequences from everything that can possibly be thought. In this sense, it is naive and primitive; it knows nothing of the irony of concepts, nor the irony of seduction. It does not ironise upon the future or destiny: it gets on with turning things into material realities.[19]

19. *ibid.*, pp95-98.

But Baudrillard's Heideggerianism, with its implicit reference to the *authenticity* of cultural forms, misses its mark if there is a switch of focus from authenticity to the specificity of a particular society. What is striking about this is the incomprehensibility of these 'old world' commentators about a 'new world' formation and its set of experiences. The language of hyper-reality, descriptively and analytically overdetermines the ways in which both different and similar structural phenomena are viewed. History, culture and society are all collapsed and transposed into the 'more real than real' of not only commodified uniformity (Eco), but also irrepressible banality and indifference (Baudrillard). The paradigmatic social form for Eco, is Disneyland; for Baudrillard it is the freeway and the car.[20] The language of hyperreality is a single story of a 'the suburbanising process' and its 'mile after mile' of uniformity so aptly portrayed not only in Baudrillard's America, but also in the following remarks by Eco:

> Baroque rhetoric, eclectic frenzy, and thus compulsive imitation prevail where wealth has no history. And thus in the great expanses that were colonised late, where the posturban civilisation represented by Los Angeles is being born, in a metropolis made up of seventy six different cities where alleyways are ten-lane freeways ... eyes are something to focus, at steady driving speed, on visual mechanical wonders, signs constructions that must impress the mind in the space of a few seconds.[21]

Disneyland and the car - in their own ways, both simulacra - simultaneously become microcosms and macrocosms of America, but in repetition of Marcuse's one-dimensionality thesis. The notion of hyperreality is a totalising meta-narrative. What goes unnoticed is the modernism in common to both continents, with its aura that combines universalism and particularism in search of a national identity. Nor is a clash of cultures and a clash of histories noticed. At the end of the twentieth century these clashes take place in the context of divergent questions and answers around the novelty of different political traditions and cultures, and not only around the production and consumption of signs. This returns us to the question of the novelty of democracy, but this time from neither vantage points of paganism nor simulation, but rather from its functionalisation. The figure, in this context, is Foucault. His strategy, though, is not so dissimilar to that of Eco and Baudrillard in their own denial of novelty; Foucault emphasises a totalisation of discurvise practices that renders novelty impossible under the conditions of modernity.

Although Foucault should not be taken as a postmodern thinker he does now haunt postmodernist concerns because he argues that totalising and functionally orientated surveillance is the predominant pattern of western modernity.[22] In an anti-foundational gesture he overlays his critique of modernity with the Nietzschean idea of power, which he sees as local, discontinuous and always transvalued. Foucault's argument in *Discipline and Punish* is that the revolutions, especially the French Revolution, which

20. Eco, 'Travels in Hyperreality', *op. cit.*, p 48, and Baudrillard, *op. cit.*, pp 54-55.

21. Eco, op. cit., pp25-26. See also Lewis Mumford, *The City in History*, Penguin, London 1984; Anthony Giddens, *A Contemporary Critique of Historical Materialism*, Vol. I, Macmillan, London 1981.

22. Foucault should not be taken as a precursor to, or as a proto-postmodern thinker, for in the end, his oeuvre concerns the sovereignty of the subject. He does not share its sensibility of 'being after'. If anything, and given his construction of an erotico-aestheticized ethics in Volume II of *The History of Sexuality*, his modenity is that of the Greek Enlightmnment'.

occurred in the name of humanity and worked with the sign of public sovereignty, are discontinuous instances that are constantly open to power-saturated re-interpretations.

In his genealogy of the French revolution, Foucault argues that 'humanity' becomes 'the respectable name given to economy and meticulous calculation'.[23] Foucault's central concern is about sovereignty and his concealed question is: once humanity becomes supposedly sovereign after Absolutism, how does it punish itself? Punishment is used as a trope, by Foucault, to investigate the curious genealogy of western forms of power, and for him, its internal relation to the humanist project. The power of reform is turned on its head; instead of reforming practices there are only punitive signs which reverse the whole temporal field of social action. The body, as a metaphor for society, becomes subject to semio-techniques which first define and codify all illegalities and then all behaviours. He extends his critique of the power of instrumentalisation or 'the micro technics of power' to society as a whole. Society becomes a panoptic carceral. Instrumentalisation, or the nexus between rationalisation and power is complete.

Foucault's critique assumes that the *res cogito*, which provided the world with 'brute facts', joined hands with the modernising state to construct only strategies of surveillance, domination and power, masked by their claim to progress and universality. In this way, Foucault's modernity is one that owes much to Descartes, Nietzsche and Durkheim. First, whilst the genealogical aspect of Nietzsche's work is important for Foucault in enabling him to critique universal history and write counter-histories, nonetheless, his reading also emphasises Nietzsche's own reading of modernity which constructs a continuity between Christianity and Enlightenment. To be sure, Foucault does not view this continuity in terms of a culture of *ressentiment*, but in a form of power as surveillance and control. Secondly, the mode of the surveillant and controlling self, for Foucault, is represented, paradigmatically by the Cartesian *cogito*, which not only cognitivistically outlaws the non-visible but also places at centre stage evidential, disengaged rationality that constructs the criteria, and thus, standard, for knowledge, and truth. Thirdly, Foucault appropriates the Marxian paradigm of production and marries it with Nietzsche's notion of the will to power. Moreover, he transposes this merger into a Durkheimian register with its emphasis on the functional division of labour. Thus, Foucault's *method* translates the functionality of the productive technique into the technique of discourse as it forges social relations of power. He can, then, take societal differentiation seriously and examine the technique of production, techniques of the juridical-political and techniques of the self.

But Foucault operates with a *double-entendre*. Like Lyotard, he constructs modernity as the modernisation of the nation state, the model and paradigm for which is the French Napoleonic one. As he says:

23. M. Foucault, *Discipline and Punish*, Penguin, London 1978.

one can place Napoleon almost exactly at the break between the old organisation of the eighteenth century police state [... characterised as a project to create a system of regulation of the general conduct of individuals whereby everything could be controlled to the point of self-sustenance, without the need for intervention ...] and the forms of the modern state, which he invented. At any rate, it seems that, during the eighteenth and nineteenth centuries there appeared ... this idea of a police that would manage to penetrate, to stimulate, to regulate and to render almost automatic all the mechanisms of society.[24]

Thus, the differentiation of society is co-ordinated by the state in which it detotalises or decentralises the constituency of power. However, Foucault combines and collapses the domains of state and society together, and turns them into differentiated and multiplicated processes of totalisation itself. Modernity is nothing but the multiplication of *differentiated* or *detotalised totalities*. Each institution becomes a functional representation of the totalising power of the Cartesian technique. For Foucault, in *Discipline and Punish* at least, this analysis begins with the transformation of the political meaning and power of the French state around the idea of sovereignty, and ends in *History of Sexuality*, Volume 1 with the medicalising discourses of both body and soul (outer and inner life), the aim of which is the control of *social* dysfunction imputed to the individual case. Scientific/medical knowledge and its truth is a representative of social norms. However, Foucault's perspective results in an image of modernity which is only functional, and he projects this functionalism as a totalising motif onto society as whole. As with the Durkheimian analysis of the organic division of labour, Parsons' construction of the social system, and Goffman's analysis of total institutions, the regime of power (the nexus between power/knowledge/truth) is a closed one that only operates according to the functional criteria of social co-ordination and the integration of the individual into society. The Foucauldian discourse swallows the subject. In other words, Foucault is unable to separate a description of modernity from his meta-theoretical principles of critique.

However, this totalising critique is certainly against Foucault's own best intentions. For Foucault, the image of freedom that is internal to projects of democracy *is* a historicisable meta-norm and is expressive - aesthetic (which is the reason he turns to ancient Greece), although in his earlier work it is portrayed as transgressive.[25] For Lyotard, and one suspects with Baudrillard and Eco, though, freedom cannot be a meta-norm - as such it is terroristic. This returns us to the perplexity of the postmodern image of novelty, and the way in which it is an attempt to escape from the clutches of continuing totalising images of society. And here, the two strains of novelty problematically combine and coalesce - the democratic and the aesthetic.

For Lyotard, the critical counter-discourses to the meta-narratives of modernity and their propensity to totalisation emerges out of aesthetics. Aesthetics produces works that are not bound by pre-established rules, they

24. 'Space, Knowledge and Power: An Interview with Michel Foucault' by Paul Rabinow, *Skyline*, March 1982, p16.

25. See Foucault, 'The Subject and Power', *Critical Inquiry*, Number 8, Summer 1982; Gilles Barbedette, 'The Social Triumph of the Sexual Will: A conversation with Michael Foucault', (trans Brendon Lemon) Christopher Street, May 1982, pp36-41; 'Space, Knowledge and Power', *Skyline*, op. cit. The functionalising dimension of Foucault's thought entraps him politically in an anarcho-maoist voluntarism which is portrayed through the language of resistance and leads to some political misjudgements, the most notorious of which is his commentary on the Iranian revolution, as well as an inability to distinguish between totalitarianism and totalisation. See 'On Popular Justice: A Discussion with Maoists', in Street, 1982, *op. cit.*,; 'Iran: The Spirit of a World Without Spirit' and Confinement, Psychiatry, Prison', both in L.D. Dritzman (ed), *Michel Foucault. Politics Philosophy Culture. Interviews and Other Writing 1977-1984*, Routledge, London 1990.

26. Lyotard, 1985, op. cit., p81.

27. *ibid.*, p82. See also Willem van Reijen and Dick Veerman, 'An Interview with Jean Francois Lyotard', *Theory, Culture and Society*, op. cit. pp277-309.

28. John Rundell, 'Marx and the Postmodern Image of Society' in *Postmodern Conditions*, op. cit., pp 58-167.

29. J.F. Lyotard, *The Postmodern Condition*, op. cit., p79.

30. Philippe Lacoue-Labarthe and Jean Luc Nancy, *The Literary Absolute*, The State Univbersity of New York Press, New York 1988: Friedrich Shlegel, 'The Atheneneum Fragments', *op. cit*; and *Dialogue on Poetry and Literary Aphorisms*, (trans Ernst Behler and Roman Struc), Pennsylvania State University Press, University Park 1968; Jacques Derrida, 'Plato's Pharmacy', *Dissemination*, (trans Barbard Johnson), University of Chicage Press, Chicago 1981. See also P.R. Harrison, 'Writing and Discourse: The Problem of Socrates in Deconstruction and in Discourse Theory', A. Milner and C. Worth (eds), *Discourse and Difference*, Centre For

are purely contingent. As we have seen, above, Lyotard extends this analysis to the very nature of democracy, itself. In an absolute anti-Kantianism, *postmodern* politics, for Lyotard, 'is not a matter of science ... [T]he only tenable position ... [is] a politics that would admit that its realm is about opinions'.[26] Postmodern politics is about the right simply to assert '*I am for, I am against*, yes, no. Assent granted or denied'.[27] In this sense, for Lyotard, postmodern politics is intuitive, it works at the level of feeling in which there is no politics of reason, neither in its sense as totalising nor as concept. There is only a 'will to power', an imaginative power to invent criteria.

However, there is an added complexity to Lyotard's position that questions the absoluteness of the present and the novelty of its creations that is given to the postmodern understanding of itself. Lyotard argues that this contingency and localism of the work had already been thematised unsuccessfully by Kant in his *Critique of Judgement*. Although stylistically Montaigne is the representative writer because he 'invent' or privileges the notion of *posthistoire*, for Lyotard, Kant's Third Critique is the first postmodern text because it explodes the horison of transcendentality. The historicity of received texts, though, is an important signal in establishing postmodernity's version of its politics and its own assumed novelty.

Taking the Appendix to the *Postmodern Condition* again as the central work, and without repeating in detail an argument developed elsewhere, Lyotard moves between two competing historical or epochal formulations of modernity.[28] In it, the postmodern typifies neither novelty nor nostalgia. Rather, it is the capacity to develop critical-counter discourses - a constant feature of the modern. It is an *attitude*. As Lyotard states: 'postmodernism, thus understood is not modernism at its end, but in a nascent state and this state is constant'.[29] Thus, for example, in the context of postmodern readings of the history of modernity and the West, the first postmodernist is Friedrich Schlegel, particularly his 'Athenaeum Fragments' for Lacoue-Labarthe and Nancy, whilst for Derrida, in the footsteps of Nietzsche, the first postmoderns are the pre-Socratics.[30] Whilst Lyotard, for one, equivocates on whether romanticism is modern or postmodern, arguing that it replicates the aristocraticism of court society (and thus homogenises taste), and, thereby, is not *pagan* enough, that is, too canonical, nonetheless his notion of politics is deeply indebted to the romantic critique of *Aufklärung*.[31] Postmodern politics is a post-romantic aesthetic politics of *positive* sublimity in which the *quest* for transcendental grounding (most recently typified by Habermas's quasi-transcendental theory of communicative action) has been replaced by a *distancing* irony. Szondi's comment on Friedrich Schlegel is, however, appropriate for the self-understanding of the postmodern attitude, but without the irony which helped to maintain Romanticism's utopic sensibility:

Irony is the clear consciousness of eternal agility, of the infinitely full chaos.' Eternal agility characterises the [person] of [post]modern times, who lives in chaos. In raising [his/her] chaotic existence to the level of consciousness, in living it consciously, he is adopting an ironic attitude towards it ... It is clear, then that in the romantic conception of irony the subject is the isolated [person] who has become his [her] own object, from whom the ability to act has been taken away by consciousness.[32]

Romantic irony is either transposed into strategy - by the concept 'game' which becomes the metaphor for theories of power, or alternatively is symptomatic of a deep cynicism towards what is constructed as the simulacra, the hyperreality of contemporary, especially, American life. Like its Romantic cousin, postmodern irony once again replaces critique as the main motif - it is its only method of distanciation from the power of attraction and aura that modernity holds. And it is an irony in which additional motifs can also find their pre-critical and malicious place. For example, there is almost a Sadian celebration of excess in Baudrillard's Marcusian anti-capitalism; likewise Eco's report on the World Cup conceals a delight in the almost infinite and senseless recklessness of the human species. For both there is an anthropological pessimism which constructs necessary and internal relations between the state and terrorism, democracy and massification. For both Eco and Baudrillard, democracy in the old world cannot survive the war between State and Terror, and in the new one becomes only proto-fascist, totalitarian once they are massified and suburbanised.[33]

However, what has emerged is neither an ironic, nor a dramatic cultural sensibility that has been termed postmodernity, but a combination of different stories in the context of *projective* analyses that are totalising and lurch toward narrative closure. In many ways, Lyotard is the most resistant to this closure through his own notion of narrative, which gives a sense of continuity, to be sure, discontinuous continuity, between the present and its pasts. However, he is unable to combine his notion of narrative with an account of the sustained differentiation of modernity, given that he, like Foucault, is committed to its representation as the totalisation and meta-narrativisation of the French state. Moreover, the relation between past and present cannot be thrown into relief in Lyotard's conceptual strategy - the texts and author's that are chosen are only markers on a path to pagan novelty. A conceptualisation of modernity is required that captures both its novelty, as well as its relation to the pasts upon which it draws. This also entails that the image of totalisation which projects itself onto differentiated modernity as a whole, thus reducing its inherent complexity, can no longer be invoked. For modernity is not one dynamic - but several, as the above discussion has intimated. Postmodernity has been the symptomatic name given to this sense of living between, in the midst of, and in tension with, not only competing modernities, but also their full visibility.

MODERNITY OR MODERNITIES OR 'FIELDS OF TENSION'?

Thus far, three sets of stories or narratives about Western modernity have

General and Comparative Literature, Melbourne 1990.

31. Lyotard, *Just Gaming*, op. cit., pp6-13.

32. Peter Sxondi, 'Friedrich Schlegel and Romantic Irony' in *On Textual Understanding and Other Essays*, (trans Harvey Mendelsohn), Manchester University Press, Manchester 1986, pp67-68.

33. Eco, *op. cit.*, J. Baudrillard, op. cit.

been outlined above: one concerning the social democratic national state, portrayed especially as a totalising one; another concerning the development of postmodern aesthetics as well as that of mass society, and another concerning democracy, which, in a postmodern register emphasised novelty and ironic detachment. What becomes apparent, though, is that each story begins to tell a tale of its own. Each story can be singled out and treated as an independent, non-reducible, yet intersecting field. It is possible to add further to this picture of the differentiation and 'creative formation' of narratives.

In this context, the question - modernity, modernities or 'fields of tensions'? - can be raised.[34] This question emerges in two ways; on the one hand, it emerges from the highly differentiated image of late twentieth century societies, an image portrayed as anchored in the dynamics and historical formation of occidental modernity itself. On the other, the image of differentiation also enables the existence of hitherto under-represented or under-theorised dimensions of modernity to come to the fore. This is particularly the case with the modern experience and interpretations of democracy. Moreover, whilst democracy is discussed within a postmodern register, what is presented is a non- or anti-foundational *gesture*, that is an aesthetics of conflict. But as Wellmer points out, in a poignant reminder of both the specificity and institutional longevity of democracy, the *recognition* of plurality and difference already has presupposed the existence of at least some common elements which concern democracy if it is going to exist beyond mere novelty and particularism. These are:

> not abstract principles, but [ ] an ensemble of shared practices, meanings and basic orientations ... What is at issue is a shared basis of second-order social habits: the habits of rational self-determination, democratic decision-making and the non-violent resolution of conflict.[35]

There remains the issue as to the label that can be ascibed the contemporary period. Here we must acknowledge its two predominant contemporary versions - the one proposed by Habermas, as one of an unfinished project - which posits the fixed plurality of contexts under the unity of reason - and Lyotard's postmodern version, which, as we have seen, posited late twentieth century society as an infinite possibility of contexts in which the social actors who inhabit them vye for strategic dominance. However, both these positions are defensible only if a dual context is either minimised or overlooked. This dual context emphasises both modernity's originality and historical formation. In the case of the former, the originality of the project of modernity consists in its ability to construct its own horisons for action and further re-interpret them, to the point of their de-legitimation. This makes the project inherently unstable.[36] Moreover, and as has been indicated above, these horisons can be differentiated and instituted as new organisational forms. Thus, from the vantage point of a project of modernity there are

34. The phrase 'field of tensions' is taken from Johann P. AArnason's counter-image of modernity that he proposes in his discussion of Habermas in 'Modernity as Project and as Field of Tensions' in Axel Honneth and Hans Joas (eds), *Communicative Action*, Polity Press, Cambridge 1991.

35. Albrecht Wellmer, *op. cit.*, p92.

36. A horizon of action refers to an indispensable and non-reducible interpretation. This interpretative horizon gives to modernity its ability to break through pre-established contexts of understanding by asking questions in need of answers (even if the answers were neither available, apparent, nor appropriate). See J. P. Arnason, 'Modernity as Project and Field of Tensions' op. cit, Hans Blumemberg, *The Legitimacy of The Modern Age*, MIT Press, Cambridge, Mass. 1986, and Agnes Heller, *Beyond Justice*, Blackwell, Oxford 1987.

both horizons of action as well as differentiated fields.

The vantage point of the historical context of modernity can be constructed in terms of the civilisational history of the West, which, following MacIntyre's argument in *After Virtue*, consists in the long shift from virtue cultures to non-virtue ones. This occurs in the context of any of the patterns and horisons of action that develop. In the light of MacIntyre's analysis, it can be argued that virtue cultures are those cultures in which there is no essential separation between the tasks that one does and living one's life as a whole. It refers to those certain human qualities that are privileged and which enable one to live one's life as a whole and live it well. According to MacIntyre, virtues, are complex sets of practices in which:

> any coherent and complex form of socially established co-operative activity through which goods internal to the form of activity are realised in the course of trying to achieve those standards of excellence which are appropriate to, and partially definitive of, that form of activity, with the result that human powers to achieve excellence, and human conceptions of the ends and goods involved are systematically extended.[37]

Within the classical Aristotelian tradition, irrespective of its specifically Greek variant, or its Medieval Christian one, there is a central and fundamental precept. For both men and women, and notwithstanding the stratification of virtues, the concept of being human 'is understood as having an essential nature and an essential purpose or function ... to be [a human] is to fill a set of roles each of which has its own point and purpose: member of a family, citisen, soldier, philosopher, servant of God'.[38] MacIntyre includes two other aspects in his complex reconstruction of the category of virtue - 'the narrative order of a single life',[39] and a moral tradition, where tradition is the intelligibility of the present as an ongoing and open commentary on the past. Virtues, then, provide both the visibility of the present, the continuity between it and the past, and the limits *and* possibilities for human action.

Leaving this aspect aside for the time being, we shall turn our attention, in this part of the paper, firstly to the fields of modernity.

From a systemic viewpoint, modernity can be characterised as a dynamic form of specific and differentiating fields, each with its own long history and historical self-understanding. It is this self-understanding that entails that the historical context cannot be separated from the way in which the field is both constituted and viewed. In other words, these fields combine both action and systemic dimensions, with the horison constituting both the point of orientation, and intersection, for, and between, them. These fields include the general and global capitalisation of social life, which revolves around a dual process of the subsumption of labour under capital, and the extension of formation of market driven economies, mediated by the money form. There is also the field and horison of industrialisation which includes the explosion of, and control over, very heterogeneous

37. Alisdair MacIntyre, *After Virtue*, 2nd Edition, Duckworth, London 1985, p187.

38. *ibid.*, pp58-59. Protestantism, following Nietzsche, Weber and Carroll belongs to the long durée of modernity. It systematically begins to problematise virtue culture along two fronts whilst leaving the shell intact. On the one side, from the vantage point of a democratisation of the church, priesthood and laity, and on the other from the vantage point of the internalisation of one's relation to God, the result of which is the anxiety of bad conscience, an early expression of the experience of contingency.

39. *ibid.*, p187.

40. The language and image of simulacra and hyper-reality belongs to the field of industrialisation. The industrialisation of the sign has a long history that belongs to the fascination with the technico-scientific imagination, its fictions and utopias.

41. J.P. Arnason, 'Modernity as Project and as Field of Tensions', *op. cit.*, pp192-193.

42. See J.G.A. Pocock, 'Virtues, Rights and Manners: A model for Historians of Political Thought', in *Virtue, Commerce and History: Essays on Political Thought and History, Chiefly in the Eighteenth Century*, Cambridge University Press, Cambridge 1985, pp37-50; and Quentin Skinner, *The Foundations of Modern Political Thought*, especially Vol 1, 'The Renaissance', Cambridge University Press, Cambridge 1978.

43. J.P. Arnason, op. cit. pp 186-189. See also John rundell, Origins of Modernity, Polity Press, Cambridge 1987, pp1-13.

44. *ibid.*, p204.

processes of machine driven technological innovation, including the technologisation of signs, and the development of the functional division of labour.[40] As indicated above, the autonomisation of art becomes a field for the destruction of the traditional aesthetics of the sacred, as the basis of its own aesthetic codes, as well as a problematic basis for a critique of other fields of modernisation.

The field of state-formation also constitutes another aspect of modernity, and within the European context, at least, consists historically in the developments of Absolutism and the nation state. These developments involved at least the following innovations: the personalisation of power, the purposive bureaucratisation of the offices of state power, the elaboration of *norm-free* or decree based forms of state-imposed and state-sanctioned legal rights, and the state's role and locus in the formation and consolidation of collective identities in terms of either nationalist orientations or revolutionary transformation from above or below.[41] The field of modern democratisation, which, itself, has its own long history, was constituted in the context of European state formation, both as a defensive argument against the state's capacity to absorb society, and as a modern innovation of, and separation from more classical traditions. Thus, it has involved debates and conflicts concerning the meaning and sovereignty of civil society, in which, mimimally, it has been viewed as a separate field from the state spatially located in cities, and thus freed from its regulatory intervention, (the liberal argument), or, maximally, as the ground from which politics and public spheres are formed. In this latter republican model, politics, rather than regulatory state power, became the model for social organisation generally. The meaning and sovereignty of persons as autonomous beings, as well as a language of universalisable rights, through which the relation between the state and the individual can be formally juridified, has accompanied this movement.[42]

Modernity can, thus, be viewed as pluri-dimensional fields in which there are irreducible tensions and conflicts between and within them. Thus, one particular field cannot be viewed as co-extensive with modernity. This tension may result, not only in a pluralisation of fields, but also in a privileging of one field against others, or a tendency towards systemic re-unification and totalisation. It is in this context that one can locate totalitarianism; it is an idiosyncratic experimental form rather than a field *per se* of modernity, in which the image and logic of the redemptive paradigm is played out in the context of the field of the modern state.[43]

As already mentioned, this multi-faceted image of the modern world is accompanied by both a pluralisation and fundamental alteration of horisons. These horisons are captured as anthropological or human self-images through which a field understands or represents itself to itself, as well as to others. Each of the anthropological images generates its own patterns or goals, as well as its horisons, of action.[44] The horison of action is the interpretation through which the anthropological image is articulated, and which (potentially) generates a surplus of meaning that is irreducible to the specific goal. Horisons of modernity are, then, constituted as anthropological shifts in which 'self-assertion' occurs that really or potentially fractures the context of the pre-existing virtue cultures. In Blumenberg's argument, the anthropological self-image through which a self-understanding of modernity is formed, and thus the world of virtues is fractured, is a cognitive one.[45] However, and for the moment leaving to one side the issue of virtue culture, we can extend Blumenberg's argument by suggesting that self-assertion not only revolves around cognition, or the image of the human being as the cognitive animal, but also the competing and differentiating images of the human being as the political animal, the economic one, the one who works, the one who creates law, or the one who creates art or culture.

45. Hans Blumenberg, op. cit, p138.

More extensively, the image and horison of the human being as the cognitive animal is concerned with epistemology and an empirically orientated reconceptualisation of knowledge formation and its truth content, whilst the image and horison of the human being as the economic one interprets needs as material goods, and then subsumes the work patterns through which these are produced under the prerogative of capital with its language of interest. The debates and conflicts concerning the question and meaning of sovereignty and autonomy are interpreted through an image and horison of the human being as a political animal, whilst the interpretion of, potentially all, relations in formal-procedural rather than substantive terms occurs through an image and horison of the human being as law maker/giver. The image and horison of the human being as the animal who works constructs this image functionally under the language of utility, whilst simultaneously emphasising humans' capacity to endlessly transform nature. The image and horison of human as artist is a motif that is constructed through which creativity, imagination and expression can be opened up, emphasised and explored.

These anthropological images become the *not uncontested* expressions of the fields themselves. A homology develops between the developmental dynamics of modernity and the anthropologically located images and horisons through which the cultures of modernity could form and gain coherence. It is here, too, that the social movements referred to above can be located. They both structure and contest specific goals and horisons specific to a particular aspect of modernisation. It should be noted, following Touraine, that social movements are neither only reactive or defensive. Rather, the fields are constituted by competing social movements which deploy a particular anthropological horison and goal of action within their particular field. In this context, social movements can draw on, or develop, a specific anthropological image and horison as the predominant cultural model within a specific field. They may also draw on other images with which to contest their specific field of action. Thus social movements can orientate themselves to the goals and horisons of, for example, democratisation, juridification, industrialisation, or may actively pursue goals

46. Alain Touraine, *The Self-Production of Society*, Chicago University Press, Chicago 1977.

and horisons of even re-traditionalisation. In other words, the anthropological images can be taken up in any of the fields, which always entails that there are interpenetrations between them.[46]

This reading of modernity, which emphasises the creative formation of anthropological horisons, and their articulation in differentiated fields, nonethless, needs to be supplemented by the long or civilisational history of the West. In the context of 'questions requiring answers', the historical innovation (although for MacIntyre it is anything but this) of creating goals and horisons of social action in terms other than virtue categories is the second historical watershed of modernity. This emphasises the clash between modernity's long and short durées. This now brings us to the shift from virtue to non-virtue cultures, as a further signpost of modernity.

The pluralisation of fields and anthropological images and horisons entails that the virtue cultures, terms, categories and forms of life are not only re-interpreted - they are also undermined. MacIntyre concedes Marx's image of a world in which 'all fast-frozen relations ... are swept away'; nonetheless, he would not celebrate the context breaking and accidental nature of a post-virtue world. For him, this post-virtue world is the result of the functionalist and individualistic images that have formed modernity and displaced virtue culture, the result of which is the impossibility of agreement even on the most basic principles or life-orientations. In other words, the development of role-based social relations, on the one side, and of transcendental formulations of epistemological certainty, sovereignty, rights and ethics, on the other, have completely altered the dynamic of social relations. In Macintyre's version, norms of good conduct are reduced and refer only to either rule governed behaviour or to an idea of the self which is constructed 'purely in terms of the presentation and maintenance

47. A MacIntyre, *op. cit.* especially chapters 6-9, and 18.

of functions.[47]

But functionalisation and individualisation are only parts of a more complex and differentiated story. Cultures of modernity are riven along the series of competing axes from the language of interest, to the dynamics of bureaucratic participation, to the now (post-transcendental) construction of the ideals of sovereignty and autonomy, to the language of limitless imagination and desire, and in being so riven each is thrown into relief. Moreover, each culture raises a clamour and a claim for the (allegiance of the) contemporary soul. The result is a dissatisfied, rather than narcissistic

48. Agnes Heller, 'The Dissatisfied Society', *The Power of Shame*, Routledge and Kegan Paul, London, 1985, pp300-315; 'On Being Satisfied in a Dissatisfied Society I and II', The Postmodern Political Condition' (with Ferenc Feher), Polity Press, Cambridge 1988, pp14-44.

or conformist, personality,who lives riven in a world of permanent tensions.[48] A modernity of the short durée, that is, of after the end of World War One, the echoes of which still reach us at the end of the century, is a post-transcendental, post-virtue anthropologically and systematically pluralised and differentiated social form — a modernity *in face of itself*.

DE CERTEAU AND CULTURAL STUDIES

Ian Buchanan

The only freedom supposed to be left to the masses is that of grazing on the ration of simulacra the system distributes to each individual. This is precisely the idea I oppose: such an image of consumers is unacceptable.

Michel de Certeau, *The Practice of Everyday Life*[1]

According to Mark Poster, of all 'the important theoretical writings in France in the 1970s and 1980s, Michel de Certeau's is most germane to cultural studies.'[2] However, judging by the weighty but negative evaluations de Certeau's work has received from two of its leading figures, namely John Frow and Meaghan Morris, it seems that cultural studies 'itself' does not agree.[3] The considerable critical interest generated by de Certeau's work has not, so far, evolved into acceptance, and it now appears that such acceptance will never be forthcoming. This conjecture is supported by the fact that John Fiske - who is the only one who uses de Certeau's work in something more than a passing manner - is criticised precisely for using de Certeau.

The problem is that de Certeau's distinctive contribution to cultural studies is yet to be determined. The reason why de Certeau's work should be taken up by cultural studies, I will argue, is that it offers a pluralist theory of power that is not constrained by the imperatives of authenticity. This reading, however, is only available to us if we read de Certeau against the background of Deleuze's notion of transcendental empiricism. As Clifford has shown, authenticity - together with its philosophical and political concomitant, negativity - today informs many contemporary ideations of cultural power. But because it cannot admit that someone can be both powerful and powerless, it is incapable of accounting for the kinds of complex power relations cultural studies, under the banners 'hybridity', 'ambivalence' and 'globalisation', is beginning to take an interest in. The way ahead, Clifford argues, is to develop a concept that can 'preserve culture's differentiating functions while conceiving of collective identity as a hybrid, often discontinuous inventive process.' Philosophically, this requires the flexibility of a notion of culture that is grounded in ways of being, not states of being. This is precisely the philosophical shift that de Certeau advocates when he gives primacy to cultural relations over their terms. As de Certeau puts it: 'Analysis shows that a relation (always social) determines its terms, and not the reverse, and that each individual is a locus in which an incoherent (and often contradictory) plurality of such relational determinations interact.'

The problem of 'Otherness' (a central concern of cultural studies, as recent work by Bhabha, Spivak, and Said attests), arises, I would argue, as a

1. Michel de Certeau, *The Practice of Everyday Life* (translated S Rendall), Berkeley, University of California Press 1984.

2. M. Poster, The Question of Agency: Michel de Certeau and the History of Consumerism', *Diacritics* 22;2, 1992, pp94-107.

3. These days it is rare for de Certeau to be mentioned in isolation. For example, 'While de Certeau's work is evidently of great interest, the dangers...have been clearly indentified by, among others, Frow', D. Morley, *Television, Audiences and Cultural Studies*, Routledge, London & NY, 1992. Similarly Grossberg subtends every mention of de Certeau with the footnote 'For an excellent critique of de Certeau see Morris...', L. Grossberg, 'Cultural Studies and/in New Worlds', *Critical Studies in Communication*, 10, 1993, pp1-22.

direct result of the non-pluralist stance that has so far prevailed in cultural studies. It usually surfaces in analyses as the problem of 'negativity': it refers to that condition of imposed silence which a subject must endure by virtue of the fact of his or her own condition of being. The Other, according to this logic, is negated by the non-Other in the process of its self-affirmation. If the Other were to speak as the Other, that affirmation would be undermined, the relation of difference would be destroyed and self-identity lost. The Other's condition of Otherness, which is at the same time the non-Other's condition of non-Otherness, precludes speech. Speech would make present what must be fundamentally absent. The problem of 'negativity' is this: how can one make one's presence known, that is speak, when one's condition of being precludes presence? Derrida's elaboration of the Heideggerian procedure of presenting the 'negative' under erasure is important for the fact that it destabilises the self-assuredness of the non-Other, but it remains unsatisfactory for a representation-based politics, finally, because the 'negative' voice is absent, even though its face may be visible. Although the Other can be perceived in their 'negativity', as it were, that state still silences them, so the problem remains. Transcendental empiricism is the solution both Deleuze and de Certeau apply to the problem of 'Otherness'. Due to the fact that 'Otherness' is treated predominantly as a moral and political issue by cultural studies, and de Certeau and Deleuze are not very up-front in this regard, they tend to be overlooked as theorists. Yet their critical and epistemological divagations, for the fact that they ceaselessly question our very understanding of 'Otherness', are enormously useful. The trouble, at least insofar as de Certeau is concerned, is that no-one has illuminated this aspect of his work, least of all de Certeau himself. De Certeau's interest in the problem of 'Otherness', though it is what makes his work vitally important to cultural studies, is buried beneath a wealth of speculative writing, and therefore virtually unknown. His elliptical style is perhaps more to blame for the misreadings that have been made of his work than anything else. The similarities between de Certeau and Deleuze - insofar as they both expound a non-dialectical, which is to say pluralist theory of relations - are important and extensive, and, as I will try to suggest, form the basis of a possible counter tradition in cultural studies. Frow's quarrel with de Certeau epitomises the reception cultural studies has given his work generally. Because it is the most sustained commentary on de Certeau yet written in the field of contemporary Anglo-American-Australian cultural studies, it can serve as our primary focus. To this end, Frow's critique is usefully reduced to three principal points of contention, which can then be addressed in turn: (1) de Certeau's use of the term transgression; (2) his lack of a non-bipolar model of domination; and (3) the impossibility of delineating exactly who or what is the subject of his analysis. The main point of contention will be that cultural studies - led by Frow, Fiske and Morris - has read de Certeau's work as though philosophically it is strictly transcendental, whereas I will argue it belongs to that order of philosophy

Deleuze has called transcendental empiricism.[4]

DE CERTEAU AND TRANSGRESSION

Frow has two main objections to transgression. The first, which I will enlarge upon here, is that transgression, either as a mode of criticism, or action, does not alter the status quo. The second, which I will deal with below in the next section, is that transgression is inescapably binarist. We can certainly sympathise with Frow here, both as concerns transgression as criticism, and as action. He is undoubtedly correct in questioning the validity of transgression as a mode of criticism. It is impossible, for instance, to theorise social change on the basis of transgression alone. Another mechanism must exist alongside it that can convert the various border crossings, the broken taboos and profaned totems, into transfigurations of the social morphology. For example, Freud, in *Moses and Monotheism* - his hypothetical exposition of the origins of society - couples parricide with guilt.[5] It is not the transgression against the despotic law of the father itself that induces change (the renunciation of instinct and the subsequent institution of democratic order), but rather the guilt that arises from that transgression. Since transgression functions as a virtual cipher for the carnivalesque, it will be as well if a number of key points of difference are highlighted. According to Rigby, de Certeau, because he challenges the standard intellectual practice of his times of concentrating on enduring cultural forms, is compelled to utilise certain ideas arising from the theory of the carnivalesque:

> If one were to try understand the culture of the people, and the creativity of the people, one would ... have to give full weight and importance to what is by definition ephemeral and instantaneous: the element of play, celebration, transgression and subversion in the life of the people, none of which tends to leave personal traces.[6]

It is not surprising therefore, that de Certeau considers 'la fete' as a quintessential element within popular culture, and as a crucial notion for understanding it. But this is still very far from a theory of the carnivalesque. The difference, as Rigby notes, is that de Certeau does not restrict 'popular culture to such exceptional moments as those which have the qualities of "la fete". The otherness of popular culture is, in fact, to be found in more mundane activities, which are far from being legitimated by the dominant culture but which form the "everyday" tissue of the life of the people.' What Rigby does not say, and I would wish to add, is that for de Certeau, as his eulogy to the common man suggests, the everyday is already extraordinary; a virtual carnival. The problem with the carnivalesque, is that its application is usually limited to events of a very singular kind. It thus distinguishes very sharply between ordinary and extraordinary. So of course it can easily be repudiated. Doubtless Sydney's gay and lesbian Mardi-Gras cannot change

4. J. Frow, 'Michel de Certeau and the Practice of Representation', *Cultural Studies* 5:1, 1991, pp52-60; J. Fiske, 'Popular Forces and the Culture of Everyday Life', *Southern Review* 21:3, 1988, pp208-306; M. Morris, 'Banality in Cultural Studies', in P. Mellancamp (ed), *The Logics of Television: Essays in Cultural Criticism*, Bloomington: Indiana University Press 1990, pp14-43.

5. S. Freud, *Moses and Monotheism* (translated J. Strachey), in Penguin Freud Library vol 13, A. Richards (ed), Harmondsworth, Penguin 1990, pp324-326.

6. B. Rigby, *Popular Culture in Modern france: A Study of Cultural Discourse* Routledge, London 1991, p18.

deeply entrenched homophobic attitudes in one night of tinsel. More damaging still, insofar as cultural studies' use of the carnivalesque is concerned, is the fact that the carnival may give rise to the illusion that change has occurred, without causing actual change, thus making it a very useful, and readily appropriated vehicle for political dissimulation. It would not be unduly cynical to say in support of this that an obviously transgressive event such as Mardi-Gras allows an otherwise homophobic governing body to divert criticism and opposition with the disarming disclaimer: 'What about Mardi-Gras?' In which case, though it may provide much needed catharsis, this particular instance of transgression in political terms is actually energy diverted from more materially meaningful goals. The carnival, despite its laudatory transgressiveness, does not, in the end bring about change by itself, which is of course one of the crucial problems that the theory of the carnivalesque is faced with. The hardline argument here, severely put, is that ostentatious instances of the carnivalesque have neither critical, nor politico-cultural value, for they do nothing, in the end, but silently and perhaps unwittingly support the very regime they apparently subvert.

What must be discovered, therefore, if the theory of the carnivalesque is to be truly useful, are the myriad ways in which the Mardi-Gras has occulted the everyday - albeit invisibly - at the level of what Raymond Williams called 'structures of feeling'. How has the Mardi-Gras enabled gays and lesbians to transform existing forms and conventions of everyday life? What, thereby, new types of relation between dominant and dominated have been entered into as a result of these perhaps minuscule, certainly quotidian, events? What happens in short, if every day/night, and not just one day/night of the year, is regarded as carnivalesque? The carnival would then be a mode, a certain style, not just an event, and this would change its meaning entirely - it would no longer be a one-off hit or miss, it would be a daily occurrence.

This is how 'la perruque' should be understood, for example. 'La perruque', de Certeau argues, is not a random act carried out by specific individuals - who might elsewhere be called felons - but an integral part of an extensive popular economy. It does not resist, by being transgressive, the imperatives of late capital; it transforms them from within by turning them to other ends. The value of 'la perruque' is that it instigates internal variation - it changes social structures from within, and is, therefore, extremely difficult to counteract. Even the most sophisticated surveillance apparatus would have trouble detecting this 'transgression' since its appearance is precisely that of conformity. As de Certeau put it: 'The actual order of things is precisely what "popular" tactics turn to their own ends ... Though elsewhere it is exploited by a dominant power or simply denied by an ideological discourse, here order is tricked by an art. Into the institution to be served are thus insinuated styles of social exchange, technical invention, and moral resistance ...' Frow dismisses 'la perruque', along with what de Certeau calls 'escaping without leaving' as the 'classic compromise of power-within-weakness'.[7]

7. Frow, 1991, *op. cit.*

The key to de Certeau's conceptualisation of popular 'resistive' practices, as Frow reveals, is: *indeterminacy*. For de Certeau, as Frow puts it: 'It is the possibility of indeterminacy, in the long run, that offers the best chance of popular resistance to technocratic rationality: not a resistance of one force or one reason to another, but an evasion of force and reason, an evasion of capture.' As we see here, Frow's interpretation of indeterminacy effectively denies it any socio-structural significance. Though he recognises its centrality to de Certeau's theoretical apparatus, Frow is not convinced that the insight is useful. Indeed, so far as he is concerned, indeterminacy is a rather pathetic and probably vain hope for social change.

As his qualification - the possibility of indeterminacy - suggests, Frow's antipathy to indeterminacy stems from the fact that he treats it as a (poorly conceived) sociological concept, which describes a certain state of affairs, and not as a philosophical concept, which articulates the conditions of possibility for that state of affairs. This reading is, I would argue, a misprision. It overlooks the fact that de Certeau explicitly locates his discourse within the Derridean critique of the proper, which, I would suggest, gives it a philosophical, not sociological, complexion. It also overlooks the quite spirited critique de Certeau levelled at Bourdieu's sociological conception of culture, which, I think, is indicative of a more general scepticism towards sociology. Viewed philosophically, in the light of the connection between Derrida and de Certeau, indeterminacy is not simply a possible source of salvation, which, like a miracle, is to be hoped for but not relied upon, a conceptualisation Frow is right to be critical of. It is rather, an inherent feature of the structure of the social which, like the faultlines in the earth's crust, poses an everpresent, and ultimately very powerful, threat to the order of things, no matter how securely entrenched. Extrapolated from Derrida's deconstruction of the orthodox, either/or distinction that obtains between a metaphor and its correlate, the literal, 'la perruque', along with 'escaping without leaving', which are both singled out for negative attention by Frow, are examples of what de Certeau describes as metaphorisation. As in the linguistic case, metaphorisation in the cultural sense refers to the inherent motility of ordered systems.

This, then, is the key to the possibility suggested above, that the everyday itself be treated as always already containing the possibility of carnival. The everyday, as de Certeau has shown, is, like metaphor, at once rule-governed, and contingent, which is why Derrida's deconstruction of metaphor is pertinent. This can be illustrated, very briefly, as follows: in order to propose a theory of metaphoricity which would treat all meaning as movement, Derrida had to postulate, at the same time, an instance of stasis. This stationary item is the proper, the literal which the metaphor surpasses, that which must be stipulated *a priori* in order to have metaphor. But it too is a metaphor, that is, *a posteriori*, in that its meaning is caught every time it is used, precisely because it is subject to use, in the flux of time - what it literally means today is not the same as it literally meant yesterday, nor will it mean the same tomorrow. The corollary is this: rules are always already put into play as soon as they are enunciated.

Even if we agree with Bateson and accept that every system contains certain limit points that cannot be transgressed without sending the entire system into irrevocable disintegration, the fact remains that the system itself - as a body of rules - has meaning only insofar as it is played with, and one of the risks of that play must be the subversion of the system.[8] More generally, a way of using imposed systems constitutes the resistance to the historical law of a state of affairs and its dogmatic legitimations. A practice of the order constructed by others redistributes its space; it creates at least a certain play in that order, a space for manoeuvres of unequal forces and for utopian points of reference. That is where the opacity of a 'popular' culture could be said to manifest itself - a dark rock that resists all assimilation. Here, I would argue, de Certeau is suggesting that the insights of deconstruction concerning the indeterminacy of meaning, are also applicable to the operations of power in everyday life. Accordingly, it is the relations between terms (the process of signification) that should be given primacy, and not the terms themselves (signifier/signified). Whether an action is strategic or tactical is thus decided not on the basis of who performs it, but rather according to the nature of the relation it establishes.

DE CERTEAU AND BINARISM

Frow's second objection to the notion of transgression stems from a more deeply etched concern with binarist theories in general. His misgiving insofar as de Certeau's work is concerned is that it does not offer anything other than a top-down model of power. Frow appears to treat de Certeau's conception of power as though it is naively Hegelian. It is precisely against this perception, for the fact that it precludes the very pluralism the concepts strategy and tactics are invested with, that I have suggested that de Certeau's work be rethought along Deleuzian lines. In what follows I will try to show how "transgression" in de Certeau might be read against a Deleuzian background in contrast to a Hegelian one. 'The peculiar ambiguity of the problematic of transgression lies' Frow writes, 'in its total dependence upon the law to be transgressed.' It means that 'I can only transgress against the state or against God if I believe in them and their authority; indeed my very act of transgression confirms them in their authority, and confirms my need of them.' Frow claims that this is exactly the meaning of de Certeau's catchphrase, 'to escape without leaving'. This, Frow says, is 'more generally true of the relation to the other, the broad model ... through which de Certeau theorises popular resistance.' Rightly Frow goes on to say that the other 'is integrated into the system it opposes, even as it undermines that system.'[9] And, as he said of Laclau and Mouffe's reformulation of the Master/Slave dialectic, which bears a strong resemblance to the construction he has made of de Certeau's terms: 'It is this that

8. In particular see 'Cybernetic Explanation@ in G. Bateson, *Steps to an Ecology of Mind*, Ballantine Books, NY 1972, pp399-411. On a more metaphysical plane, Blanchot has described these points in everyday life as 'limit experiences', M. Blanchot, *The Infinite Conversation* (translated S. Hanson), University of Minessota Press, Minneapolis 1993.

9. Frow, 1991, *op. cit.*, p57.

constitutes the model's efficacy, but only at the price of a repetition of the Same: on this interpretation, populist antagonism can never break the cycle of power because it is never more than a mirror image.' These comments alert us very clearly to the urgent need to disassociate de Certeau from Hegel.

In his response to Frow, Schirato too reflects on the problem of transgression, but the course he takes is different from the one outlined here. I have tried to show that 'transgression' in de Certeau's work is an exceptionally problematic term and that its use there is far from casual. I would add that if it is not to fall prey to precisely the criticisms Frow has made, then its very specific range of meanings must be tightly monitored.

In comparison, and much more ambitiously, Schirato attempts to repudiate Frow's definition of transgression. His rebuttal, however, is prevented from becoming a serious challenge to Frow because of its neglect of two points: first of all, it makes no significant mention of metaphorisation; second, and most seriously, it does not engage with the Hegelian master-slave dialectic which is implicit in the definition of transgression that Frow supplies. Schirato begins by saying Frow presumes, 'quite incorrectly, that an awareness of power of the state is the same as a belief in the natural authority of the state; or again, that a consciousness of the power exerted by those who speak in the name of God is the same as belief in God.'[10] He goes on to argue that it 'is patently not the case' that an awareness of authority corresponds to a belief in its insuperability. What he is arguing then is that when Frow asserts that belief in either the State or God is necessary in order to think transgression he is in fact claiming that acknowledgement of authority is equivalent to subservience. This, however, is not Frow's meaning at all. He does not conflate these two processes - acknowledgement of authority and subservience - as Schirato thinks. Strictly speaking, Frow claims only, and without controversy, that recognition of an other as a governing force is the necessary precondition for the transgression of that force. The position of subservience is a product of an acknowledgement by one of the authority of another, and that transgression works only within this economy. The implication of this, which concerns us, is that de Certeau's notion of transgression mirrors this Hegelian model and is similarly trapped into a dialectical ideation of power. This is what Frow means when he points out that it is only possible in de Certeau's fabulation of power to transgress against the State, or against God, if first their authority is believed in. The state must be recognised, to use the more familiar Hegelian term, as an authority before that mastery can be challenged either openly or covertly. It is through this recognition that the self-identity of master and slave is formed. 'They *recognise* themselves as *mutually* recognising one another.'[11] The trouble with this conception, is that the definitions of Self and Other it makes available are too superficial; they lack complexity, and have a tendency to group together under one rubric quite distinct classes. The Self, for example, might be composed entirely of White people, while the Other

10. T. Schirato, 'My Space or Yours? De Certeau, Frow and the Meanings of Popular culture', *Cultural Studies* 7:2, 1993, pp282-291.

11.G.W.F Hegel, *Phenomenology of Spirit* (translated A.V Miller), Clarendon Press, Oxford 1977, p112.

may be composed entirely of people of Colour, which does not take into account class structure, to give but one important nuance. This is why Frow wants de Certeau's notion of 'the people' which he sees 'as a unified bloc, the composition of which transcends class differences' restored to its full diversity of fractions and factions. Something which is not possible within the manifestly uncomplicated binary of transgressor-transgressed he imputes to de Certeau. Thus, Frow can write apropos 'power' in de Certeau: 'Nowhere in his work is there anything other than a polar model of domination, according to which sovereign power is exercised by a ruling class (or, more often, by an "elite"; or else by a technocracy or a technocratic rationality defined without reference to class) over a mass of oppressed popular subjects who lack all power.' He concedes that the oppressed operate 'an art of the weak' which can at times be seen to attenuate the affects of oppression, 'but the flow of power is nevertheless all in one direction and from a singular source. Rather than being defined by complexity, diversity, and ambiguity, the struggle for social power is thought in terms of a simple pathos of resistance.'[12] In Frow's view, it is preferable to formulate the dominated and dominant as separate, but of course intersecting, forces, or better still, classes according to a logic of what he describes as an incomplete, or at least more complex, correlation. But this still demands processes of identification, which are vulnerable to precisely the critiques he has directed at de Certeau. In contrast to this, as I will argue below, what de Certeau offers with strategy and tactics is a means of analysing culture without recourse to such a blunt and inflexible instrument as identity. This criticism of de Certeau, that he lacks something more subtle and sophisticated than a top-down model of power, has had considerable influence. Indeed, it has provoked some astonishingly misguided assertions. Hermes, obviously extending Frow's derogation of de Certeau's (alleged) reliance on transgression, writes that de Certeau, in the context of the socio-political cultural sphere, 'closes off all possibilities of change using a polar model of domination that is strengthened rather than changed by the tactics "ordinary" people use'.[13] Here, Frow's fear that the transgressive is recuperated in advance by the putatively transgressed is reiterated. So too is the assumption that de Certeau's template uncomplicatedly reflects the established standard of the Hegelian model of Self and Other. Hermes' principal complaint against de Certeau (and for that matter Frow), is that his theorisation of the social, apart from being unacceptably romantic, 'totally discounts that viewers will try to explain and legitimise their media use.' 'The issue', Hermes says, 'is to understand the relative importance of the media text and media use.' But as the following citation will show, this does not contradict anything de Certeau has said.

> [O]nce the images broadcast by television and the time spent in front of the TV set have been analysed, it remains to be asked what the consumer makes of these images and during these hours. The thousands of people

12. Frow, 1991, *op.cit.*, p57-58.

13. J. Hermes, 'Media, Meaning and Everyday Life', *Cultural Studies* 7:3, 1993, pp493-506.

who buy a health magazine, the customers in a supermarket, the practitioners of urban space, the consumers of newspaper stories and legends - what do they make of what they "absorb", receive, and pay for? What do they do it with it?[14]

14. de Certeau, 1984, *op.cit.*, p31.

Indeed, far from contradicting him, it might be argued that de Certeau has influenced Hermes. According to Silverstone it is precisely this avenue of inquiry, the relation between media and media-user, that de Certeau has done the most to open up, and is at his most valuable. Silverstone thus contends that de Certeau's arguments 'allow us to think more critically about the precise role of television in the mediation between everyday life and the places occupied by the Other (that is science, politics or the generically inaccessible) but they also offer a possible route for the exploration of the relationship between television as medium, as institution and as technology, with its audience.' Although it turns out that Hermes' real gripe is against cultural critics who denigrate, or otherwise eschew, the use of viewer interviews, the fact remains that his perception of de Certeau's model of power as a polar model of domination is attributable to Frow. De Certeau himself does not address this issue, which he designates a 'problematics of repression'. In fact, he deliberately situates his project outside it.

Unfortunately, because it transcribes strategy and tactics as dominant and dominated, John Fiske's affirmative use of de Certeau's apparatus far from providing a source of much needed relief actually contributes to the problem. Fiske writes:

> The central paradox on which I wish to focus ... is that for the last four centuries in European and European produced societies those with power ... have failed to construct the subordinated people into their own image.[15]

15. J. Fiske, 'Popular Forces and the Culture of Everyday Life'. *Southern Review*, 21.3, 1988, pp208-306.

The people, in other words, have preserved their own. They have done this via 'a never-ending series of resistances, evasions and counter attacks: popular culture as guerilla warfare'. Highlighting the importance of the background against which de Certeau is read, the structure of Fiske's argument, manifestly dialectical, makes his polarisation of de Certeau practically inevitable. It is of course de Certeau who initially proposed that popular culture might be understood as a form of 'guerilla warfare'. Therefore Fiske writes: 'Let me introduce two of his crucial oppositions: strategy and tactics, place and space.'[16] Fiske then suggests that strategy and tactics, which he correctly identifies as the primary terms, can be productively compared to the structuralist binaries, langue and parole, and enonce and enunciation. The implication is that strategy is a cultural system, and tactics its use. This would be fine, though it would still be an occultation of de Certeau, except that strategy and tactics are cast in opposition by Fiske. To follow Fiske, we would have to claim that one can have, either the system of language, or its use, meaning that each is separable from the

16. *ibid.*

other, which is impossible. If parole is the instantiation that a particular language-system makes possible, then it cannot be in opposition to langue since langue is its condition of possibility. The fact of this doubtless inadvertent solecism is, however, less important than the image it projects. Fiske's reconfiguration of de Certeau creates the impression that de Certeau is an exponent of precisely what he rejects (i.e., a 'problematics of repression'). The problem with Fiske's rendering of de Certeau is that he does not draw a sharp enough distinction between use and user. An activity which invests a product, or a phenomenon, with individuality is correctly referred to as tactical, but the agent performing that activity is not. Likewise, the systematic consolidation of power, such as one finds in the Benthamite panopticon, is correctly referred to as strategic, but the administrators of that regime are not. What effectively Fiske does is ontologise strategy and tactics: he transforms into users what de Certeau determined very particularly to be 'ways of using'. A strategy is the 'calculation (or manipulation) of power relationships', while a tactic 'is a calculated action determined by the absence of a proper locus.' Strictly speaking, it is only possible to operate tactically or strategically; one cannot be tactical or strategic. It is this feature of his apparatus, the fact that it does not require any process of identification, that enables de Certeau to operate outside of the imperatives of dialectics. Because of it, he no longer has to identify 'top' or 'down', and can therefore show without contradiction that the manifestly powerful are vulnerable to the manifestly weak. So, far from top-down, de Certeau's conceptualisation of power is pluralist. And pluralism, Deleuze argues, is simply another word for (transcendental) empiricism.

THE SUBJECT OF DE CERTEAU'S ANALYSIS

17. Frow, 1991, *op. cit., p59*.

Frow's third point of contention is that de Certeau's analyses are diminished by the fact that they lack 'a definite and graspable object'.[17] This is dangerous, Frow argues, because in its absence 'the analyst will inevitably reconstruct such an object.' The trouble with definite and graspable objects, de Certeau would argue, however, is that they are invariably constructions of the analyst's own making. As in a workshop or laboratory, the objects produced by an inquiry result from its (more or less original) contribution to the field it has made possible. They thus refer to a 'state of the question' - that is, to a network of professional and textual exchanges, to the 'dialectic' of an inquiry in progress (if one takes 'dialectic' in the sixteenth-century sense of the movement of relations among different procedures on the same stage, and not in the sense of the power assigned to a particular place to totalise or 'surmount' these differences). Doubtless, de Certeau would agree with Frow that cultural studies is perpetually threatened with 'a politically fraught substitution of the voice of middle-class intellectual for that of the users of popular', but would not exculpate himself as Frow apparently does.

Morris's sense of disquietude with de Certeau's analyses of everyday life too concerns his 'imprecise' construction of a research object. Morris contends that this 'object' is entirely masculine. There is, she avers, no space for women in the confines of de Certeau's discourse. As she puts it: 'feminist critique of *The Practice to Everyday Life* would find ample material to work with. De Certeau's Muse - the silent other to whom his writing would strive to give voice is unmistakably The Ordinary Man.'[18] Though Morris may be said to adumbrate the feminist response to de Certeau, it is worth noting that recent works by feminists, Lois McNay and Elspeth Probyn, suggest, despite her concerns, that there is much in de Certeau to interest feminism. This is particularly so for current reconsiderations of the body. For instance, McNay argues that de Certeau's concept of consumption offers a more concrete theorization of the practices of self than does Foucault's aesthetics of self. Probyn finds de Certeau's concept of the tactic useful as a means of theorizing the feminine in the active voice; it offers feminism, she says, 'a mode of speaking that engages with the taken-for-granted and underestimated ways in which women express themselves at home and in the family'. Thus, it is the fact that the object is not determined in advance, which makes de Certeau's analyses useful to feminist applications.

Morris is also disturbed by the fact that she finds in de Certeau what she calls a 'unifying myth of a common otherness'.[19] This is an extension of the point made above. Because de Certeau does not essentialise his research object, he can be accused of emptying it. While de Certeau recognises the existence of a community of othered peoples, he does not determine otherness (in the ontological sense) on the basis of this fact of being othered (in epistemological terms, though, this is precisely how the other comes to be). The community exists only insofar as each of its constituents conform to a particular style of action. The epistemological other is what the discursive system excludes in its search for homogeneity, literally for the sake of purity. The other corresponds, then, to those messy contingencies which disrupt or disprove the rule. Otherness, in the ontological sense, however, refers to a state of being, rather than a way of being.

De Certeau's other is defined by a certain way of operating, a stylistic inflection of an imposed syntax - way of being - and not according to inherent traits - state of being. Since its 'otherness' is consequent upon its own actions, and not subsequent to another's impositions, the Other can only ever be becoming, it cannot have already become. Therefore the Other cannot be determined in advance. So rather than bemoan the absence of a clearly delineated object, what de Certeau would suggest we should do is question the possibility of such a thing as an object of inquiry. Is it possible, given the immensity of its possible field, for cultural studies to have an object that is not also a reduction, or an abstraction? This is the real question. Not *who* or *what* is de Certeau's subject matter - but is a subject matter (object) possible? How does the research item (man, woman, television viewer, romance novel reader, consumer, star-gazer, wanna-be) come to be? What procedures are involved in the textualising of the practices of everyday life - what must be

18. M. Morris, *op. cit.*, p36.

19. *ibid*, p35. Morris also argues that de Certeau's procedure in *The Practice of Everyday Life* 'invokes a troubling reinscription of a theory/practice opposition - semantically projected as "high" versus "low".' But this is simply a repetition of a previously encountered failure to recognise the significance of AND as opposed to either/or.

done to make the everyday sayable? It is the methodology, the decisive means by which the elusive practices of daily life are converted into knowledge, that is de Certeau's quarry. His agenda does not include within its ambit, however, the search for a perfectly unbiased apparatus, nor even for an objective means apprehending a subject matter (two things he rejects unequivocally). It is the 'violence' of textualising that needs to be made the focus of a rigorous examination: how does a literature come to be?

To date, all of de Certeau's commentators within the cultural studies field have treated his schemata (strategy and tactics) as though they should be configured according to the traditional pattern of A and not-A. Yet it is this very structure that he is at the greatest pains to escape. Because it is governed by the law of noncontradiction (i.e., either/or), the relation between A and not-A is secondary to the terms themselves. The agonistic predicament it gives rise to is dominated, therefore, by a problematics of mutual exclusion. For example, strategy and tactics can only be read as strategy or tactics - either strategy, or tactics - not strategy *and* tactics. The problem here is that separating strategy from tactics, is like separating, as Deleuze might have put it, the wasp from the orchid; it ignores the fact of the double capture: 'the wasp AND the orchid'.[20] As Proust has memorably shown in the opening pages of *Cities of the Plain*, it is not the wasp (Charlus), or the orchid (Jupien), that is primary, but the relation. What is strikingly absent from this scene, which the dialectical configuration A and not-A deems must be present, is any evidence of subservience; neither Charlus nor Jupien could be said to occupy a dominant position to the other's subordinate one. We surmise then, that since it necessarily casts one term in a subordinate role - even when such subordination is not in evidence - and another in a dominant role, it is the A and not-A configuration itself that condemns the Other to eternal silence.

The problem with this dialectical model is that, in spite of the fact that it is used by Hegel to demonstrate that the essential nature of lordship is 'the reverse of what it wants to be' and that 'servitude in its consummation will really turn into the opposite of what it immediately is', it binds the master and slave together so fully that it is impossible to think of one outside of the other; which is to say, in a non-relation to the other. The slave subtends the master's self-consciousness by precisely being a slave, and although that alters the truth of slavery as a problem of being, it does not alter the condition of being a slave. Still, the master can only gain power through the subordination of an other. Though Hegel ultimately shows that domination in philosophical terms is a vicious enterprise, always involving loss, to the extent that there can be no absolute, he is nevertheless incapable of escaping the snare of polarity. The precession to *Aufhebung* is irreducibly and irretrievably polar: negation and affirmation. Moreover, even if the subsequent lifting up eliminates them both, it nonetheless begins with two poles. The process then starts all over.

To escape it Deleuze says, one must escape 'the operation of the negation'

20. G. Deleuze & C. Parnet, *Dialogues* (translated H. Tomlinson & B. Habberjam), Athlone, London 1987. The fullest treatment can be found in Deleuze, *An Essay on Hume's Theory of Human Nature*, (translated C.V. Boundas), Columbia University Press, NY 1991.

and take up instead 'a theory and practice of relations, of the AND'. A non-bipolar model of domination, which this move toward the AND heralds, has been the ambition of philosophy since the earliest times as Foucault has shown in relation to sexuality (the problem, in other words, of 'A Boy's Honour'), but it is only now that we are beginning to see how this might be possible: transcendental empiricism.[21] Deleuze's empiricism, is of a very particular variety: it is only in Hume's empiricist philosophy - and not in either Locke's or Berkeley's - that the significance of AND can be discovered.[22] As Deleuze put it: Of course, every history of philosophy has its chapter on empiricism: Locke and Berkeley have their place there, but in Hume there is something very strange which completely displaces empiricism, giving it a new power, a theory and practice of relations, of the AND, which was to be pursued by Russell and Whitehead, but remains underground or marginal in relation to the great classifications, even when they inspire a new conception of logic or epistemology. The key to Deleuze's empiricism, as his monograph on Hume reveals, is the proposition: 'Relations are external to their terms'. The principal implication of this is as follows: the relation is primary, not the term. In fact, it is the relation itself that gives the term, wasp/orchid, its distinctive character. The same is true of strategy and tactics: it is the relation between the two that determines the one as strategic and the other as tactical. This discovery of the AND, so crucial to Deleuze's later elaboration of such concepts as stammering and the rhizome, is fundamental to empiricism's 'escape' from the negativity ordinarily and necessarily entailed by dialectics.

For Deleuze AND is an efficient way of side-stepping Hegel. The conjunction, according to Deleuze, 'is neither a union, nor a juxtaposition, but the birth of a stammering, the outline of a broken line which always sets off at right angles'.[23] By which he means to suggest a way of 'philosophizing as a novelist, of being a novelist in philosophy.'[24] In less poetic terms this implies the elaboration of an agonistics that is conceptually grounded in the relation between terms, not in the terms themselves. Rather than the Hegelian duologue of A and not-A, it operates according to a logic of A AND B.

Strategy and tactics occupy the position of the AND: what they do in fact is typologise relations. Tactics then, precisely as a way of operating, specify a type of relation between two terms. As such, the art of the weak does not necessarily require that its operator *be* weak. What is tactical, and therefore belonging to an order of the weak, is only the action, the relation not the agent. And that relation is always doubled, at least. In the example of the master-slave dialectic, we see that this must be the case.

The master has a particular, that is to say, singular, style of relation with the slave; and, by the same token, the slave has his or her own peculiar style of relation with the master. The master attains mastery not through the process of identification wherein the slave recognises the master, but, more forcefully, by entering into that type of relation. Here the essential axiom of transcendental empiricism, that relations are external to their terms, means

21. M. Foucault, *The Use of Pleasure: The History of Sexuality Volume 2* (translated R. Hurley) Harmondsworth, Penguin, 1992.

22. Deleuze, 1991, *op. cit.*

23. Deleuze & Parnet, *op. cit.*, 1987, pp9-10.

24. *ibid*, p54.

that the relation pre-exists its eventual instantiation. Structurally, the master-slave relation necessarily involves the active subordination of an other, but this other is not the negative remainder of a dialectics of dominance. It is an actual, already constituted identity, an*other* rather than an *Other*, which is subjugated. Because it retains its identity within this heterologically configured agonistics, the other (properly designated now as B instead of not-A; or better, as the Different instead of the Other) is able to enter into its own relation with the dominant term. This relation, B AND A is tactical not because the other, A AND B, is strategic, but because it is the more opportune. It is judicious to operate tactically, not obligatory. This is what Deleuze means by double capture: master AND slave.

This is a crucial difference. Hegel's ontologically configured agonistics determines the nature of the relation on the basis of the terms themselves, thus a master IS masterly, and the slave IS slavish, therefore the relation between them (master/slave) is inalterable. With transcendental empiricism this is not the case. The dominated, at the risk of annihilation, can operate strategically, but will, as is prudent, usually choose not to. And as it is the relation which determines the terms, the tactical is never completely divested of power - even if theirs is the lesser form - because the tactical relation of B to A (B captures A); or, to use Deleuze's terminology, even as B deterritorialises A, A reterritorialises B (A *captures* B). The apparently single relationship between A *and* B is in fact multiple. A multiplicity of relations obtain between A AND B, each with their own affective character. 'The multiple is no longer an adjective which is still subordinate to the One which divides or the Being which encompasses it. It has become a noun, a multiplicity which constantly inhabits each thing.'[25]

25. *ibid*, p57.

What de Certeau's work offers, because it is structured according to the precepts of transcendental empiricism, is a pluralist theory of power. Not founded on positives and negatives, or on any other such binaristic forms; strategy and tactics do not divide the social between the powerful and the powerless, but rather discriminate between different types, or modalities as it might also be put, of power. This means that strategy and tactics are adjacent rather than complementary; they distort and ramify one another, but they do not depend on one another. The most persistent and damaging distortion of de Certeau's theory has been the enshrining of the idea that strategy and tactics are oppositions in the dialectical sense. This misperception can be attributed, as we have seen, to the background against which de Certeau has so far been read, which suggests that a new background needs to be developed. The primacy of the conjunctive though deeply embedded, is a crucial postulate of de Certeau's infrastructure. If its significance is not immediately apparent, this is doubtless due to the fact that de Certeau does not himself devote any attention to developing verbatim this facet of his work. However, if we continue to ignore this aspect of his work, then de Certeau's true contribution to cultural studies will never be known.

'THE DEATH OF PSYCHOANALYSIS'?:
FOUCAULT ON LACAN

Lee Grieveson

The notion of problematisation gradually came to occupy a central place in Foucault's thought. There is a history of thought because a domain of action or thought loses its familiarity and becomes uncertain. What was it, in the experience of madness, illness, criminality or sexuality, for example, that presented itself in such a problematic way that this experience both could be thought about and had to be thought about? By the second volume of *The History of Sexuality* this question was addressed to the thought of being. The point is not to analyse 'behaviours or ideas, nor societies and their "ideologies" but the *problematisations* through which being offers itself to be, necessarily, thought'.[1] For Foucault here, it seems, there is a subject because of the historical rise of particular ways in which human beings problematise what they are and what they do. This re-introduction of the problem of 'what is termed "the subject"' (2:6) marks a significant shift in Foucault's work, the consideration of an axis of ethics (the relation to the self, the forming of oneself as a subject, the governing of the self) beyond - though enmeshed with - the axes of knowledge and power (which can now be conceived of as the relation to things and the relation to others). In the much earlier essay 'Nietzsche, Genealogy, History', for example, truth and being - which ostensibly 'lie at the root of what we know and what we are' - are conceptualised as 'but the exteriority of accidents'.[2] Similarly, in the roughly contemporaneous *The Archaeology of Knowledge* the subject is defined as a 'space of exteriority in which a network of distinct sites is deployed'.[3] By *The Use of Pleasure*, however, truth and being are reconsidered not simply as products of an accidental exteriority but as contingent products of an ethical problematisation of the self *qua* self.

In the spirit of Foucault's work on problematisation, my starting point here will be the question: what problem does Foucault's re-problematisation of the subject respond to? What is Foucault's account attempting to make uncertain, to re-question, and to de-familiarise? Let me state in advance the answer that I will try to prove here: psychoanalysis, or, rather, the subject of psychoanalysis. Further than that, I will suggest, this subject became inextricably associated with Lacan's return to Freud, through which the notion of a split, divided and decentred subject would become central to the axioms of critical discourse. An account of Lacan will become central to Foucault's project to historicise the practices of the self in relation to sexuality and desire, and the concomitant reintroduction of the problem of the subject

1. Michel Foucault, *The Use of Pleasure, The History of Sexuality Volume 2*, trans. Robert Hurley, Random House, New York, 1985, p10. All subsequent references to specific volumes in (The History of Sexuality will be given by volume and page number in the text . They include *The History of Sexuality, Volume 3*, (trans. Robert Hurley, Random House, New York, 1978 and *The Care of the Self, The History of Sexuality. Volume 3*, trans. Robert Hurley, Random House, New York, 1986.

2. Foucault, 'Nietzsche, Genealogy, History', trans. Donald F. Bouchard and Sherry Simon in *The Foucault Reader*, Paul Rabinow (ed), Penguin Books, London 1984, p389. This essay was first published in *Hommage a Jean Hyppolite*, Presses Universitaires de France, Paris, 1971.

3. Foucault, The Archaeology of Knowledge (trans. A.M. Sheridan Smith), Tavistock Publications, London, 1972, p55. Originally published as *L'Archeologie du Savoir*, Editions Gallimard, Paris, 1969.

beyond its conceptualisation as subjected to forces of exteriority. Lacan will become the crucial pivot around which Foucault's history of sexuality, desire and the subject will swivel. At any rate, it is this I will endeavour to argue here by, firstly, tracing out Foucault's critique of Lacan in the first volume of *The History of Sexuality* and, secondly, by pursuing this critique through Foucault's subsequent reformulation of that project in its shift onto a history of desire and 'desiring man'. What account of Lacan is produced by Foucault's genealogies? What history does psychoanalysis have in Foucault's account? In a broad sense this will finally be a question of *inheritance*: what is inherent - what inheres - in psychoanalysis? Can psychoanalysis inhere?

Let me start with the issue of desire and law, for this will allow me to quickly focus on Foucault's problematisation of psychoanalysis, indeed on the irreducible core of difference between these two important theoretical endeavours. The positioning of Freud as an event in the dissolution of repression, and the theorisation of repression that exists in (certain of) Freud's texts, is possible only if sex is seen as antithetical to power and, then, as temporally prior to the imposition of power. Sex is repressed by power. Sex will be, in this account, inextricably linked to the truth of the subject. Freud will go to great lengths to maintain the primacy of sexuality, understood as object-desire or libido, in the process installing a subject of desire as foundational.[4] Foucault's critique of this model of repression is well known: power in its various discourses and institutions cultivates sex in the image of its own normative construction such that there is no 'sex' ontologically immunised from power to which a supervening Law attends but that 'sex' is produced by that monitoring. Furthermore, that 'sex' is produced as that which calls to be monitored and regulated. In order to exercise and elaborate its power, a regulatory regime will generate the very object it seeks to control such that there is no temporal lag between production and regulation.

This much is well known. The problem for Foucault's archaeology of psychoanalysis here though becomes what to do with the moments that exist in Freud's work which allow for a quite different reading of repression, or, for example, with Lacan's conception of the super-ego not as a repressive, juridical law but precisely as an injunction to enjoy.[5] In the abstract, the question that confronts Foucault's account is this: what is inherent in psychoanalysis? Foucault's response is interesting. In a curious passage roughly halfway through the first volume of *The History of Sexuality*, in response to an imaginary figure questioning his account, Foucault chides himself for 'feigning ignorance of the fact that a critique [of this model of repression] has been mounted from another quarter and no doubt in a more radical fashion: a critique conducted at the level of the theory of desire'. It is worth pausing over Foucault's characterisation of this theory:

In point of fact, the assertion that sex is not 'repressed' is not altogether new. Psychoanalysts have been saying the same thing for some time. They have challenged the simple little machinery that comes to mind

4. For a detailed reading of Freud's maintenance of the primacy of sexuality at the expense of a mimetic or identificatory definition of desire see Mikkel Borch-Jacobsen's *The Freudian Subject* (trans. Catherine Porter), Stanford University Press, Stanford, California, 1988.

5.See, for example, Freud's re-reading of repression in the 1926 *Inhibitions, Symptoms and Anxiety* XX (1926d), in *The Standard Edition of the Complete Psychological Works of Sigmund Freud*, James Strachey (ed), The Hogarth Press, London, especially pp163- 4. For the development of this reading of Lacan see Slavoj Zizek's *Enjoy Your Symptom! Jacques Lacan in Hollywood and Out*, Routledge, London, 1992.

when one speaks of repression; the idea of a rebellious energy that must be throttled has appeared to them inadequate for deciphering the manner in which power and desire are joined to one another; they consider them to be linked in a more complex and primary way than through the interplay of a primitive, natural and living energy welling up from below, and higher order seeking to stand in its way; thus one should not think that desire is repressed, for the simple reason that the law is what constituted both desire and the lack on which it is predicated (1:81).

This conception of the complex spiral between a form of power and desire which reduces the temporal lag between production and regulation seems to take on the critique Foucault aims at repression. Psychoanalysis is not a totality; a *return to* Freud can figure as a *going beyond* Freud.

Psychoanalysts have been saying the same thing for some time. Which psychoanalysts? What is the temporality Foucault invokes? My reference to Lacan's famous slogan, put forward in Vienna in 1955, is not unwarranted here. The characterisation of a theory of desire which sees the Law as constitutive of desire and the lack on which desire is predicated seems to quite explicitly reference Lacan who, for example, in the 1959-1960 Seminar VII on *The Ethics of Psychoanalysis* would assert that an object of desire becomes the object of desire only in so far as it is prohibited. Desire needs Law, which is to say, there is a direct identity of desire and Law.[6]

Foucault's critique of this theory of desire will effectively centre on the question of power. Foucault will associate both a theory of repression and a theory of desire with a juridical conception of a power that has its 'central point in the enunciation of the Law' and is thus emanational - emerging from some centre and transmitting itself downwards - and ultimately prohibitive (1:90). This notion of power inheres in psychoanalysis, and though differences may be seen in other regards - for example, in 'the way in which they each conceive of the nature and dynamics of the drives' (1:83) - there is this fundamental and problematic continuity. These two moments that exist in psychoanalysis in relation to repression and desire, which I am reading here as the 'moments' of Freud and Lacan,

6. See Jacques Lacan, *The Ethics of Psychoanalysis*, Routledge, London, 1992.

> both rely on a common representation of power which depending on the use made of and the position it is accorded with respect to desire, leads to two contrary results: either to the promise of a 'liberation', if power is seen as having only an external hold on desire, or, if it is constitutive of desire itself, to the affirmation: you are always already trapped (1:83)

Foucault's reconceptualisation of power in the first volume of *The History of Sexuality* will lead to a reconsideration of the subject beyond an understanding of a truthful residue in the subject which may be liberated and, crucially, beyond an understanding of the subject as trapped within and by its own desire. In this latter version of psychoanalysis, the subject is inevitably subjected to the Law: 'Confronted by a power that is law, the subject who is constituted as subject - who is "subjected" - is he who obeys' (1:85).

The subject subjected to law and desire. Foucault's critique will challenge the formulation of desire in terms of negativity, and the related conceptualisation of the subject as derivative of the relation to the Other and the function of a lack. In line with what might, in the abstract, be seen as a Nietzschean critique of a Hegelian negativity, Foucault's account will pursue power and subjectivity in its positivity, or rather, the positivity of the subject after, and leading, from the positivity of power. This at least is how Foucault's analysis progressed, with the consideration of an axis of ethics following from, and closely connected to, the axes of knowledge and power (and it is, incidentally, the specificity of these connections that render any critique of this later work on ethics as upholding the 'autonomous subject' within a 'humanist-elitist tradition' redundant).[7] The first volume of *The History of Sexuality* is effectively sited in the interstices of this crucial shift, conceptualised by Foucault as either 'a re-elaboration of the theory of power' or as a contribution to the axis of ethics.[8] As such it sets in play the intricate analyses of the chiasmatic connections between government and self-government that emerge in Foucault's later work on the whole theme of 'governmentality'. The re-elaboration of power beyond law, pleasure beyond the negativity of desire, would become central to Foucault's re-problematisation of the subject.

It is well known that the conception of the Law of the Symbolic as constitutive of a structural and ontological 'fact' of desire will emerge in Lacan - more precisely, the Lacan of a certain period - via the translation of Freud's fictive anthropology of the primal horde, through Levi-Strauss's work on the prohibition of incest and the rule of exogamy in the reproduction of culture. Such a prohibition will institute a primordial repression that is constitutive of the split subject. This primary repression constitutes desire as a lack, a response to an originary separation; desire, in Lacan, is the expression of a longing for a return to the origin which, if realised, would necessitate the dissolution of the subject itself. The repression of Oedipal desires, a founding prohibition, survives in desire as the Law of the signifier; the paternally enforced prohibition against incest is, for Lacan, coextensive with language itself. In short, and to simplify matters somewhat, Lacan's account, perhaps psychoanalysis 'itself', will centre on the prohibition - or the failure of the prohibition - of incest in the human subject. It is no coincidence that in the first volume of *The History of Sexuality* Foucault will outline a genealogy of how the incest prohibition could come to be seen as central to the truth of the subject. Foucault's attention is directed there to the 'always already there' prohibition of desire, inscribing Lacan's understanding of 'The tangential movement towards incest that has

7. Respectively, Mladen Dolar, 'The Legacy of the Enlightenment: Foucault and Lacan', *New Formations* 14, Summer 1991, p54, and Slavoj Zizek, *The Sublime Object of Ideology*, Verso, London, 1988, p2. For Foucault's insistence of the connections between these axes see, for example, 'The Return of Morality' in Sylvere Lotringer, *Foucault Live: Collected Interviews. 1961-1984*, (trans. Lysa Hochroth and John Johnston, Semiotext(e), New York, 1996, p466.

8. Foucault, 'The History of Sexuality' in Colin Gordon (ed), *Power/ Knowledge*, Pantheon, New York, 1980, p187. This interview was conducted in 1977. For the latter position see Foucault, 'On the Genealogy of Ethics: An Overview of Work in Progress', in Paul Rabinow (ed), *The Foucault Reader*, p352. This interview was conducted in 1983.

manifested itself ever since the coming of a universal community' into a form of history.[9] What kind of history can there be of incest?

A history that outlines the putting into play of a form that may itself have universal form. Foucault's account of the historical dissonance between juridical and bio-political registers is directed at this. The shift from a juridical register where the political order of the sovereign, the differentiation into orders and castes and the values of descent lines were predominant, to a bio-political configuration where the mechanics of power were addressed to the body, to life, and to mechanisms which will sustain it, figures as the 'birth' of a deployment of sexuality. The overall dissonance between juridical and bio-political registers is linked then to a split between a deployment of alliance and a deployment of sexuality. Both deployments connect circuits of sexual partners but in diametrically opposed ways. The deployment of alliance is a system for the fixation of kinship ties, of transmissions of names and possessions, having as one of its objectives 'to reproduce the interplay of relations and maintain the law that governs them' (1:106). The deployment of sexuality operates according to polymorphous and contingent techniques of power, engendering a continual extension of areas and forms of control. The issue of governmentality in Foucault's later work would pursue this dissociation between sovereignty/legality and power mechanisms associated with norms.

9. Lacan, *Ecrits: A Selection*, trans. Alan Sheridan, Tavistock, London, 1977, p66.

For Foucault, various mechanisms figure as switchpoints in the recodification of sovereignty and law in the newly unstable politico-epistemic configuration associated with the emergence of a deployment of sexuality. The family, in the form in which it came to be valued in the course of the eighteenth century, became the interchange of sexuality and alliance, making it possible for the main elements of the deployment of sexuality to 'develop along its two primary dimensions: the husband-wife axis and the parents-children axis' (1:108). It is in this way that 'sexuality' is, from the start, incestuous, thoroughly saturated with strategies of power. Foucault writes:

> It may be that in societies where the mechanisms of alliance predominate, prohibition of incest is a functionally indispensable rule. But in a society such as ours, where the family is the most active site of sexuality, and where it is doubtless the exigencies of the latter which maintain and prolong its existence, incest - for different reasons altogether and in a completely different way - occupies a central place; it is constantly being solicited and refused; it is an object of obsession and attraction, a dreadful secret and an indispensable pivot. (1:109)

The Oedipus complex, through its imagining of an incestuous desire at the base of the subject and its positioning of the father as sovereign, legislator and pure negation of desire, figures as the rediscovery of 'the law of alliance, the involved workings of marriage and kinship, and incest at the heart of this sexuality' (1:113). Though the patient is separated from the family, the family emerges within the patient, so that the guarantee that one would find the parent-child axis at the root of sexuality - as the root of sexuality - ensured that sexuality remained inextricably enmeshed with the law of alliance. Psychoanalysis will figure as an *indispensable pivot*, stitching back together historically dissonant deployments of power.

To return via this, to Lacan, is intriguing. In Lacan's reading, there is no incestuous desire prior to the prohibition of incest. Such a prohibition is formative of psychic autonomy and the structure of sexual desire itself, which can then only be enmeshed with its prohibition. Foucault's analysis seems to want to direct attention to the nature of the prohibition that in Lacan figures as Symbolic Law, associated with the indelible rules of kinship which 'from the dawn of history' have represented law, culture and language through the figure of the Father.[10] We can perhaps imagine Foucault's question, for it will be a question dictated by Foucault's nominalism and Lacan's realism. Simply: what creates this Law? Such a question will ultimately be inadmissible within the conceptual parameters of psychoanalysis and as such motivates Freud's movement backwards to the myth of the primal band and Lacan's problematic appropriation of Levi-Strauss's notion of the 'symbolic' and the reformulation of this in structural terms.[11] For Lacan, the Law must be excluded as a symbolic foundation, opposed to the symbolic structure it founds. Foucault's analysis would suggest that what Lacan described as an *a priori* law of human desire was a problematic hypostasis of a deployment of alliance that was no longer relevant. As such, the theoretical effort of psychoanalysis - for which we can now add proper names, Freud and Lacan - 'to reinscribe the thematic of sexuality in the system of law, the symbolic order, and sovereignty' will effectively mean that psychoanalysis will be, from its 'birth', out of date. There can be no return to Freud because psychoanalysis 'is in the last analysis a historical "retro-version"' (1:150), consigned forever to re-interpreting and re-reading the moment of its birth without ever being able to account for the historicity of a desire and Law it takes as a starting point.

It will be the historicity of this conception of desire as the truth of the subject, and its links to the articulation of a law, that will become central to Foucault's revised *History of Sexuality*. This connection has gone largely unnoticed in the recent proliferation of discussion of Foucault's late work. It is well known that Foucault's project to historicise sexuality changed significantly from the plan he had sketched out in the first volume. Instead of analysing in more detail the deployment of sexuality, the project shifted focus, moving back in time to an analysis of the practices of the self in the cultures of classical Greece and the later Greco-Roman period, attempting now to find out how, for the subject 'itself', the experience of its sexuality as desire had been constituted. Foucault's account of this shift accords a central place to the theory of desire. Thus, in the introduction to the second volume, Foucault notes that to speak of sexuality as a historically singular experience it was necessary to be able to analyse the three axes that constitute it, those

10. *Ibid*, p67.

11. This issue is addressed, from a different perspective, by Mikkel Borch-Jacobsen in 'The Oedipus Problem in Freud and Lacan', trans. Douglas Brick *Critical Inquiry 20*, Winter 1994.

being the formation of sciences that refer to it, the systems of power that regulate its practices, and the forms within which individuals are able and obliged to recognise themselves as subjects of this sexuality (2:4). Foucault's previous work enabled the analysis of the formation of disciplines and power relations but the third axis was more difficult, the 'problems were much greater'. Why so? Because of a theory of desire. 'At the time', Foucault writes, 'the notion of desire, or of the desiring subject, constituted if not a theory, then at least a generally accepted theoretical theme' (2:5). In short, the primary theoretical tool available for the analysis of the interiority of the subject centred on a theory of desire.

Is this the same theory of desire referenced and critiqued in the first volume? The answer is surely yes, for Foucault goes on to note that the acceptance of this theory, or variations on it, 'was found not only at the very centre of the traditional theory, but also in the conceptions that sought to detach themselves from it' (2:5). This re-states the dichotomy that Foucault had broached in the first volume and ultimately dismissed. For Foucault's alternative account of desire and sexuality this theory of desire, which is Freud's *and* Lacan's, will ultimately be ineffective because it withdraws 'desire and the subject of desire ... from the historical field' (2:4). The evacuation of desire from history ultimately denies the 'historicity of forms of experience'.[12] Foucault's later work on sexuality would be directed precisely at outlining how an 'experience' came to be constituted that caused individuals to recognise themselves as subjects of a 'sexuality'. Experience is here understood as conjoining fields of knowledge, collections of rules, and a mode of relation between the individual and him/herself. Following this latter perspective, the analysis of forms of experience can proceed from an analysis of 'practices' so long, Foucault writes, 'as one qualifies that word to mean the different systems of action *insofar as* they are inhabited by thought'.[13] For Foucault, it is clear, the theory of desire, and of desire as constituted by the law, is unable to provide the tools for an analysis of the formation, development and transformation of practices of the self and forms of experience.

Foucault's genealogy of desire will not then be a history of the successive conceptions of desire but rather an account of

the practices by which individuals were led to focus their attention on themselves, to decipher, recognise, and acknowledge themselves as subjects of desire, bringing into play between themselves and themselves a certain relationship that allows them to discover, in desire, the truth of their being, be it natural or fallen (2:5).

The subjectivity of desire is found in a relationship to desire, and Foucault suggests that in the relationship that developed throughout 'our' history desire in its distance to the subjects who were to govern it was recognised as the truth of our being. This history cannot be written via Lacan's conception

12. Foucault, 'Preface to *The History of Sexuality*, Volume II', trans. William Smock, in Rabinow (ed), *The Foucault Reader*, p334.

13. *Ibid*, p335.

of desire, via an ever more complex hermeneutics of desire and law, because this conception must itself be placed within that history (which, in the broadest sense, may be seen as a contribution to a history of truth (2:6). Foucault will want then to ask: why has desire come to be seen as central to the truth of the subject? What historical processes have installed desire as truth? And, further than that, for genealogy must always begin from a question asked in the present: what contemporary theoretical practices continue the triad desire/truth/subjectivity?

Foucault's account will ultimately suggest a link between a theory of desire and Christianity. As Foucault's analysis demonstrates, early Christianity brought several important modifications to ancient asceticism, intensifying the form of the law and re-orientating the practices of the self in the direction of a deciphering of the self as a subject of desire. Law and desire become interlinked. As Foucault remarked in an interview, 'The articulation of law and desire appear to be rather characteristic of Christianity'.[14] Before the heteronomy of a Universal Law associated with the historical event of Christianity the subject cannot possibly measure up, and is thus forced to watch 'its' desires, confess them and ultimately renounce 'itself' as sinful. In short, 'subject' itself to the law. This articulation of desire and law and concomitant subjection is historical, with 'an ontology of deficiency and desire' obliterating an earlier ethics of sexual behaviour. Foucault writes:

14. Foucault, 'The concern for Truth', trans. John Johnston in Lotringer (ed), *Foucault Live*, p459.

> we do have an example of an ethical experience which implied a very strong connection between pleasure and desire. If we compare that to our experience now, where everybody - the philosopher or the psychoanalyst - explains that what is important is desire, and pleasure is nothing at all, we can wonder whether this disconnection wasn't a historical event.[15]

15. Foucault, 'On the Genealogy of Ethics: An overview of Work in Progress' in Rabinow (ed), p347.

It is no coincidence that Foucault quotes Aristotle asserting that desire is always 'desire for the agreeable thing', and not for the Other or the desire of the Other (2:43). It seems clear, more generally, that Foucault's call for 'bodies and pleasures' in the first volume of *The History of Sexuality* and the questioning of pleasure and desire in this late work on ethics constitutes a sustained attempt to move beyond an historical articulation which was still visible in contemporary theoretical debates. For Foucault, the issue would not be around desire and law but pleasure and the multiplicity of power. This I shall return to.

The final question I want to address here which emerges from Foucault's historicisation of the desire/law relation centres around morality. Simply, how does one conceptualise morality and conscience beyond the articulation of the law? This is effectively the question Joan Copjec addresses to Foucault in her recent pitting of Lacan against the 'historicists'. If the law is conceived of as primarily positive, the fact of conscience cannot be explained. As Copjec suggests, 'the experience of conscience and the interiorisation of the law through representations is made superfluous by [Foucault's] theory of law'.[16] In Lacan's account, conscience forms only as primal repression and primal law fall under the aegis of the paternal metaphor. The inner demand of the moral law is not with us from the start but is internalised through the mechanisms of the Oedipus complex. As we have seen, Lacan's structural account of this complex suggests that it is only through figures of interdiction that we come to represent in and to ourselves the primal or structural fact that we are constituted through repression of our desire.

Foucault's account would look very differently but would not deny the 'fact' and 'experience' of conscience, as Copjec suggests. Nothing is further from the truth. In these final works on the techniques of the self the reconceptualisation of morality and conscience became central to Foucault's re-problematisation of the subject. Indeed, in the short text in which Foucault announced this shift from the analysis of power to the 'history of the different modes by which, in our culture, human beings are made subjects' it was conceptualised in relation to the issue of conscience.[17] The word 'subject', Foucault suggested, could be understood in two ways: 'subject to someone else by control and dependence' or 'tied to his/her own identity by a conscience or self- knowledge'.[18] It was this latter conception that Foucault's work on ethics would address. For Foucault, then, moral conduct could no longer be simply understood as action conforming to some norm. Instead, morality effectively consists of two elements: codes of behaviour and forms of subjectivation (the way in which the individual establishes their relation to these codes). On the one hand, emphasis might be placed on the systematicity of the code and on the enforcement of this code. Here 'subjectivation occurs basically in a quasi-juridical form, where the ethical subject refers his conduct to a law, a set of laws' (2:29). On the other hand, the strong and dynamic element of the morality is to be found in the forms of subjectivation and the practices of the self. Schematically, Foucault discerns a shift from Greek ethics to the establishment of the heteronomy of a universal law associated with the formulation of the Christian doctrine and pastoral ministry regarding the flesh (for Foucault's more detailed consideration of the links and transformations see chapter three of *The Use of Pleasure*). This shift is reflected in the mode of subjectivation, where a care of the self and a use of pleasure shifts to a hermeneutics of the self, a shift in the mode of subjection (*mode d'assujettisement*) to divine Law, and a shift in the ethical substance - that part of the individual which is the prime material of their moral conduct - from acts and pleasures to 'desire and its purifying hermeneutics' (2:254).

Summarised in this way, and bearing in mind all that Foucault has to say about confession in the first volume of *The History of Sexuality*, it is clear that Foucault associates the Lacanian theory of law as constitutive of desire with the heteronomy of a universal law associated with Christianity. Both accounts place an emphasis on the systematicity of the code and, as such, imagine subjectivity in a quasi-juridical form. The subject is involved in an endless

16. Joan Copjec, *Read My Desire: Lacan Against the Historicists*, The MIT Press, Cambridge, Massachusetts, 1994, p26.

17. Foucault, 'The Subject and Power' in Hubert L. Dreyfus and Paul Rabinow, *Michel Foucault: Beyond Structuralism and Hermeneutics*, Harvester Wheatsheaf, London, 1982, p208.

18. *Ibid*, p212.

hermeneutic quest to 'read' its desire. In a different historical configuration, however, morality is not implanted by law but emerges through practices of the self - through relations with the self, through exercises by which the subject makes itself an object to be known, and through the practices that enable the subject to transform its own mode of being (2:30). Moral conceptions in Greek and Greco-Roman antiquity were much more oriented toward practices of the self and the question of *askesis* (a training) than towards the codification of conducts and the strict definition of which acts were permitted and which were forbidden. (Foucault notes that though incest was prohibited in Greece the elaboration of this prohibition was of little interest to philosophers and moralists - its elaboration could be at the heart of Sophocles' tragedy but was not at the centre of moral reflection).[19] '[T]o form oneself as a virtuous subject in the use he makes of pleasure', Foucault notes of classical Greek thought, 'the individual has to construct a relationship with the self that is of the "domination-submission", "command-obedience", "master-docility" types (and not, as will be the case in Christian spirituality, a relationship of the "elucidation-renunciation", "decipherment-purification" type)' (2:70). Elucidation-renunciation and decipherment-purification take place, Foucault would suggest, in relation to 'the timeless operation of prohibition, or the permanent form of law' (2:251). Beyond this permanent quasi-juridical form one must conceptualise the *mode d'assujettisement* in a fundamentally different fashion; the point is not to have a 'theory of the subject' in relation always to its subjection before the law, or in relation to the residue that may escape that subjection, but to pursue instead a history of subjectivisations.

It is this question of a 'beyond' that seems to haunt Foucault's account of psychoanalysis. How do we imagine the 'beyond' of the deployment of sexuality and psychoanalysis? Foucault will suggest, at moments in the first volume, that a 'multiplicity of pleasures' can exist beyond the artificial unity of bodily functions associated with the deployment of sexuality. This comes perilously close to the emancipatory discourse he was critiquing (and, indeed, Judith Butler has observed that this reading is 'not so far afield from the psychoanalytic postulation of primary polymorphousness').[20] On a different level, Foucault suggests that the deployment of alliance precedes sexuality. This deployment itself has no history in Foucault's account and its dissolution, considering the pivotal position it occupies in Foucault's argument about the rise of a bio-political configuration, is only summarily dealt with via the invocation of a diffuse non-discursive causality (1:106). What is needed here, as Foucault would acknowledge in a later interview, was a more precise genealogy of biopower, which was addressed in the 1978 and 1979 lectures at the *College de France* but subsequently dropped out of the project to historicise sexuality.[21] Foucault's account here does not adequately resolve Freud and Lacan's impasse before the question, what comes before the law?

This question seems to me though to become increasingly central to

19. See Foucault 'The Concern for Truth' in Lotringer (ed), *Foucault Live*, p460.

20. Judith Butler, *Gender Trouble: Feminism and the Subversion of Identity*, Routledge, London, 1990, p96.

21. Foucault, 'On the Genealogy of Ethics: An overview of Work in Progress' in Rabinow (ed), *The Foucault Reader*, p344. For more details on Foucault's lectures during these years see Ann Laura Stoler, *Race and the Education of Desire: Foucault's History of Sexuality and the Colonial Order of Things*, Durham, Duke University Press, 1995.

Foucault's revised *History of Sexuality*, which in effect associates this law with Christianity and inscribes that in history in accordance with a standard Foucauldian practice - tracing out a historical and conceptual moment from both sides of the break, following the lines of force that produce such an eclipse. The genealogy of this positioning of Christianity in Foucault's history is worthy of our attention (such a genealogy of the eight-year project to historicise sexuality must certainly follow Foucault's own prescription for genealogy, operating as it does 'on a field of entangled and confused parchments, on documents that have been scratched over and recopied many times').[22] In the original plan for *The History of Sexuality* Foucault included a study on Christianity as the second volume (the title given on the back cover of the original French edition of the first volume was *Le Chair et le Corps*). The Christian hermeneutics of the subject of desire would be the point of departure of the modern experience of sexuality. In an interview given around the time of the publication of the second and third volumes of Foucault's revised history, he pointed out that he had written the fourth volume on early Christian experience first and only then had moved backwards.[23] This fourth volume, seemingly titled *The Confessions of the Flesh*, is announced in the introduction to *The Use of Pleasure* but has yet to appear. In the revised plan, then, Christianity would emerge also as the point of departure for the analysis of the ancient problematisation of sexual practices.

In effect, the rise of Christianity emerges for Foucault as a crucial hinge point around which his analyses will swivel. It seems clear, as I have suggested, that Foucault's interest is in tracing out the particular articulation of desire and law which emerges historically with Christianity, tracing this out both before its emergence and in its modern configuration. This articulation for Foucault institutes a particular configuration of subjectivity, inscribing desire as the truth of the subject who is forever subjected before a law which produces desire. Psychoanalysis, more specifically Lacan, emerges as the continuation of this configuration par excellence. As such, Foucault's attempt to outline the genealogy of this configuration is inextricably enmeshed with a genealogy of Lacan. Lacan is sited as the crucial pivot around which Foucault's attempt to historicise sexuality and desire, and to re-problematise the subject, swivels, and this despite the fact that Lacan is never referenced throughout *The History of Sexuality*. It was, after all, Foucault who pointed out that

> Silence itself - the things one declines to say or is forbidden to name, the discretion that is required between different speakers - is less the absolute limit of discourse, the other side from which it is separated by a strict boundary, than an element that functions alongside the things said, with them and in relation to them within over-all strategies (1:27).

Further, Foucault would also suggest that 'it's important to have a small number of authors with whom one thinks, with whom one works, but on whom one doesn't write'.[24] It seems clear that Lacan figured as such an

22. Foucault, 'Nietzsche, Genealogy, History' in Rabinow (ed), *The Foucault Reader*, p76.

23. See Foucault, 'The Return of Morality', trans. John Johnston in Lotringer (ed), *Foucault Live*, p472.

24. *Ibid*, p470.

author for Foucault. Ultimately this must then be conceptualised in two ways. Firstly, in relation to the problematisation that Foucault enacts on Lacan. Secondly, in relation to the problematisation that emerges in Foucault's project which necessitated the considerable re-problematisation of the subject visible in this late work on ethics which developed, as I have suggested here, in close connection with a genealogy of psychoanalysis and Lacan.

Finally, it is certainly the case that these issues centred around the question - what is beyond psychoanalysis? - are not alien to psychoanalysis 'itself'. Freud's *Beyond the Pleasure Principle*, for example, may be seen as suffused with questions about the inheritance of psychoanalysis, of what can exist of psychoanalysis beyond Freud. Certainly, as Derrida's reading of Freud's witnessing of the *fort/da* game suggests, the issue of repetition emerges as central, as this becomes a game through which Freud asks himself whether his achievement, in being bound to the uniqueness of his name, can be repeated and inherited.[25] Lacan himself would continually question the inheritance of Freud, the unsurpassibility of Freud and yet the problematic necessity of going beyond him. This double bind preoccupied Lacan throughout the 1970s. In 1975, the year before the publication of Foucault's first volume, Lacan claimed 'I am Freud's heir', punning though on 'heretic' (*here-etique*).[26] Just as the *haeresis* (Greek: choice, from *hareein*, 'to take') of the Christian heresiarchs was to break with the 'lived experience' of the institutionalised Church in a return to the text of scriptural doctrine, so Lacan chose to bracket off the whole field of post-Freudian analytic endeavour to begin again with a reading of the foundational texts of psychoanalysis. Lacan's heresy will be intertwined with inheritance, a ceaseless tussle between the *fort* and the *da*. Foucault's project will be somewhat different. Standing to one side of the inheritance that Lacan pursues Foucault will ultimately want to site his heretical project beyond repetition and identification - though that certainly exists and, in a sense, must exist - and instead as a movement of separation.

These questions from *Beyond the Pleasure Principle* and from Lacan's rereading, questions of separation and loss, of inherence, of inheritance as continued existence, bring me back, at the close, to the title of this paper, a title taken from an imaginary book not yet written. It is a book imagined by Jacques Alain Miller - himself not untouched by these questions of inheritance - who, commenting on the apparent shift in Foucault's account of psychoanalysis from the 1966 *The Order of Things* to the 1976 first volume of *The History of Sexuality*, writes:

25. See Derrida's 'Coming Into One's Own' in Geoffrey Hartman (ed), *Psychoanalysis and the Question of the Text*, John Hopkins University Press, Baltimore, 1978 and *The Post Card: From Socrates to Freud and Beyond* (trans. Alan Bass), Chicago University Press, Chicago, 1987.

26. Lacan, Seminar of 18 November 1975, *Ornicar?*, 1976. This translation by Luke Thurston. See also Luke Thurston, ' *From Parletre to Sinthome:* Lacanian Subjects' in Lee Griveson and Howard Booth (eds), *Proceedings of the Subject Conference*, University of Kent, Canterbury, 1995.

27. Jacques Alain Miller, 'Michel Foucault and Psychoanalysis' in Timothy J. Armstrong (ed), *Michel Foucault: Philosopher*, Harvester Wheatsheaf, London, 1992, p59.

> it might well be that a future archaeologist will place one Foucault text from 1966 and another from 1976 at the beginning of a book called *The Death of Psychoanalysis*.[27]

Miller will, of course, suggest such a book is unwritable. Psychoanalysis inheres. Foucault's heresy will have been to pursue an analysis of the subject, of the interiority of the subject, without and beyond psychoanalysis, asking: how can we begin again the analysis of the subject beyond psychoanalysis? What other strategies can we use to imagine different ways of being than that concretised by psychoanalysis? These questions underlie Foucault's return to a historical moment where 'forms of relation to the self [were] different from those characterising the experience of sexuality', a return that was ultimately a way of historicising the subject of desire and imagining a way of moving beyond it, of effecting 'kinds of virtual fracture which open up the space of freedom understood as a space of concrete freedom, i.e. of possible transformations'.[28] The flip-side of Foucault's genealogy, which begins from a question asked in the present, will then be this: what might come after psychoanalysis? What would happen if the faces of Freud and Lacan were drawn in sand by the edge of the sea?

For Foucault, the death of psychoanalysis would enable new ways of being human, new ways of setting up and developing relationships with the self, for self-reflection, self-knowledge, self-examination, new ways of organising the contingency of our selves.

Numerous conversations with both Elizabeth Cowie and Luke Thurston helped enormously with the writing of this article. My thanks to them and also to Vanessa Martin and Howard Booth.

28. Foucault, 'Preface to *The History of Sexuality* Volume II' in Rabinow (ed), *The Foucault Reader,* p339 and Foucault, 'Structuralism and Postmodernism: An interview with Michel Foucault', *Telos* 55, Spring 1983, p206.

How Ideas Spread

Alan Durant

Dan Sperber, *Explaining Culture: A Naturalistic Approach*. Blackwell, Oxford 1996. pp175; £35.00 cloth, £13.99 paperback.

Dan Sperber's perhaps most influential work is *Relevance: Communication and Cognition*, co-written with the linguist Deirdre Wilson and first published by Blackwell in 1986 (recently re-published in a revised edition). That work offers a critique of 'code' models of communication (prevalent in linguistics and semiotics), and suggests a compelling alternative framework based on a combination of coded and inferential interpretation; in doing so, the book simultaneously offered persuasive answers to a number of problems in semantics and pragmatics, and also addressed the question how human communication fits with cognition more generally and with evolution-based accounts of the human species. Alongside that work, however, Sperber has also published a series of anthropological studies, from an early account of structuralism in anthropology onwards, through *Rethinking Symbolism* (1975) and *On Anthropological Knowledge* (1985), up to the present book: a collection of essays written over the last ten years outlining what Sperber calls an 'epidemiology of representations'.

Compared with other French thinkers such as Foucault, Bourdieu, or Baudrillard, Sperber remains relatively unknown in cultural studies in Britain. Given broad trends in the field, that is unsurprising. This collection should serve, however, if not to make Sperber's work more widely understood, then at least to present a serious challenge to those who ignore it without having answers to most or all of the important theoretical questions he asks: questions about the variable diffusion of representations in society; questions about ontology and causation in cultural theory; and questions about variation and species-invariants in human cultures.

Despite some repetition of central concepts and themes, the collection presents formidable arguments for considering population-scale macro-phenomena, such as myths, fashions, rituals, or traditions, as the cumulative effect of micro-processes involving individually analysable causal events. Such events consist principally of the production of physical, 'public' representations which are derived from cognitive representations (what we describe informally as 'expression' or 'cultural production'), and the derivation of mental representations (attributions of meaning) from such public representations. Sperber contrasts investigation of causal *chains* of micro-processes of this kind (which he describes as 'naturalistic', in virtue of its compatibility with disciplines in the natural sciences) with most existing work in social science. More commonly in the social sciences, he points out, holistic approaches are adopted which explain one macro-phenomenon in terms of another (Sperber's preferred illustration is explaining religion in terms of economic structure). But approaches which attribute causal properties to ideal or abstract objects (of the kind macro-phenomena inevitably are), Sperber argues, fail in a number of respects: they do not sufficiently distinguish types from tokens; they submerge issues of ontology with falsely attractive notions of 'cultural autonomy'; they allow formal properties to assume inexplicable causal interaction with the world; and in many cases they proclaim a materialism which is at best illusory.

By contrast, Sperber characterises his own general approach as an 'epidemiology of representations', readily acknowledging that the term involves an element of metaphor or analogy. But what, more precisely, does this expression convey? An epidemiological approach should describe and explain, according to Sperber, the distribution of representations. Representations, he argues, take two forms: either mental states in human minds, or physical products (such as books, utterances, or institutions) which are the traces of human production and exist in the environment of human minds. What we loosely call culture consists of patterns in the circulation of these two kinds of representation, where 'circulation' means a vast number of local events of interpreting, remembering, re-telling, and reworking of representations.

'Cultural phenomena are ecological patterns of psychological phenomena.' So proclaims one highly condensed statement in perhaps the collection's key chapter: a reprinted, already-influential Malinowski memorial lecture from 1984 entitled 'Anthropology and Psychology: Towards an Epidemiology of Representations'. One interesting implication of this statement is that cultural phenomena are not a distinct set of entities, such as might be prescribed in a standard curriculum topic list, but unevenly distributed and varying patterns of representations which are then carved up into distinct objects of study (such as myth, ideology, pop music, or literature) more for interpretive convenience than on theoretical, explanatory grounds. There is on Sperber's account no clear-cut distinction between what we usually think of as private mental representations (one-off desires, personal memories or meditations) and deep or enduring cultural traditions. The two simply involve different degrees of 'cultural-ness'. How far any representation acquires 'cultural-ness' depends on its suitability to do so, within a given ecology or environment. It is also that suitability, coupled with environmental factors, which locates any given representation along a continuum that ranges from little or no distribution outside an originating human mind, through what might be thought of as representational 'epidemics' (such as fashions or discussion of current affairs), to cultural 'endemics' (long-lasting and pervasive cultural traditions, such as canonical literary works, proverbs, and religious rituals).

The medical analogy introduced by the term 'epidemiology' signifies, among other things, two distinct but related approaches. For cultures to exist at a larger macro-level of description and interpretation, both intrasubjective (psychological) and intersubjective (public) processes are required. The 'epidemiology' analogy accordingly draws a two-level parallel: between viral or bacterial infection and individual pathology, in the case of disease, and cognitive processes such as memory, attention, and attainment of relevance, in the case of representations; and between identifiable social conduits for transmission of infection, in the case of disease, and ecological or environmental processes, such as whether writing is available, in the case of representations.

For Sperber, however, there is a key *difference* between an epidemiology of diseases and one of representations. Viruses and bacteria mutate only relatively seldom, while at almost every step in the millions of interpretive events involved in the social distribution of representations some degree of non-random transformation is introduced, even in cases where the physical means of circulation themselves - by recording, e-mail forwarding, or another technological means of reproduction - ensure exact replication. Crucially, such transformation is the result of the specific cognitive endowment of humans, which Sperber examines in terms of dispositions (or positively adapted evolutionary capabilities) and susceptibilities (or indirect consequences of dispositions which may or may not have any adaptive role). Endowment imposes specific *constraints* on cognitive abilities, such that we have for instance limits on memory, a need to prioritise information to prevent cognitive overload, and a psychological readiness to search for maximal relevance at cost of minimal effort (as Sperber illustrates convincingly with his examples of Gödel's theory, a 20-digit number, and the story of Little Red Riding Hood). At this point, the connection between Sperber's epidemiological arguments and Relevance Theory more formally is especially evident: the extent and direction of the transformation of representations which takes place in the chain of interactions between representational tokens (which in turn collectively constitute large-scale cultural phenomena) are shaped by what best fits with human psychological capacities.

Concern to examine cultural phenomena within historical and evolutionary time-spans obliges Sperber to address questions surrounding the acquisition of cultural concepts (as well as, in the previously unpublished Chapter 5, to investigate statistical and other claims surrounding notions of selection and attraction in evolutionary theory). After reviewing arguments about acquisition of basic concepts (including claims about innate abilities in the case of elementary colour discrimination, and the development of an encyclopaedic database of concepts, such as natural kind terms, as a sort of default from ostension), Sperber develops a more specific hypothesis: that humans have, perhaps as part of a controversially extended modularity of mind (cf. Fodor), what he calls meta-representational abilities. Such abilities allow incomplete concepts to be embedded in fully-formed reporting or meta-representational attitudes of disbelieving, wondering, doubting, etc. Sperber suggests that such incomplete concepts (one of his illustrations is a child's belief that someone has died being held simultaneously with recognition that she doesn't understand what dying means) are retained on the basis of the authority to which they are attributed, and relevance subsequently sought for them. Some of these half-understood concepts are later understood more fully (for instance as the child gradually enriches her notion of dying), while other such concepts remain perplexing and unresolved mysteries.

Among such mysteries, Sperber interestingly claims (as he has done since *Rethinking Symbolism* in the 1970s, where he called such incomplete representations 'semi-propositional knowledge'), exists a sub-class of mysteries which are particularly evocative. Such mysteries are both especially well-suited to cognitive abilities such as remembering and also generate a large number of relevant thoughts; they become established, Sperber suggests, as a culture's recognised myths, religious conventions, and cultural beliefs. This is in itself a highly suggestive and thought-provoking contention, best developed in Chapter 4, 'The Epidemiology of Beliefs'. But what makes the claim interesting theoretically is a related hypothesis: that humans have an evolutionary *disposition* to expand learning with meta-representational concepts, and as a result also an inherent *susceptibility* to retain for later understanding mysteries produced as a by-product of learning, which, as it turns out, provide the stuff of religious beliefs, superstition, ideology, and aesthetic pleasure.

As Sperber emphasises repeatedly in *Explaining Culture*, especially in the brief Introduction and Conclusion (where general issues in social science research are addressed), an account of culture along these lines does not preclude or devalue descriptive and interpretive work; rather, it redraws the terrain for theoretical explanation and encourages research pluralism. Sperber's emphasis on frameworks which are explanatory is not in a general sense polemical (though his irony on specific points is biting, as is well illustrated by his pastiche analysis of Little Red Riding Hood and *Hamlet* as in a relationship of 'structural inversion', or his critiques of functionalism, organicism and proclaimed materialism in the social sciences). Throughout, Sperber insists that no unified, grand theory of culture is likely to be possible; research and theory need to remain heterogenous and modest, not only because of the scale and difficulty of the questions to be asked, but also because so little is genuinely understood at present.

Many people in cultural studies are unlikely, I imagine, to enjoy this book much. Some will not get past the word 'naturalistic' in its sub-title. That will be a pity. Apart from its wealth of insight, cogent arguments, apposite illustration, and lucid and entertaining prose, *Explaining Culture* also offers a glimpse of what cultural study might be: rather than foreclosing possibilities on the strength of received wisdom or a selective interdisciplinarity which rules out so much interesting thinking, it makes its own start on the formulation of fresh, apparently basic but at the same time far-reaching research questions.

INDIVIDUAL REGIMES

Barbara Cruikshank

Nikolas Rose, *Inventing Our Selves: Psychology, Power, and Personhood.*
Cambridge University Press, Cambridge,1996; pp222 , £35.00 cloth

With one exception, the essays by Nikolas Rose collected in *Inventing Our Selves*, are previously published; in some cases several versions of the same essay are in print and appear here in revised form. Those familiar with the earlier work of Rose will find several surprises in these collected essays, as well as some further reflections on the arguments made in *Governing the Soul* and *The Psychology Complex*. In those earlier works, Rose adapted Michel Foucault's genealogies of the modern subject to tell his own stories about how human interiority became knowable and governable. Only one of the essays in this new volume continues that line of inquiry with a fascinating survey of early 20th-century social psychology as a science of democracy. Rose deftly explains that in the USA and UK, references to democracy in social psychology were more than rhetorical flourishes. Group psychology and public opinion research, for example, offered solutions to the problems of government by and for the people as well as techniques for governing democratically. By rendering the subjective will of the demos visible and calculable, government could be conducted in alignment with the desires and choices of the governed. Rose does not overestimate the role of *psy* in making the liberal arts of government practicable. He does not argue that psychology is part of a state apparatus of social control, domination, or a discourse of legitimation. Rather, he makes a compelling case for treating the heterogeneous histories of *psy*, psychological expertise, and social scientific techniques as a 'regime of the self' that invents and re-invents, rather than discovers, the self.

In the other essays collected here, the reader will find Rose more concerned with our current regime of the self. In its own way, each essay builds upon the historical hypothesis drafted by Foucault, that disciplines with the psy prefix originated in 'a reversal of the political axis of individualization' (p105). Where once only heroic and privileged lives were individualized and put into descriptive narratives as individuals, with the advent of psy, the individuality of ordinary people was rendered visible, objectified, and differentiated by the regulatory norm of autonomy. With that historical backdrop, Rose questions the emergence of new constructions of interiority and normativity such as 'enterprising selves' and the possibilities for 'assembling ourselves.'

The first four chapters grapple with the question, how should we do the history of *psy*? These chapters will be of interest to anyone looking for ways to account for particular histories of power-knowledge and they are essential reading for historians of the social sciences. Readers interested only in psychology itself will be impatient with these essays for in addition to being repetitive, each is deeply reflective and critical of psychology. However, to those facing the history of the social sciences, it will seem that some things do bear repeating. While it is an annoying academic convention, Rose cites himself repeatedly to direct the reader to texts where the historical method under discussion is actually utilized. In that sense, one might consider them a primer for reading Rose's earlier works; but they are much more than that. These essays say as much about how to do the history of psychology as how not to do it.

Rose presents a persuasive case that it is not enough to look at the history of *psy* discourses in terms of the epistemic possibility of uttering a truth claim about mental health or an ethical claim about what is good for us. The history of *psy* cannot be told without accounting for its distinctiveness in relation to other ethical, medical, and religious discourses. Rose argues that the unique success of psy rests not in the ideological or scientific force of its discourses, but in its techniques for visualizing human subjectivity, identity and difference into science as a known and calculable object. Nor can the institutionalization and dispersion of psy be attributed to the ontology of its object, the self. A geneology of the self must be carried through without presuming the self as an object of analysis. Rather than tell us what the self is, that is, rather than practicing psychology, he tells us how the self is made. Rose draws on Bruno Latour to explain that *psy* is not merely a conceptual apparatus applied to human being, but a method or *techne* for inscribing human subjectivity. Despite its heterogeneity, Rose argues, what distinguishes psy from other disciplines are its techniques for inscribing and disciplining human difference, for making human subjectivity governable. In these and the remaining chapters, Rose characterises and enlivens three contemporary themes.

First, Rose reminds the reader that the current proliferation of challenges to the unity of the self coming from disparate movements (feminism, genetics, medicine, cybernetics, among others) make human-being appear more and more to be a product of invention. Alongside these challengers, Rose adopts a critical-historical approach throughout that disrupts the self-evidence of psychological thinking, as he terms it, by thinking against the present. Without pronouncing the dawn of a new age, Rose makes it clear at every critical juncture that the current regimes of the self are an unstable mix of practices, knowledges, and institutions. In the gravity of that mix, it is not possible to simply 'disinvent' the selves we have become; but it is possible to contest the current regime of the self and to struggle to invent ourselves otherwise. Each of the essays is charged by that possibility.

More suggestive than definitive, Rose examines the disparity between the disappearing unity of the self in social theory and the persistence of the self in regulatory practices from self-realization to the enterprising self. Rose uses the conception of folding found in the writing of Gilles Deleuze to explain how it is possible to act as if we are coherent selves while at the same time relating to or acting upon ourselves; how is the boundary between the self and the exterior traversed without shattering the apparent unity of the self? Rose rejects the idea that subjects are constituted linguistically and narratively, without any exterior apparatus other than language. He suggests looking at the relationships of interiority to external authority, apparatuses and powers.

A second theme coheres at the point where psy meets liberal democratic government, in the history of invention in myriad locales of techniques for governing the interiority of human-being. This theme is thoroughly developed in *Governing the Soul* and here appears more as an undercurrent than as an argument in itself. As noted above, one chapter considers social psychology as a science of democracy. Also, in an essay titled, 'Governing Enterprising Individuals,' Rose illustrates a recent set of programmes for governing human autonomy and freedom in new ways termed neoliberal. Part of a much larger set of challenges to the liberal welfare state from both the left and the right, Rose argues that neoliberalism succeeded in operationalizing new techniques for governing without the paternalistic intrusions of social workers and legislative bodies into the autonomous choice and decision-making of individuals conceived as entrepreneurs. Here, Rose is at his best, identifying what is discontinuous, and thinking critically against the current movements in liberalism.

The third theme is that the regime of the self is heterogeneous. This is no history of ideas nor of the powers that be, but of how incredibly complex, local, and heterogeneous the regime of the self is which dominates our present conception of ourselves. That regime of the self does not invent or force uniformity, Rose argues, but practices a common normativity for measuring all selves against the regulatory ideals of choice, autonomy, and self-realization. From his vantage point, even materialist history looks surprisingly superficial. None of that history was necessary or inevitable; the role of psy in regulating the freedom of the modern self is a question that cannot be explained with reference to the self as a given, but only as a product of invention. The implications for future research are that a great deal of meticulous and localized study must be undertaken without the promise of discovering who we are. Without the driving force of discovery, we are faced with the daunting task of inventing our selves.

SPACE EXPLORATION

Gail Low

Caren Kaplan, *Questions of Travel: Postmodern Discourses of Displacement*, Duke University Press, Durham and London, 1996; pp238; £15.95 paperback, £47.50 cloth

If the past decade established the academic study of travel writing as a legitimate, albeit marginal, adjunct of colonial and postcolonial cultural studies, the last few years have seen how 'travel' and 'displacement' have become major tropes in the representation of postmodernity. Contemporary theory's preoccupation with space and place within the politics and poetics of identity has meant that its discourse is permeated with metaphors of dis/placement in terms such as migration, nomadism, exile, tourism, cosmopolitanism, diaspora, position, location and the margin. Caren Kaplan's monograph attempts to provide a historical and political map of the use and abuse of such geographical representations in critical practice. The book is divided into four chapters; the first two explore the construction and rhetorical use made of a metaphor (nomadism), or opposing metaphors (exile/tourist), while the final two look at the language and politics of both 'disaporas' and 'locations'.

The opening chapter guides a reader through different aspects of a critique of the Euro-American modernist celebration of exile as cosmopolitan internationalism. Firstly, there is a 'critical promotion of exile as aesthetic gain' where 'exilic displacement' operates in inverse proportion to contemplative and aesthetic creativity. Existential alienation and melancholia is constructed as an 'enabling fiction': 'the activity of writing and the professional legitimation of authorship provide a form of recompense for the loss and uncertainty of the modern condition' (p38). Secondly, the critical institutionalisation of these writers contributes to an 'ideology of modernism' which has the effect of de-politicising and de-historicising modernist aesthetics. 'Dislocation' is translated as 'detachment' and the nationalism/internationalism debate is narrated as a freeing of artists from the 'worldly locations of nation-states' for 'loftier pursuits'. Thirdly, Kaplan considers modernism's complicity with imperialism. Here, the quest for new aesthetic forms is impelled by nostalgia and a search for authenticity located elsewhere in other worlds. The modern subject travels (physically or mentally) to other locations in time and space to appropriate and incorporate. Employing Renato Rosaldo's term, 'imperialist nostalgia', Kaplan argues that the narrativisation of Euro-American past as another country, culture or time is central to the 'conquering spirit of modernity'. Focusing on Malcolm Cowley's *Exile's Return* and Paul Fussell's *Abroad*, she shows how they both produce and are produced by the primary tropes of Euro-American modernisms.

Kaplan's argument takes an interesting turn in this chapter when she deliberately positions Dean MacCannell's *The Tourist* against the elitist focus on exile as a privileged signifier in the paradoxical relation between time and space in modernity. MacCannell's postmodern tourist also embodies the modern subject's ambivalent relation to the past and quest for authenticity. In an unevenly developed global economy, the tourist 'confirms and legitimates' the First and Third World categorisations: 'created out of increasing leisure time in industrialised nations and driven by a need to ascertain identity and location in a world that undermines the certainty of those categories, the tourist acts as an agent of modernity' (p58). Functioning as an emblem of modern man, the formulation of the tourist in MacCannell enables a powerful critique of modernity. However, Kaplan does not simply displace the exile for the tourist but focuses her analysis on their structural similarities and their central role in the production of Euro-centric discourses.

The postmodern turn leads Kaplan to consider the 'nomad', recently cast as the figural embodiment of a progressive poststructuralist theorisation of displacement. In this second chapter, the work of Baudrillard, Deleuze and Guattari are argued to be imbued with a modernist ahistorical romanticisation of exile. Kaplan's Baudrillard is revealed not as the postmodernist theorist's theorist; his travelling theory invokes modernist poetics. Reading *America* and *Cool Memories* as instances of travelling theory, Kaplan looks at how Baudrillard's texts contain structural similarities with the Euro-centric discourses of exploration, heroism and imperialist nostalgia. His 'theoretical cruising' employs the stereotypical narrativisation of woman as the obscure object of desire and the space of theoretical formulations. In this light, 'the theorist as nomadic subject in the poetics of space is situated through and against Others' (p74). Deleuze and Guattari's theory of 'deterritorisation' promises a politicised theory of postmodern subjectivities; they hold out the possibility of alternative political practices to the nationalist, humanist and liberal agenda. Their version of the nomadic subject and their employment of the rhizomic metaphor constitutes 'an anarchic relation to space and subjectivity, resistant to and undermining the nation-state apparatus' (p87). But as Kaplan also points out, their generalised poetics of displacement is at its best utopian. At its worst, they reproduce a kind of 'theoretical tourism' which enacts 'a kind of colonial discourse in the name of progressive politics.' Becoming minor is a strategy that only makes sense if you are not already dispossessed. Celebrating hybridity and alterity without addressing the transnational and global nexus of power and capital simply constitutes the margin as a 'linguistic or critical vacation' while producing a 'new poetics of the exotic'. In contrast, Gayatri Spivak, Lawrence Grossberg and Janice Radway's calls for the analysis of the subject positioning (or positions) of theorists and intellectuals points the way forward for a less blind and more productive critical practice.

Kaplan argues that Euro-American modernist deployments of displacement often work to mystify and to homogenise historically specific encounters, travels and circuits of exchange. They also mask economic and social differences in a generalised celebration of cosmopolitanism. Travelling theories and theorists are part of the legacy of imperial history and Kaplan traces - to use a mixed metaphor - the impassioned polarisation of exile/ expatriate and immigrant/cosmopolitan in cultural theory. The shift from modernist exile to postmodern cosmopolitan diasporas also enables her to concentrate on the work of Edward Said and James Clifford - two theorists who are very much concerned with thinking through multiple positions, locations, border crossings and the politics of transnational cultural production. In Said's work, Kaplan sees a productive tension between politics and aesthetics, location and exile, the local and the cosmopolitan, neutrality and affiliation, and 'cataclysmic loss and critical possibility'. Exile functions in Said's texts as 'a reading strategy, a definition of a historical condition, a precept, a political or cultural program, and a specific zone for the exploration of the relationship between nation, identity, and location' (p117). In relation to Clifford's work, Kaplan focuses on three separate areas: his engagement with the poetics of displacement and the writing of culture, his call for 'the politics of theory as a historical relationship between cultural production and reception' and his turn to 'diaspora' as a term that confounds 'essentialist nationalisms in favour of transnational [and postmodern] subjectivities and communities'. Yet as with the celebration of nomadism, Kaplan warns against erasure of difference and suppression of material histories; these absences of the histories of collective displacements, and absenting of refugees and immigrants in favour of the 'diasporic' and the 'hybrid' tell us more about 'the social construction of Euro-American theory than about the historical and cultural conditions of migration' in modernity. Transnationalism has both positive and negative effects; it may refer to new diasporic identities, the construction of 'dynamic border zones' as well as 'hegemonic aspects of globalisation and transnational corporate exploitation' (p135).

As part of the exploration of metaphors of displacement, Kaplan's arguments conclude with a consideration of location and placement in the production of feminist discourses of identity and subjectivity. That geography and typography have impacted on contemporary cultural theory can be seen in relation to the proliferation of spatialised metaphors of location, locale, place and position used in the theory and praxis of 'emergent identity formations and social practices'. Yet the recourse to geography must not be at the expense of history; coming to terms with the complex circuits of postmodernity involves both a temporal and spatial dimension. The question of 'how to negotiate or mediate space with time or vice versa' forms the central preoccupation of theories of spatial politics or the politics of location.

Political and cultural resistance in postmodern theory can take the form of a valorization of the local and regional; Kaplan argues that, especially for feminist and postcolonial theory, 'the privileging of the local' is 'produced in a context of increased concern about hegemonic cultural and economic practices ... fomented and disseminated by transnational capital and its diversely pervasive effects' (p146). Challenging the homogenisation, abstraction and aestheticisation of the worst totalising excess of theory, feminist discourses have sought to offer complex and differentiated subjects and 'material analyses of lived experience and gendered divisions of labor'. Kaplan offers a brief history of Euro-American feminism's interrogation of global feminism and the naturalisation of 'woman'. Adrienne Rich's first use of the term 'the politics of location' was to deconstruct hegemonic uses of the word 'woman' and to foreground the position of the theorist. From Nancy Hartsock's somewhat conservative coining of 'standpoint epistemology', and gender as a 'singular standpoint' for feminist practice, to Chandra Mohanty, Ruth Frankenberg and Lata Mani's theorisation of location as 'discontinuous', multiple and 'traversed' by diverse historical and material formations, Kaplan traces a complex and paradoxical field where postmodernism and postcolonial discourses of feminism intersect. Location, she concludes, should be thought less as a place than an 'axis'. Such a change in metaphor admits to an 'uneven, discontinuous, yet open process [and] allows for the alignment of identity at the intersection of axes not as the monumental erection of a stable site but as a temporally spatialized location - a paradoxical space of historicized effects' (p184).

Kaplan's book presents an excellent exploration of how metaphors and specific terms bring with them particular ideological formations. Her account of differences and similarities across the field of cultural theory in the Euro-American academy offers the reader a useful mapping of discursive relations. Her final two chapters, which focus less on particular texts or theorists and more on situating significant theorists and theories within the field of postcolonial and feminist cultural production, provide especially admirable and nuanced conceptual histories. My only reservation is that *Questions of Travel* calls for a history of the production and reception of theory and critical practice, but this call should not be restricted to a literary or representational history. Kaplan's brief references to the historical contexts of theoretical discourses and practices (for example, the 'geopolitics and cultural conventions of the cold war era', the 'rock 'n'roll and pop culture of 1950s and 1960s America that ties Baudrillard's *America* to the French reception of American popular culture in the aftermath of World War Two) made me wish for different kind of book to be written. A book that moves from the close circuit of theory towards a more 'empirical' account of how theory shapes and is shaped by history and culture.

Imported Goods

Keith C Hampson

David Howes (ed), *Cross-Cultural Consumption: Global Markets, Local Realities.*
Routledge, London, 1996; pp224; £13.99 paperback

David Howes has assembled a collection of essays which, though written
largely from an anthropological tradition, should be of value to all disciplines
concerned with the cultural, economic and political implications of the global
movement in cultural commodities.

While each of the nine essays (plus an introduction and epilogue) address
a particular case of cross-cultural consumption, what gives this publication
its considerable coherence is the shared desire among the theorists to
reconsider two assumptions common within cultural anthropology: (a) that
subordinate, marginal cultures are by and large defenceless against the
imposition of dominant cultural production ('cultural imperialism') and
dominant consumption practices ('cultural appropriation'); (b) that, 'for
the sake of analysis', intrusions by such outside forces can and should be
distinguished from the 'original' or 'genuine' culture. Whether examining
the usurpation of the symbols of a subjugated culture or the rapid
deployment of Western production and marketing into a previously
'untouched' cultural environment, scholarly work within anthropology has
tended to both minimize the resistive capacity of subordinate cultures and
to downplay the evolving, incorporative quality of cultural formation.
According to this view, then, commercial practices such as the international
expansion of brand names Coke, McDonalds, and Disney, or the cultural
'poaching' in developing nations by Western tourists has led to the erosion
of local differences and to the subsequent rise of global consumer capitalism
as a way of life.

While the essays in this book recognize the potentially devastating effects
of global capitalism on the economic, environmental, health-related and
cultural conditions of marginal cultures, they emphasize the importance of
the practical and discursive conditions in which these interventions operate,
and how these conditions may serve to creatively defend and reconstitute
the subordinate culture in light of such developments. Drawing on recent
work in anthropology, cultural studies and post-colonial theory, the studies
recognize, to varying degrees, the negotiatory role of culture and the capacity
of individuals and communities to rework commodities in accordance with
their unique objectives, interests and values. The reception and ultimate
impact of global capitalism is shaped, thus, by local, historically-specific

forces which can only be understood by way of consideration of the particularities of the context of consumption. Howes suggests that:

> ... the assumption that such goods, on entering a culture, will inevitably retain and communicate the values they are accorded by their culture of origin must be questioned. When one takes a closer look at the meanings and uses given to specific imported goods within specific 'local contexts' or 'realities', one often finds that the goods have been transformed, at least in part, in accordance with the values of the receiving culture. (p5)

This notion of the 'active consumer' is a very familiar one within cultural studies. Several theorists have advocated a recognition of the creative, resistive nature of everyday culture. Indeed, the debate surrounding this issue became something of an obsession for cultural studies in the late 1980s and early 1990s. Despite the familiarity of the book's fundamental theoretical perspective, though, *Cross-Cultural Consumption* provides a number of excellent analyses which pose new and relevant questions of global consumer capitalism which could, in turn, stimulate the revaluation of cultural studies.

For example, the considerable attention paid within cultural studies to consumer capitalism has not often been extended to non-contemporary, Western urban settings. While it may be the case that cultural studies should be cautious about over-extending its geographical reach - to not be all things to all people - it may also be the case that as consumer capitalism continues to evolve into a borderless activity, maintaining such restrictions may become increasingly difficult. Secondly, the concrete empirical character of many of these studies contrasts with the relatively loose application of the ethnographic method often found within cultural studies. As many of the essays in this book illustrate, the study of individuals, groups and contexts in substantive detail can provide an insightful account of the complexity and uneven nature of the economic and material conditions through which real people live.

Finally a number of these studies pose refreshingly new questions of the weary concept of 'resistance'. David Howes, for example, asks if cultural resistance can be productively recast in legal terms. He suggests that, despite the Anglo-American bias of the legal system, the Native American Hopi may be able to employ legal measures as a means of defending against the appropriation of the traditional Hopi cultural practices and symbols by dominant, non-native cultures. Similarly, Marian Bredin considers how alternative applications of communication technologies among Canada's northern First Nation communities may be shaped (and potentially inspired) by exposure to southern, urban and non-native media. The unique employment of media technologies can be understood, then, as responses to the subordinate culture's experiences as consumers.

If there is a shortcoming to this publication it is the omission of a discussion of the ways in which global capitalism increasingly launches production and marketing efforts which cater to the peculiarities of local tastes, traditions and values. In those instances in which this tactic is central to production and consumption processes, the very relevance of the 'cross-cultural consumption' issue is upset. The degree to which multinational consumer capitalism can assume a 'local' or 'authentic' status within specific contexts, regardless of the actual origins of the products and services, is fundamental to questions of its reception and ultimate significance. The growing corporate emphasis on sophisticated, detailed market research enhances the capacity of companies to locate, understand and secure the customer, 'to get us where we really live'. Within North America the accuracy with which this tactic is carried out is increasing dramatically. It is safe to presume that these efforts will be extended to other, non-Western markets as well. The development of this issue requires attention if only to be discounted.

Why not Subscribe?

New Formations is published three times a year. Make sure of your copy by subscribing.

SUBSCRIPTION RATES FOR 1997/98 (3 ISSUES)

Individual Subscriptions
UK   £35.00
Rest of World   £38.00

Institutional Subscriptions
UK   £70.00
Rest of World   £75.00

Please send one year's subscription
starting with Issue Number _____

I enclose payment of _____

Please send me _____ copies of back issue no. _____

I enclose total payment of _____

Name _____

Address _____

_____ Postcode _____

Please return this form with cheque or money order (sterling only) payable to *Lawrence & Wishart* and send to:
Lawrence and Wishart, 99a Wallis Road, London E9 5LN

THE LEGACY OF THE FRANKFURT SCHOOL IN CULTURAL STUDIES

A two day interdisciplinary Conference organised by the European Studies Research Institute, University of Salford in association with **New Formations. March 31st - April 1st, 1998**

CALL FOR PAPERS

THEMES WILL INCLUDE:
THE HIGH/LOW CULTURE DEBATE, THE POLITICS OF SPACE AND TIME, UTOPIANISM, THE CRITIQUE OF THE ENLIGHTENMENT, QUEER AESTHETIC THEORY, IDENTITY AND THE CITY, DIALECTICS AND DECONSTRUCTION
Keynote speakers: J. Bernstein (Essex University), Neil Lazarus (Brown University), Simon Critchley (Essex University)

Selected papers to be published by New Formations
A 200 word abstract should be sent by 31st December 1997 to either Scott McCracken, s.m.mccracken@english.salford.ac.uk, or Antony Rowland, a.c.rowland@english.salford.ac.uk, at Depatment of English, University of Salford, Salford M5 4WT.
Tel: 0161 295 5133 or Fax: 0161 295 5511

The time is ripe for a reassessment of the influence of the Frankfurt School in Cultural Studies. With an eye on the critical element in Critical Theory, the conference will explore the influence of figures like Theodor Adorno, Max Horkheimer, Walter Benjamin, Ernst Bloch, Hannah Arendt and Leo Lowenthal in current debates on mass society, the new geography, postmodernism, postcolonial theory, feminist criticism and queer theory. The conference will refocus attention on the legacy of the Frankfurt School in the contemporary theory and practice of cultural studies.

new formations

NUMBER 32   **LEGAL FICTIONS**

EDITED BY SALLY LEDGER AND STELLA SWAIN

Jeremy Bentham took the view that there was far too much 'fiction' in the legal system. Fictions, he said, 'carried into every part of the system the principle of rottenness.' In direct opposition to this position, this volume explores legal fictions: from the challenge of seeing law as language, text rhetoric and interpretation, to the exploration of how subjectivities and narratives produced in legal discourse are represented, reproduced or resisted in cultural practices. Contributors include: Ian Ward on law, literature and history, Steven Connor on the trials of the voice, Peter Fitzpatrick on Freud's Totem and Taboo, Ruth Robbins on Oscar Wilde, David Glover on aliens, anarchists and detectives, Maria Aristodemou on ethics and the imagination, Josaphine McDonagh on child murder and national identity and Sally Munt on the lesbian outlaw.

Entertaining the Third Reich
Illusions of Wholeness in Nazi Cinema
Linda Schulte-Sasse
". . . sets new standards in the domain of the analysis of ideological mechanisms at work in cultural products."
—Slavoj Zizek
Post-Contemporary Interventions
408 pages, 67 b&w photos, £17.95 paper

The Third Eye
Race, Cinema, and Ethnographic Spectacle
Fatimah Tobing Rony
". . . an extraordinary contribution to both film history and the theorization of the ethnographic gaze."
—Lisa Cartwright
328 pages, 50 b&w photos, £16.95 paper

Chinese Modernism in the Era of Reforms
Cultural Fever, Avant-Garde Fiction, and the New Chinese Cinema
Zhang Xudong
Offers both a historical narrative and a critical analysis of the cultural visions and experiences of China's post-Mao era.
Post-Contemporary Interventions
496 pages, 12 b&w photos, £20.95 paper

Sex Scandal
The Private Parts of Victorian Fiction
William A. Cohen
Never has the Victorian novel appeared so perverse as it does in these pages—and never has its perversity seemed so fundamental to its accomplishments.
Series Q
272 pages, £15.95 paper

Gaze and Voice as Love Objects
SIC 1
Renata Salecl and Slavoj Zizek, editors
"A marvellous collection of essays . . . [ranging] over an amazing topography of issues."—John Mowitt
SIC
304 pages, 9 b&w photos, £15.95 paper

Questions of Travel
Postmodern Discourses of Displacement
Caren Kaplan
Explores the various metaphoric uses of travel and displacement in literary and feminist theory,
Post-Contemporary Interventions
256 pages, £15.95 paper

The Repeating Island
The Caribbean and the Postmodern Perspective
Antonio Benítez-Rojo
Translated by James E. Maraniss
Benítez-Rojo, a master of the historical novel and critical essay, continues to confront the legacy and myths of colonialism.
Post-Contemporary Interventions
376 pages, £16.95 paper

The Lettered City
Angel Rama
Translated and edited by John Charles Chasteen
A vitally important work by one of Latin America's most highly respected theorists.
Post-Contemporary Interventions
176 pages, £13.95 paper

Science Wars
Andrew Ross, editor
The essays in this volume are sharply critical of the conservative defense of a value-free science.
352 pages, £15.95 paper

Vampires, Mummies, and Liberals
Bram Stoker and the Politics of Popular Fiction
David Glover
Vampires, Mummies, and Liberals reconstructs the cultural and political world that gave birth to *Dracula*.
240 pages, £15.95 paper

Cultural Institutions of the Novel
Deidre Lynch and William B. Warner, editors
In a far-reaching blend of comparative literature and transnational cultural studies, this collection shifts the study of the novel away from a consideration of what novels are, to what they do.
472 pages, £20.95 paper

Immigrant Acts
On Asian American Cultural Politics
Lisa Lowe
Lowe argues that understanding Asian immigration to the United States is fundamental to understanding the racialized economic and political foundations of the nation.
264 pages, £15.95 paper

The "Real" Thing
Testimonial Discourse and Latin America
Georg M. Gugelberger, editor
Examines *testimonio*, presented as the authentic testimony of the disenfranchised, the colonized, and the oppressed.
328 pages, £16.95 paper

*Duke University Press
c/o AUPG, 1 Gower Street
London WC1E 6HA
Tel: (0171) 580 3994
Fax: (0171) 580 3995
email: monk@easynet.co.uk*

BACK ISSUES

1 **Peter Wollen** on fashion and orientalism / **Denise Riley** on 'women' and feminism / **Dick Hebdige**'s sociology of the sublime / **Laura Marcus** on autobiographies / **John Tagg** should art historians know their place? / **Franco Bianchini** on the GLC's cultural policies / **Homi K. Bhabha, Stephen Feuchtwang** and **Barbara Harlow** on Fanon

2 **Mary Kelly, Elizabeth Cowie** and **Norman Bryson** on Kelly's Interim / **Greil Marcus** on subversive entertainment / **Georgina Born** on modern music culture / **Geoffrey Nowell-Smith** on popular culture / **Ien Ang** on 'progressive television' / **Alan Sinfield** on modernism and English Studies in the Cold War / **Tony Bennett** on Eagleton.

3 *TRAVELLING THEORY* – **Julia Kristeva** on the melancholic imaginary / **David Edgar** on carnival and drama / **Kobena Mercer** black hair – style politics / **Jacques Rancière** on journeys into new worlds / **Peter Hulme**'s Caribbean diary / **Bill Schwarz** on travelling stars / **Ginette Vincendeau** on chanteuses réalistes / **Steve Connor** on Springsteen / **Christopher Norris** on Gasché's Derrida.

4 *CULTURAL TECHNOLOGIES* Out of print

5 *IDENTITIES* – **Homi K. Bhabha** on the commitment to theory / **Philip Cohen** on Tarzan and the jungle bunnies / **Glenn Bowman** on Palestinian nationalist consciousness / **Kristin Ross** on Rimbaud and spatial history / **Kaja Silverman** on liberty, maternity, commodification / **Adrian Rifkin** on Carmenology / **Margaret Sotan**'s epistemology of the wandering woman / **Andrew Benjamin** on psychoanalysis / **Gill Davies** on heritage / **Les Back** on soundsystems.

6 *THE BLUES* – **Jacqueline Rose** on Margaret Thatcher and Ruth Ellis / **James Donald** how English is it? / **Benita Parry** on Kipling's imperialism / **John Silver** on Carpentier / **Mitra Tabrizian** and **Andy Golding**'s blues / **Barbara Creed** on *Blue Velvet* / **Joseph Bristow** on masculinity /

Graham Murdock on Moretti's *Bildungsroman* / **Edmond Wright** on post-Humptydumptyism.

7 *MODERNISM/MASOCHISM* – **Victor Burgin**'s Tokyo / **Linda Williams** on feminine masochism and feminist criticism / **John Tagg** on criticism, photography and technological change / **Geoff Bennington** l'arroseur arrosé(e) / **Emilia Steuerman** on Habermas vs Lyotard / **Paul Crowther** on the Kantian sublime, the avant-garde and the postmodern / **Mark Cousins** on Lévi Strauss on Mauss / **Iain Chambers** being 'British' / **Adrian Forty** on lofts and gardens / **Lisa Tickner** on Griselda Pollock.

8 *TECHNO-ECOLOGIES* – **Peter Wollen** cinema: Americanism and the robot / **John Keane** on the liberty of the press / **S.P. Mohanty** on the philosophical basis of political criticism / **David Kazanjian** and **Anahid Kassabian** naming the Armenian genocide / **Paul Théberge** the 'sound' of music / **David Tomas** the technophilic body / **Félix Guattari** the three ecologies / **Margaret Whitford** on Sartre.

9 *ON ENJOYMENT* – **Slavoj Zizek** the undergrowth of enjoyment / **Peter Osborne** aesthetic autonomy and the crisis of theory / **Rachel Bowlby** the judgement of Paris (and the choice of Kristeva) / **Joseph Bristow** being gay: politics, identity, pleasure / **Gail Ching-Liang Low** white skins black masks / **Christine Holmlund** I Love Luce / **Line Grenier** from diversity to indifference / **Mark Cousins** is chastity a perversion? / **Simon Critchley** review of Christopher Norris.

10 *RADICAL DIFFERENCE* – **McKenzie Wark** on the Beijing demonstrations / **Paul Hirst** on relativism / **Cindy Patton** African AIDS / **Anna Marie Smith** Section 28 / **Tracey Moffatt** something more / **Susan Willis** Afro-American culture and commodity culture / **Hazel V. Carby** on C.L.R. James / **David Lloyd** on materialist aesthetics / **Peter Redman** Aids and cultural politics.

Back issues cost £14.99 each
Make cheques payable to *Lawrence & Wishart* and send to:
Lawrence & Wishart, 99a Wallis Road, London E9 5LN